ENEMIES
WITHOUT
GUNS

ENEMIES WITHOUT GUNS

THE CATHOLIC CHURCH IN THE PEOPLE'S REPUBLIC OF CHINA

by

James T. Myers

A PWPA Book

PARAGON HOUSE
New York

Published in the United States by
Professors World Peace Academy
481 8th Avenue
New York, New York 10001

Copyright © 1991 by Professors World Peace Academy

A Professors World Peace Academy Book

The Professors World Peace Academy (PWPA) is an international association
of professors, scholars and academics from diverse backgrounds, devoted to issues concerning world peace. PWPA sustains a program of conferences and
publications on topics in peace studies, area and cultural studies, national and
international development, education, economics and international relations.

Library of Congress Cataloging-in-Publication Data

Myers, James T.
    Enemies without guns / James T. Myers,
    p. 334   cm.
    "A PWPA book."
    Inclucles bibliographical references and index.
    ISBN 0-943852-90-0 (hard.) — ISBN 0-943852-91-9 (pbk.)
    1. Catholic Church—China—History—20th century.   2. Persecution—
China—History—20th century.   3. China—Church history—20th century.
4. China—Politics and government—1940–   Title.
BX 1665.M45   1991
282' .51' 09045—dc20   90-23647
                                                        CIP

After the enemies with guns have been wiped out, there will still be enemies without guns; they are bound to struggle desperately against us, and we must never regard these enemies lightly.

Mao Zedong
"Report to the Second Plenary Session of the Seventh Central Committee of the Communist Party of China" (March 5, 1949).

For
CHRISTINA
and in memory of
her beloved Papa,
my buddy,
PETE

CONTENTS

FOREWORD

The heroic faith and courage of many Catholics in the People's Republic of China is an inspiration to their brothers and sisters throughout the world, especially those of us who have never lived under such difficult circumstances. The survival and growth of the church there during the last fifty years is remarkable. It confirms the insight of St. Jerome many centuries ago: "Persecutions have made the church of Christ grow; martyrdoms have crowned it."

It is very important that the story of the Catholic Church in China during the last five decades be told with objectivity and accuracy. Despite shorter works and histories of certain religious communities in China, until now there has been no comprehensive, up-to-date work on the subject. We are grateful, indeed, to Professor Myers for his masterful study.

The relationship of Catholics in the People's Republic to the universal Church is both complex and controversial. It is essential that we in the West better understand the culture and worldview of the Orient, especially of China. This book makes a significant contribution to that task.

I pray that the Church will continue to grow in China and that it will contribute to the development of that society.

Joseph Cardinal Bernardin
Archbishop of Chicago

AUTHOR'S PREFACE AND ACKNOWLEDGMENTS

This is a book about the Catholic Church under Communist rule in China, but it is, hopefully, about more than that as well. While the treatment of Catholics was in some ways unique, Catholics also represented one of the many "United Front" groups from which the new government of the People's Republic of China sought cooperation after 1949. Part of the story of the early years of Communist rule in China in the 1950s, is the story of how these United Front groups were squeezed and eventually discarded by the ruling party when it believed that they were no longer needed as allies. The details of this process varied, but the patterns were the same, and in this sense the Catholic Church may serve as a metaphor for all those groups of patriotic and well-meaning Chinese who might have been so very useful to the state in its modernization efforts.

I have attempted in the pages which follow, to discuss the policies of the Chinese government toward the Catholic Church not in a vacuum, but to show how those policies shifted and evolved with the ebb and flow of political events in China over more than four decades. One of the themes which emerges from this study is that the Communist Party of China, compelled by the logic of its ideology, sought to destroy many of the groups and individuals in China which could have been most useful in national construction. But in the heady revolutionary environment of the early years, national construction eventually took a back seat to the romantic revolutionary vision of Mao Zedong and his effort to transform his nation and his countrymen according to this revolutionary vision. Religious believers were a special target of Mao's revolutionary ideology because their faith represented an alternate version of truth. It was only after Mao's death, with the beginning of the "reform" era about 1980, that the Chinese government attempted to resurrect and revitalize the concept of a United Front in their efforts to bring China into the modern world. Even here, however, the problem of alternate versions of truth—Communist and Christian—continued to be a problem.

As another theme, the book tries to correct the widespread misperception that most of the violence to organized religion in China was done by the Cultural Revolution which began in 1966. In fact, the truth is far different. By the time the Cultural Revolution broke in the late summer of 1966, there was very little of the Catholic Church left to destroy. The Church had suffered a relentless series of attacks, beginning in some parts of China even before the government of the People's Republic was established for the entire mainland of China in 1949. The government's effort, of which no secret was made, was to penetrate, control, and eventually eliminate religion from Chinese life. Foreign missionaries were expelled, Church properties were confiscated, schools, hospitals, orphanages and the like were taken over by the government. Eventually, when the foreigners were all gone, the Chinese authorities systematically rounded up all of the native clergy and lay people who remained loyal to Rome and who refused to cooperate with the government-established "Patriotic" Church. Many of these people were killed, while others were confined for decades in prisons and labor camps. It is not a pretty story.

Another theme which emerges from these pages is the persistence of religious faith and belief even in the face of the most severe persecution. Many outside observers, even those who hoped for the best, believed that the Church in China had been dealt such a serious blow that it would be decades, at least, perhaps centuries, before it could possibly recover. What we learned in the 1980s was quite different, and many who knew both the Church and China quite well were astonished at the vitality and resilience exhibited by a Church which many had feared was all but dead. These years have also given us stories of remarkable courage and heroism in the face of almost unbelievable brutality. Some of these stories are told in the chapters which follow. Indeed, one of the privileges I have had in writing this book has been to meet some of these brave people and to learn their stories first-hand.

In the end, the story of the Catholic Church in the People's Republic of China is but a small story in a vast land of more than one billion people. But it is an important story of the triumph of the human spirit in the face of persistent hostility, brutality and massive governmental power bent upon its destruction. It is also, in microcosm, the story of the Chinese Communist revolution itself, and especially of the failure of that revolution to realize the early promise which many believed it offered.

Many talented and knowledgeable people have helped me in this effort, including a number who know the subject at hand far better than the author. My colleague, Ambassador Richard L. Walker, who generously agreed to contribute an introduction, has read the entire manuscript more than once and offered many valuable suggestions and insights. My friend, Abbot Christian Aidan Carr, O.C.S.O. of Our Lady of Mepkin Trappist Monastery, has likewise read and edited the entire manuscript. He has also provided moral support and wise counsel over a number of years. I owe a tremendous debt of gratitude to Fr. Angelo S. Lazzarotto, P.I.M.E., Director of the African and Asian Section of the Centre for Missionary Animation of the Italian Bishops' Conference. When he was at the Cathedral in Hong Kong, Fr. Lazzarotto permitted me to photocopy his complete set of the *China Missionary Bulletin*. More recently, despite his own heavy schedule of responsibilities, he has taken the time to read and comment upon the entire manuscript.

I have profited greatly from my many conversations with Most Reverend Ernest L. Unterkoefler, recently-retired Bishop of the Diocese of Charleston, South Carolina. Bishop Unterkoefler has also read and commented on the entire manuscript. He has, in addition, been patient and gracious in explaining the intricacies of canon law to an author whose talents are no match for the Bishop's powerful intellect.

This book probably could not have been written without the help of Fr. Laszlo Ladany, S.J. China scholars know Fr. Ladany as one of the greatest of all "China-watchers." He founded, and for more than twenty-five years was editor of *China News Analysis* in Hong Kong. His friends also knew him as a man of great warmth, wit and humility, and of great generosity when it came to sharing his wisdom and documentary resources. Fr. Ladany was very interested in this study. He read and commented extensively on nearly the entire manuscript. I deeply regret that he did not live to see the book in print.

I owe a similar debt to Most Reverend Dominic Tang Yiming, S.J., Archbishop of Canton. Over the years that I have known him, he has been an absolutely unfailing source of friendship, advice, materials, contacts and support. He is, now in his eighties, a true human dynamo, and one of the most remarkable human beings I have ever met. It was in the Archbishop's office that I first met Catherine Ho, the young woman introduced here as "Wang Xiaoling," whose moving account of her prison experiences in China is woven through the chapters which follow. She has been kind enough to permit me to draw heavily on those experiences for this book. Through Catherine I was introduced to Margaret Chu, who has also graciously permitted me to reproduce the account of her own courageous struggle with life in a forced labor camp.

Other friends, colleagues, and correspondents who have assisted me in many ways, both great and small, include Fr. Norbert Pieraccini, O.F.M., Fr. W. Aedan McGrath, Fr. Ivar McGrath, Fr. Michael J. McKiernan, M.M., Fr. Franco Belfiori, S.J., and Fr. Patrick J. Scanlan. Fr. Bernard J. Shields, S.J. has been most helpful in obtaining for me the sometimes obscure documents on Church affairs which find their way to Hong Kong. He has also gone far beyond the call either of duty or friendship by providing a detailed critique of the entire manuscript. Dr. Audrey Donnithorne has been a source both of information as well as inspiration. Fr. Benedict Chao and the Trappist community of Our Lady of Joy at Lantao, Hong Kong, have several times received me and offered both assistance and solitude. Prof. June Teufel Dreyer has faithfully kept me supplied with clippings, documents and information which I might otherwise have missed. My friend John Connick, Editor of *The Catholic Banner*, has for the last several years regularly supplied me with Catholic wire service reports on China-related matters.

I am deeply grateful to Joseph Cardinal Bernardin for the foreword which he has graciously contributed to this study.

I also want to express my thanks to Dr. Gordon L. Anderson

of Professors World Peace Academy for the personal interest which he has expressed in this project since its inception.

I would be remiss if I did not acknowledge my debt to my friends of the Trappist community at Mepkin Abbey. Much of the early thinking about this book was done during short weekend stays there. A considerable amount of writing was done there as well. Over the years the monks of Mepkin Abbey have made me and my family feel like a part of their family, and they have provided for me a place of solitude and serenity in which much writing and thinking about writing has been accomplished. My debt to Abbot Christian Aidan was noted above. It is probably unfair to single out for special mention any of this rare group of men who have all become my friends, but I would like to thank my dear friend, Brother M. Joseph, whose life is a constant reminder to me of my own inadequacies as a human being.

Over the life of this project, critical financial support has been provided by the Earhart Foundation, the Pacific Cultural Foundation, and the China Studies Program of the University of South Carolina's Institute of International Studies. I am deeply indebted to all of these for their assistance.

Finally, no one could possibly sustain the effort needed to finish a project of this length without firm support on the home front. My family has been unusually patient and understanding, especially during the rather hectic final rush to complete the manuscript, when the author was frequently distracted, crabby and out of sorts. I want to thank my family for their love and support, my children Townsend, Amy and Aidan, and my wonderful wife Christina. She is once again, and ever, my joy and my blessing.

A Note On Romanization

The romanization of Chinese names has presented a bit of a problem in this study. Many of the older sources cited rely on the Wade-Giles system of romanization, while some of the more recent sources use the *pinyin* system developed in the P.R.C. For those not familiar with Chinese names, or with these systems of romanization, the differences can appear puzzling indeed. In the former system, for example, the name late Chinese leader is written Mao Tse-tung, while in *pinyin* it becomes Mao Zedong. Teng Hsiao-p'ing in Wade-Giles becomes Deng Xiaoping in *pinyin*.

This alone is difficult enough, but confusion is added to difficulty by virtue of the fact that, in the past, and in the mission chronicles which form so important a source of information for this study, many Chinese names were romanized in an English spelling which followed no convention at all, or which attempted to reproduce the sounds of a local dialect. The Catholic complex at Shanghai, for example is variously given as Ziccawei, Zi-ka-wei, Hsuchiahui (Wade-Giles) and Xujiahui (*pinyin*). The Bishop of Canton who appears prominently in these pages spells his name Tang Yi-ming (or, sometimes, Yee-ming), though his surname in standard or Mandarin Chinese would be romanized as Teng (Wade-giles) or Deng (*pinyin*). Similar problems exist with respect to placenames which are usually cited in older accounts of events in China according to conventional map spellings which do not follow either of the standard systems of romanization. Thus, for example, we have cities like Peking (Beijing in *pinyin*), Tsingtao (Qingdao) and Canton (Guangzhou), and provinces Shensi (Shaanxi), Hupeh (Hubei) and Chekiang (Zhejiang).

I have adopted *pinyin* as the standard system of romanization for this study. Were other sources are cited, such as the *China Missionary Bulletin*, which use older or non-standard spellings of personal or place names, the *pinyin* spelling is also provided in most cases. There are instances, however, where in the absence of Chinese characters for reference, it is simply impossible to translate non-standard, dialect spellings into the correct Mandarin-*pinyin* spelling. In the case of personal names, I have tried to retain the spelling commonly used by the individual in question. Thus, I have through out the book referred to the Bishop of Canton (Guangzhou) as "Tang" which reflects the Cantonese pronunciation of his name, rather than using "Deng" as some writers do, representing the correct Mandarin pronunciation and *pinyin* spelling of his surname. In all of those cases where more than one spelling of a personal or place name have been used, entries are cross-referenced in the index.

INTRODUCTION

Ambassador Richard L. Walker

While flying from Hong Kong to Burma during the Korean War, my companion in the seat beside me was a Catholic missionary father returning to Italy. He had been expelled from China after a period of imprisonment and torture at the hands of the new communist regime. Given the grisly tales he had to relate, I could only marvel at his quiet composure and philosophical perspective. I explored with him his views about China and where the Mao regime was leading the Middle Kingdom. He was convinced that although the communists were self-confidently sure that they could remake all of China and its people, they would not succeed. He stated the new rulers, even though Chinese, did not understand some of the basic faith of their culture. The people really do have an abiding faith in the human spirit, the existence of which the communists denied. He felt that their battle would be long but in the long run unsuccessful. They could not compete with the Confucian legacy and its belief in the essential goodness of man.

His own faith gave him a sense of detachment from the traumas of his recent agonies. He shared with so many other missionaries an admiration for the Chinese people and a conviction that Mao's doctrines of materialism and class struggle would not find permanent roots in China's soil.

In the intervening four decades I have drawn inspiration from my journey with the courageous and learned Catholic priest. Like some in my own family, who had been missionaries in China, he was convinced we had much to learn from China's rich culture, that it has a persistence and unique integrity.

I told my companion on the flight that he should write of what he had told me, the world needed to have a record of the details which he could provide regarding this important moment in China's modern history. He said he had already given a full account to the Catholic Center in Hong Kong where he had recovered for several months from the violence to which he had been subjected. Naturally his story brought into focus for me the importance of the fate of the Catholic Church in China. Over the following years I became acquainted with many of the China scholars at the Hong Kong Center. They have been a source of inspiration.

Thus it is with great enthusiasm that I have followed the work of my friend and colleague, Professor James T. Myers, and his determination to tell the story of the Catholic Church in China. I know the story has needed telling, and he is ideally equipped for the task.

Professor Myers has a background of training with some of the foremost China scholars. He studied and worked with, among others, Karl A. Wittfogel whose works on despotism and Liao Dynasty China are classics; with Franz Michael, a specialist in Manchu China and modern Chinese politics; and with Hsiao Kung-chu'uan, one of the world's leading scholars of traditional institutions of control in Chinese society. Myers has lived in China and travelled throughout the People's Republic many times. A Catholic himself, he can empathize and relate with the people whose stories he tells so vividly. In this volume he displays a capacity for thorough research and a knowledge of the nature and style of communist rule in China.

Readers will come away from reading *Enemies Without Guns* with a better appreciation of the dynamics of the communist system which Mao Zedong attempted to impose on his people. As Professor Myers makes clear, the horrors of the Cultural Revolution (1966–1976) were already abundantly present in the early Maoist operational code. Within the thought control system, which he organized for the domination of the world's most populous nation, Mao was able to present a "we-they" approach toward all human activities. Thus anyone who did not accept the Maoist version of "truth" became an "enemy of the

people"; they were "enemies without guns." Marxism-Leninism-Mao Zedong Thought does not acknowledge those two
essential ingredients which set humans apart—compassion and
concern for the spirit. In the Maoist apocalyptic view of the
world, and especially as it applied to China, "neutrality is only
a term for deceiving people."

Professor Myers chronicles the massive convulsive movements which were carried out under Mao's rule and details the
role and fate of the Catholic Church in China during those
tragic years. He notes:

> ...all these campaigns, this immense release of systemic energy
> was wasted in the futile effort to transform the character of the
> Chinese people according to Maoist revolutionary image, not at
> making China more prosperous or more modern...the revolutionary
> true believers who came to power with Mao Zedong in 1949 believed
> that such a revolutionary transformation could be more or less
> rapidly achieved. It was hubris, therefore, the pride and conceit of
> the revolutionary true believer, coupled with some stunningly bad
> political management, which can account for the failures of the
> Chinese communist revolution.

It was not surprising that Mao and his colleagues should
focus on the Catholic Church as a major enemy target for their
attempt to remake China. It offered a magnificent opportunity
to exploit traditional Chinese xenophobia, not only because of
the presence of foreigners and the linkages with the outside
world, but also because church doctrines and scriptures were
non-Chinese. The Church also constituted a formidable challenge in that it possessed its own internal organization and
communications system. These constituted an enemy fortress
to be destroyed by the Maoist true believers.

From the time of Matteo Ricci's arrival in China at the end
of the 16th century, Catholics played an important role in Chinese history. French Jesuits were members of the Manch ad-
ministrations of the Kang Hsi, Yung Cheng and Chien Lung
emperors in the 17th and 18th centuries. Although there were
less than 4 million Catholics in China in 1949, when Mao came
to power the influence of the church had been built through
its remarkable record in the fields of public service, human-
itarian institutions, medicine, and education. Chinese Catholics,
well educated and comforted by their religion of compassion,

became respected and influential community leaders.

The Maoists could never quite decipher how and why the Catholics remained so stubborn in their faith. But then, perhaps they did not appreciate that anyone who lived before Karl Marx or Chairman Mao was of any significance.

James Myers has woven a compelling tapestry of the 40 years of suffering and martyrdom of the Chinese Catholics under the Maoists. He shows in painstaking detail how the fate of the Church has been closely intertwined with the twists and turns of Chinese domestic politics. It is a story which helps us much better to grasp the nature and underlying ethos of the Maoist legacy in China.

Readers will be especially impressed by the documentary Appendices which have been added after several of the chapters. They carry a sense of immediacy and help to convey the human dimensions of this story of persecution and oppression of the Church. They also convey vividly the courage and integrity of the Catholic faithful among the Chinese.

No reader of Professor Myers' thorough and impressive work on the four decades of communist struggles with their rival "true believers" of the Catholic faith in China will be surprised by any accounts of the horrors of the Cultural Revolution. Again, the reader of *Enemies Without Guns* will understand the background and rationale of the system which Deng Xiaoping was supporting when he authorized turning guns on students seeking democracy in Tiananmen Square in Beijing on June 4, 1989.

Perhaps it is surprising to some that this complete story of the Beijing regime's struggle against the Catholic Church in China has not been told before. Of course, there are many individual accounts and memoirs and there are monographs which relate to the Church's fate during the many drives and campaigns that have been the essential pattern of Maoist rule. There are several reasons for the neglect. First, initially the communists exploited guilt complexes of westerners over their early imperialism and continuing privileges in China. Second, many Christians and western scholars were hesitant to antagonize the rulers in Beijing with seemingly negative accounts which could further encourage Chinese isolation. Again, there was always that "hope which springs eternal" that the communists would change their convictions and that faithful from the West could return to the China which they had cared about so much. Also, many of the sources have been scattered, and it has taken a formidable effort to pull them together.

This is what Professor Myers has done. He has drawn upon his many years as one of our respected China specialists and his many contacts among Chinese intellectuals and Catholic Church leaders. He has devoted unsparing energy to the travel and research necessary for this volume. In it he has combined his understanding of Chinese politics, communist patterns, and Catholic institutions.

The story is not a pleasant one, nor are the prospects for the Church in China at all encouraging as long as the Chinese Communist Party remains in power. But the resurgence of the Christian faith in the Soviet Union and Eastern Europe along with the loss of the communist faith there offers a bit of hope for the future of Chinese Catholics. As James Myers makes plain, they are capable of sustaining their faith through long trials.

(Dr. Richard L. Walker is one of America's most eminent specialists on East Asian Affairs. He was Ambassador to the Republic of Korea from 1981–1986. Walker is currently the James F. Byrnes Professor and Ambassador in Residence at the University of South Carolina.)

ONE

PORTENTS

The beginning of the end had come a week earlier with the arrests of Father Chrysostomus and Father Seraphim, and their trial before a people's court. Now, seven days later, on July 9, 1947, eighteen priests and their brother monks of Our Lady of Consolation Trappist Abbey gathered at 4 A.M. to celebrate Holy Mass. Though they could not yet know it, this would be the last time the monks would celebrate Mass together in their monastery. Thus began an ordeal which would finally see the magnificent monastery reduced to rubble and 33 of the monks become martyrs to their faith.[1]

Northwest of Beijing, about eighty miles, in the rugged mountains of what was formerly the southern Mongolian province of Chahar, a thousand meters above sea level, lies the stony plateau of Yang Jia Ping. It was here that the Trappist Cistercians came in 1883 to establish the first monastery of their order in the Far East. They gave their foundation the name "Our Lady of Consolation." In the Trappist tradition, the area chosen by the monks, near one of the numerous sections of the Great Wall protecting the approaches to Beijing, was remote and difficult to reach. Indeed, Yang Jia Ping was sufficiently isolated that a journey of three days by mule was required to reach the abbey from the nearest railway stop. When the Trappists first came to their hundred square-mile foundation it was virgin wilderness, and the early monks frequently encountered tigers and leopards. Over the years, the monks built a sizeable complex of buildings, surrounded by a wall twelve feet high. From a distance, the abbey resembled a good-sized village. The centerpiece of the abbey was its immense chapel, built in the Gothic style of the 13th century, twenty by fifty meters in size, and

1

supported by granite pillars one meter in diameter. The whole of the expansion of the monastery in the 1920s was overseen by a remarkable priest-architect named Alphonse Moerloose. Father Moerloose had already supervised the construction of one cathedral in China when he came to Yang Jia Ping in 1902. He was to stay there among the Trappists, living the life of a hermit, for more than 25 years.

As the years passed, the monastery prospered. Groves of almond and walnut trees were planted to provide for the support of the monks, and a huge cave, twelve feet wide and more than one hundred yards deep was hollowed out of the side of a mountain to provide storage for fruits and vegetables during the winter months. In the mid-1920s the community had grown to more than one hundred monks and it was decided that the site for a new foundation should be sought. By 1928 the new foundation was ready, near Shijiazhuang in southern Hebei Province. On April 29 of that year, seven monks from Our Lady of Consolation officially opened the monastery of Our Lady of Joy (Liesse).

Our Lady of Consolation was spared destruction during the anti-foreign and anti-missionary violence of the Boxer Rebellion (1899–1901), and the monks suffered few difficulties at the hands of the conquering Imperial Japanese Army. Though the monks encountered the Japanese army during its sweep through northern China, the Japanese never attempted to establish control over the rugged, mountainous area around Yang Jia Ping. From the fall of 1937, though, the monks found themselves increasingly in contact with units of the Chinese Communist Eighth Route Army under the command of General Ho Long, which had become active in the rural areas of north China.

The communist forces had seized the opportunity of the Japanese invasion of China to expand the scope of their operations in north and northwest China. From their rural base in Yan'an, Shaanxi Province, where they had settled following their epic 3,000-mile "Long March," they began to rebuild their shattered forces. Relying heavily on anti-Japanese patriotic sentiment, they rebuilt the Red Army, and soon began to enjoy successes in guerrilla operations over wider areas of northern China. As the areas under communist control grew in size, the communists' experience in civil administration increased as well. One of the first two communist border region governments was established in early 1939 in the Shaanxi-Hebei-Chahar border region, roughly including the area in which Yang Jia Ping was located. And it was in October of that year that the monks of Our Lady of Consolation had their first serious encounter with General Ho Long's troops.

Though the Communist army had grown in size and effectiveness, it remained an army which was poorly armed and equipped. Many soldiers, in fact, had no weapons at all. Thus, when it was rumored that the monks had a small arsenal of weapons at Yang Jia Ping, units of Ho Long's army were dispatched to demand that the weapons be surrendered. An army of 8,000 soldiers surrounded the monastery and negotiations began between the communist commander and the Trappist superior. The monastery did have a small cache of weapons intended to defend the community from roving bands of bandits. The monks, in fact, may have been better armed than the peasant army which confronted them. But fighting was not their way of life, and even had they somehow contrived to drive away the communist army, their situation in the midst of an area increasingly controlled by the Red Army would have been untenable. In the end, despite the misgivings of some members of the community, the arms were surrendered. Those monks who expressed such misgivings were quickly vindicated. As soon as the weapons were turned over, soldiers entered the monastery to make a thorough search for any arms which might have been held back. Father Anthony, who served the monastery as cellarer (the monk in charge of business and provisions for the community), and two of the monks who assisted him, were arrested. They were stripped of their clothing and hung on trees in the bitter cold, their thumbs and big toes tied together behind their backs. Soldiers fired rifles past their heads in order to frighten them into revealing the existence and location of additional stores of arms. There were no more arms, though, and at last, satisfied that they had obtained all that Our Lady of Consolation had to offer, the troops left Yang Jia Ping. In departing, however, the communist authorities left behind political cadres to keep an eye on the monks. As

Father Stanislaus Jen, historian of the community, later wrote, "The monks were now like silent lambs driven to slaughter."[2]

Many of the monks feared the end of monastic life under communist authority, and indeed, the education of the oblates—young men who lived in and served the monastery but had not taken monastic vows—was stopped at this time. Interference and harassment by communist officials was so great following the disarmament of the monastery that the abbot secretly devised a plan to send thirty of his monks south to Our Lady of Joy. This he did in the summer of 1940, though a brief period of relative harmony between the monks and the communist authorities persuaded him to call them back in 1941. No sooner were the monks back at Consolation, though, than the entire community was put under house arrest and prohibited from moving outside the immediate area. This condition of house arrest and surveillance continued up to the fateful summer of 1947.

By 1946 the final phase of the civil war between communist and nationalist forces for control of the Chinese mainland had begun. The nationalists enjoyed some apparent successes in the battle for north China by capturing in late 1946 the important railway terminal at Kalgan (Zhang Jia Kou), about 70 kilometers distance from Yang Jia Ping, and by overrunning the communist stronghold at Yan'an in March 1947. Such nationalist victories did little to weaken the communists significantly, however, and by the summer of 1947 the newly-renamed Chinese People's Liberation Army (PLA) was ready to launch the counteroffensive which would ultimately bring it to final victory. Communist military action was always accompanied by political agitation to raise the consciousness of the peasantry—especially the poorest of this group—in order to create a reliable base of rural support. The Chahar border region had been no exception to this practice, and the political cadres had spared no effort to turn the peasants against the monks.

Still, the Trappists had befriended the local people over the decades in time of need, and the peasants had been reluctant to seize monastic property for their own cultivation, or to cut wood in the land around the monastery. Perhaps for this reason, fearful of alienating the local populace, which was still seen as friendly to the monks, the communists had been reluctant to move more forcefully against the monastery. By mid-1947, however, the situation had changed. Political agitation and re-education efforts which had persistently painted the monks as feudal oppressors ruling over land rightfully belonging to the peasants, probably aided by a combination of pressure and fear, had started to bear fruit; and the peasants began to abandon their reluctance to take what they wanted from monastic lands. Perhaps this fact was merely coincidental and did not represent the removal of the last check on the communist authorities. Whatever may have been the reasons and motives of the communist officials, the summer of 1947 marked the end of the uneasy standoff between the Trappists and the PLA.

On July 1, two lay brothers who managed a small herd of cows and goats near the monastery were summoned before a People's Court. They were sentenced as "oppressors of the people," and made to hand over a number of animals. Members of the community saw this as a preliminary skirmish, and a test by the communists of the peasants' reliability. The following day, Fathers Chrysostomus and Seraphim were arrested and brought before another people's court for a trial which lasted for one week. Father Chrysostomus Chang was only 29 years old, but he had proven himself both able and sophisticated, and when the abbot had left China for Europe, he had designated Father Chrysostomus to care for the community should anything happen to the superior. In addition, Father Chrysostomus served the monastery as procurator, in which capacity he had been responsible for the seemingly endless negotiations with the communist officials. Father Seraphim was about ten years older than the young monk, and served Father Chrysostomus as an assistant in charge of the lay brothers.

The charges against both men were somewhat obscure as they involved "crimes against the people" going back to the Boxer Rebellion. The foreign powers had invaded China in 1900 to relieve the siege by the Boxers of the foreign legations in Beijing. By this act, the foreigners were said by the communists to have oppressed the people of North China, and somehow, it was charged, the monastery had been involved. Yang Jia Ping, in fact, had not been touched by the Boxer Rebellion, but one of the communists' other charges appears to have been partially true. It was alleged that Our Lady of Consolation had been built with funds provided by the indemnity which the Chinese Imperial Government had been forced to pay to the foreign powers under the terms of the Boxer Protocol of 1901. Because much of the Boxers' violence had been aimed at foreign missions, religious authorities received shares of the indemnity, and though the monks had suffered no violence at the hands of the Boxers, the Bishop of Beijing apparently used a portion of his share of this money to finance the new building at Yang Jia Ping in the 1920s.

But both of the priests were Chinese, not foreign. Indeed, only five of the 75 monks living at Consolation at the time were foreigners, so the aim of the court could not have been to relieve the area of the "foreign" domination of the monastery. The communists' motives appear to have been both more simple and more complex. As the trial ended on July 8, the monks were sentenced to hand over the furniture of the monastery, and later that evening, they were "fined" fifty blankets. Eventually, the monastery was completely vandalized and plundered. The simple motive thus appears to have been to loot the monastery of everything of any possible use. The more complex motive apparently involved drawing the local peasantry into a psychological commitment to participate in the violence against the monks who for so many decades had been their friends. This strategy of drawing peasants into an alliance or commitment against a common enemy would be repeated many times during the period of the land reforms following the communist victory in 1949. The commitment to violence—the stoning to death of landlords during the land reforms, for example—was the key commitment, for it represented the break with cultural attitudes, fears, and attachments of the old order and bound the actor somehow to his communist liberators, and to the values of the new order which the liberators represented.

That evening, July 8, peasants from some thirty nearby villages descended on the monastery to collect the fines. Monks were rousted out of their sleep as the bedding was dragged from their straw pallets. Virtually every scrap of cloth that could be carried away was taken, including the spare clothing of the monks. Soon the crowd turned to the church and its sacristy. Sacred vessels were seized along with the vestments of the priests. It was later learned that Christians had been among the looters, and that the sacred vessels and the best of the Mass vestments had been taken by faithful Chinese Catholics to be hidden for safekeeping. As the mob departed, a saddened community gathered for what would be its last celebration of Holy Mass. The Mass was barely ended, however, when the looters returned. This time mattresses were stripped from the beds for the valuable cloth which they contained, and napkins and eating utensils were taken from the hands of the monks as they ate their simple morning meal in the refrectory.

By dawn, a large company of soldiers had arrived, demanding entry to the monastery's storeroom. The monastery was renowned for its stores of foodstuffs. In past times of famine, as many as 3,000 hungry peasants had been provided food by the monks. Indeed, memorial tablets given to the monastery over the years by grateful peasants, and displayed on its walls, carried sentiments such as, "The benefits you have brought us are as weighty as the mountains." There were no grateful peasants to intercede for the monks now, however, as the troops carted away some ten tons of foodstuffs, all intended, presumably, for use by the army. Later that morning, with little left to take from the monastery, the soldiers turned their attention to the monks. The entire community was gathered together into the chapter room and imprisoned there. For several days they were kept in the now bare room under armed guard, sleeping on the stone floor and eating only one meal of weak soup each day.

At last, after five days, their captors were ready to bring the monks to trial. Two-by-two they were marched to a nearby field on the side of the mountain, where yet another People's Court—this with more than 1,000 spectators—awaited them. Once again the court focused its anger on Father Chrysostomus Chang and Father Seraphim Shu, this time together with Father Augustine Faure who was acting superior of the community. The charge against the monks was the same as it had been previously: that somehow the monastery had been responsible for the suppression of the Boxer Rebellion by the foreign powers. Father Seraphim was the first to be tried. He was questioned for several hours and repeatedly beaten, but he steadfastly refused to admit his guilt of the crimes of which he was accused. Finally, he was declared guilty and it was the turn of Father Chrysostomus. In addition to his other crimes, Father Chrysostomus was said to be guilty of having usurped the monastic lands and lived off the people. He, too, found it impossible to plead guilty, and though he was repeatedly beaten and clubbed, he refused to change his plea. When it came the turn of Father Augustine, the court had already levied fines against the monastery so enormous that the 70-year-old acting superior doubted they could be paid by ten monasteries the size of Our Lady of Consolation, and this he told the court. In return for his outspokenness, the judge ordered him clubbed as well. With the trial thus ended, the community was led back to the monastery where they were imprisoned under guard once more.

As before, the monks slept together on the stone floor and ate their one simple meal of thin soup each day. For ten days they went on in this fashion until, on the morning of July 23, they were led together into their chapel. They found the choir stalls filled with soldiers and the Church transformed into a courtroom. Under the sanctuary lamp, which was now extinguished, the communist officials had installed a table at which were seated the judges of the court. The rest of the Church was filled with spectators. Once again, Fathers Chrysostomus and Seraphim were questioned and beaten. A new charge was leveled against Father Seraphim. He was accused of going to certain villages during the anti-Japanese war to gather information which he then passed to the enemy. When the priest denied this new accusation, he was savagely beaten. The court then produced a witness against Father Seraphim. Maria Chang worked as a catechist in one of the nearby villages. She had apparently been told what was expected of her as a witness, yet when she was questioned on the witness stand, she refused to condemn Father Seraphim. It was not the accused priest, she said, but another priest who had already gone away from the monastery. And that priest did not come to her village to gain information for the Japanese enemy, but to bring the Sacraments to the dying. So enraged was the judge by this testimony which contradicted the charges against Father Seraphim, that he ordered Maria Chang chained to a pillar and clubbed. The soldiers beat the unfortunate woman with such enthusiasm that she soon sank unconscious to the floor. Both monks and soldiers assumed—incorrectly as it turned out—that Maria Chang had been beaten to death. They threw a cover over her body and dragged it from the church.

Father Chrysostomus was now interrogated, and when he once again refused to confess his crimes and those of the abbey, he, too, was savagely beaten. So severe was the beating administered to the young priest that two of his brothers rushed forward in despair to shield his body with their own. It was near the end of the day now, and time for the judge to pass sentence. After consulting the opinion of the crowd, the entire community of monks was sentenced to death. The sentence could not be carried out immediately, however, as it was necessary for the local officials to have the death penalty approved by higher authority. Meanwhile, the monks were stripped of their belts, scapulars, and religious medals. Those who wore glasses had already been forced to give them up. Many of the monks were shackled and all were put under armed guard to await confirmation of the death sentences.

During the ensuing two weeks, many of the monks were tried and interrogated individually, and the beatings and maltreatment continued. Finally, on August 12, the monks were gathered together again, not to be executed but to be led out of their monastery. Word had reached communist officials that nationalist troops were moving on the Kalgan rail-line toward the monastery. The communist commander proposed to lead his troops away from Yang Jia Ping and take the monks with him. It is still not entirely clear why the communist troops did not simply abandon the monastery and slip away into the mountains. The stated reason for taking the monks on what would become known as their death march was to show them the tremendous changes which had taken place in the surrounding villages under communist administration. It is certainly possible that some communist officials held the sincere belief that the mentality of the monks could be changed if only they were exposed to the truths of Marxism and the benefits of communist administration. The years ahead would witness many such apparently sincere attempts to change the mentality of unreconstructed Christians. The brutality exhibited toward the monks by their captors, however, would seem to indicate that the ultimate aim of the communist officials was not to win the Trappists over to the cause of Maoist communism.

The column set out at night, the priests and brothers loaded like pack animals with the food supplies which the army had taken from the monastery. The monks, many of them elderly, stumbled over the rugged terrain until noon the following day when they were finally allowed to rest and eat. Here, however, the plans changed. The nationalist forces, learning that the monastery had been abandoned, apparently halted their advance, and the communists decided to return to Yang Jia Ping. The communists waited with the monks in an abandoned house until August 18, and then began their march back to the abbey. On the return march to Yang Jia Ping, one of the elderly monks, an 82-year-old lay brother, succumbed to the hardships of the march. He was buried without ceremony.

Back at the abbey, those monks who had not previously been shackled were placed in manacles, and when there were no more manacles, the monks had their wrists bound with wire. Within ten days, two more elderly lay brothers had died. Suddenly, on the night of August 28, the monks were once again herded together and dragged outside. News had reached Yang Jia Ping that the nationalists were once more on the move, and the communists again decided to evacuate the monastery and take the monks with them. As before, the monks were loaded with heavy packs, and the company set out at a rapid pace. Most of the monks were still bound with wire or manacled, and they slipped and skidded over the narrow, rocky trails.

The monks were forced along all night and all of the next day without rest. By the end of the day they had travelled some thirty miles south of Yang Jia Ping to a village called Da Long Men near a section of the Great Wall. The following day the weather added to the monks' misery. All day they climbed steep, rocky trails in a torrential downpour accompanied by fierce, howling winds. The hardships of the march and the brutality of the guards were beginning to take their toll. The weakest and most elderly of the monks began to fall out, and their brethren had to make litters to carry them. For several more days the party was driven into the mountains of Hebei Province. When they stopped in villages to pass the night, the monks were forced to sleep in pigpens.

By September 8, the monks had been marched as far as the village of Deng Jia Yu. Along the way they had lost the French priest, Father William Camborieu. One of the bearers carrying Father William's litter had slipped on the rocky trail, allowing the priest's head to be cut open on a jagged rock. The old monk bled to death as the party hurried on through the dark. At Deng Jia Yu the monks were kept for 25 days. Most were housed in tumbled-down buildings with little protection against the bitter north China cold. Others, including Father Chyrsostomus, were again forced to stay in pigpens. About ten of the monks were kept in solitary confinement. All lived in conditions of incredible filth, and those who had their hands unbound tried to help their shackled and bound brothers remove lice and other vermin from their unwashed bodies. It was later reported that several of the monks whose hands were bound had almost literally been eaten to death by the vermin which afflicted them.

At Deng Jia Yu the public trials were resumed. The monks once again had to face the same charges and endure the same brutal beatings. The hardships and brutality at Deng Jia Yu claimed the lives of five more Chinese lay brothers and three priests. One of the priests, Father Alphonsus L'Heureux, was the object of special brutality. Father Alphonsus was a former Jesuit theologian who had received permission from his Order to retire to Our Lady of Consolation to live the remainder of his life in prayer and penance. Perhaps it was his Jesuit training and the force and clarity with which he defended his faith that earned him the special wrath of his captors, for he had been one of the most outspoken critics of the mistreatment of his brothers. Father Alphonsus' hands had been bound together behind his back with steel wire for more than one month when he arrived at Deng Jia Yu. His wrists had swollen, and the bones were visible in the horrible wounds. In addition, Father Alphonsus had developed a serious case of dysentery. Because he could not help himself, and no one else was allowed to help him, his pants, which he was not permitted to change, were covered with his own feces. He was made to live apart from the other monks, in the open, without shelter or cover, though for a time one of the younger monks was permitted to help him eat. When it became apparent that his spirit was not yet broken, his captors prohibited the other monks from helping Father Alphonsus, forcing him to eat his meager rations from a bowl like a dog.

At last, when it became clear that Father Alphonsus was near death, one of the guards took pity, unbound his hands, and permitted the monks to carry him into a hut with Father Sebastian. Father Sebastian heard the old priest's confession and gave him absolution. A few moments later he died. The scene has been recorded by Father Patrick J. Scanlan, once a member of the community of Our Lady of Consolation, and a close friend of Father Alphonsus, based upon letters from eyewitnesses. When the young Chinese guard went to tell the other monks of Father Alphonsus' death, he was said to have stated: "That man died very peacefully. He looks like the other man on the 'ten-figure' frame (the Chinese character for ten is a cross) in the Yang Jia Ping chapel." Father Sebastian wrote: "We took him out and laid him on a stretcher. He did not look like a corpse at all, smiling as he was, with both hands crossed over his breast. Bending on one knee, we took up the stretcher and as we walked, we looked at his smiling face and we prayed for him. When we reached the slope of the mountain, we dug a hole only about one foot deep and buried him, because it was raining and the soldiers would not wait."[3]

It was about the time of Father Alphonsus' death that word reached the prisoners that the monastery at Yang Jia Ping had been destroyed. Indeed, the communists made the special effort to have three of the younger and stronger monks marched back to Yang Jia Ping to confirm the destruction with their own eyes. Even with the passage of so many years, it is still not entirely clear who was responsible for reducing the monastery to ruins. Most believed the Red Army to be responsible for mining and burning the monastery. But there is also the possibility that Our Lady of Consolation may have been destroyed by nationalist commanders who feared that it might be turned into a stronghold by the communists.

The beginning of October was nearing, and it seems to have become clear that the communist authorities who held the monks were not going to receive permission to execute them all. Consequently, they began making plans to get the monks off their hands. First, the entire group was moved to another village, and then small groups of brothers and lay brothers began to be released. None of the priests were released, however, and in the months that followed, a number of them met death. Two, Fathers Augustine and Antonious, are believed to have been poisoned. Others succumbed to infections brought on by their wounds, or to various diseases resulting from the beatings, hardships, and exposure. For two, at least, a more formal end awaited.

The two unfortunate priests, Father Chrysostomus and Father Seraphim, together with four brother monks, were marched back to a village near Yang Jia Ping to be tried once again by a People's Court. Both priests and the four brothers persisted in their refusal to cooperate with their captors, and once again they were sentenced to death. It appears that the local communist authorities must have had permission to treat this small group as special because, in the end, the sentences were carried out. One account of the executions has the condemned killed by having large stones dropped on them, crushing their skulls. Another account has them dragged to death. It seems most likely, however, that the six were simply shot.

Thus ends the story of the abbey at Yang Jia Ping. It would not rise from the ashes of destruction to be reestablished elsewhere, as was later the case with its sister house, Our Lady of Joy, which eventually found a new home at Lantao (Hong Kong). Of the nineteen priests at the abbey, fourteen were killed, together with nineteen brothers. Four of the surviving priests from Our Lady of Consolation made their way to Beijing, which was not yet under communist control, where they established a dairy. With the help of a number of their brothers from Our Lady of Joy, and the addition of several new monks, they tried to carry on their lives in the Trappist-Cistercian tradition.

The Trappist dairy prospered, even reportedly providing milk for Mao Zedong after 1949, until it was confiscated by the government in 1954.

The destruction of Our Lady of Consolation was not, however, merely an isolated incident. Nor were the Trappists the only victims of anti-Catholic violence during the bloody winter of 1947–1948. On August 31, 1947, in Chifeng Prefecture about 200 miles north of Beijing, Father Paul Shih Kuang-chiu, a prisoner of local communist authorities, was stripped to the waist. A man sat on his chest while others dragged him by a rope tied to his feet. He was dragged over rough paths, rocks, and *gaoliang* (sorghum) stubble for two hours, part of the time by Christians who were forced to participate. Finally he was shot dead.[4] Father Joseph Chang suffered the same fate. For his refusal to apostatize, Father Chang was made to stand motionless for days and nights, and then to sit over a coil of burning cord until his skin blackened and cracked. Finally, along with Father Shih, he had a rope tied around his ankles and was dragged over rough ground until he died.[5] Father Francis Chu of a nearby village was dragged for twelve hours in order to force him to apostatize. He, too, was later killed.[6] Father Camille Hsia, a 70-year-old priest was dragged over the fields in the same way. Witnesses reported that his body was covered with blood and his flesh badly torn, but it was not known for certain if he died. All together in the diocese of Chifeng, seven priests were known to have been killed and four others jailed or missing.[7]

On January 17, 1948, in the Fushun Diocese of Manchuria, Father Maurus Pai was shot and killed by communist soldiers and his body thrown into a ditch.[8] On February 15, about fifty miles from Beijing, Fathers Joseph Li and Simon Li were shot and killed after being paraded through villages and humiliated for several days.[9]

In Linxing Prefecture, Shandong Province, the violence began in the summer of 1947 as it had at Yang Jia Ping. On July 12, three priests were arrested and taken to the county jail. On July 23, two of the priests were taken out for a public trial. At the trial, one of the men, Father Ch'en Hsing-hua, was struck on the head with an axe and while unconscious, was beaten to death with sticks. His companion, Father Li Tung-ming was taken back to jail. At the beginning of September, Father Li was again taken out of jail. This time his communist captors arranged no trial. He was flogged with thorn-imbedded scourges and then dragged to death. The third priest remained in jail, his death deferred until a later date.[10]

In Shanxi Province, a Franciscan priest, Father Leonides Bruns, was killed on October 25, 1947. He was brought to public trial, and when he refused to confess the crimes of which he was accused, he was beaten violently with sticks, many of the bystanders being forced to participate. When it was believed that the priest was dead, six other people were tried and executed in the same way. Following these executions, it was learned that Father Bruns still lived. He was thereupon killed with a bayonet, decapitated, and his heart cut out.[11]

These incidents represent only a small sample of the cases of reported anti-Catholic persecution in the communist-controlled areas during the period prior to the final victory over the nationalists in 1949. Indeed, the Shanghai journal *China Missionary* in July 1948, published an "incomplete" list of 87 priests and other religious who had met death at the hands of the communists over the previous eighteen months.[12] By the fall of 1948, however, the anti-religious violence had subsided. In May of that year, Mao Zedong had moved his headquarters and those of the Party Central Committee from northern Shaanxi to Hebei Province in anticipation of an early victory over the nationalists. At this critical juncture in the Chinese Civil War, as nationwide victory for the communist forces appeared ever more likely, the harsh and aggressive persecution of Catholics and other Christians abated.

In his long 1945 work "On Coalition Government," Mao Zedong had written: "All religions are permitted in China's Liberated Areas, in accordance with the principle of freedom of religious belief. All believers in Protestantism, Catholicism, Islam, Buddhism, and other faiths enjoy protection of the People's government so long as they are abiding by its laws. Everyone is free to believe or not to believe; neither compulsion nor discrimination is permitted."[13] As we have seen from the treatment of Catholics in the liberated areas, this policy was honored more in the breach than in the observance. Yet, as the likelihood of a final communist victory over the nationalists loomed ever larger, the policy of freedom of religious belief was apparently seen as one which should, as a practical consideration, be more strictly enforced than had been the case during the brutal period just ended.

Mao had always been a cautious and practical man, and beginning in January 1948, he had authored a series of essays and directives which dealt with the problem of "leftist adventurism," by which he meant the tendency of communist cadres toward incautious acts attempting to push the revolution forward too rapidly.[14] As he began to see nationwide victory within his grasp, Mao turned his attention to the problems of Party consolidation, increasing agricultural production, and building the broadest possible base of support for the final stage of the civil war. Though he did not mention this fact in his writings, it is entirely possible that Mao had his eye on the Americans during this period as well. The United States, in an effort of deep soul-searching, was in the process of disengagement from the Chinese Civil War. Severe disillusionment with the nationalist war effort and with the leadership of Generalissimo Chiang Kai-shek was evident both in Washington and in the U.S. Embassy in Nanking. By mid-1948, Ambassador John Leighton Stuart would cable Secretary of State George C. Marshall: "Within the last month the prestige and authority of the Central Government has sunk to an all time low."[15] Under such circumstances, the last thing Mao would have wished for would be greater, rather than less, U.S. involvement in China on the side of the nationalists. And dragging helpless missionaries over the ground until they were dead was an activity which could only serve to inflame the passions of U.S. politicians.

Mao also looked forward to the critical period of national consolidation which would follow victory, and domestically, therefore, for the present he sought not to alienate unnecessarily even those groups such as merchants, rich peasants and intellectuals with whom he would deal brutally when the time was more propitious. One of his directives Mao opened with the words, "Do not be impetuous."[16] "Reactionaries must be killed," he said, "but killing without discrimination is strictly forbidden."[17] And he further warned that, "In trying criminals, a People's Court or democratic government must not use physical violence."[18] By such admonitions, Mao expressed no moral revulsion at the idea of large-scale killing, rather he articulated a tactical principle intended to enhance the success of his movement. In early 1948, Mao could already write that, "the enemy is now completely isolated." But, warned Mao, "his isolation is not tantamount to our victory. If we make mistakes in policy, we shall be unable to win victory. To put it concretely, we shall fail if we make, and do not correct, mistakes of principle...."[19] As we shall see, the principles to which Mao referred were tactical and opportunistic, not, as some Christians dared to hope, principles of some higher ethical or philosophical order which would have made possible a more permanent accommodation between Christians and communists. The editors of *China Missionary* asked whether the end of the persecution in 1948 might "signify an awakening of the communist leaders to the fact violent persecution of religion always backfires, by disillusioning supporters at home and antagonizing public opinion abroad."[20]

It did not, and the bloody winter of 1947–1948 was only a portent of things to come.

NOTES

1. The story of the destruction of Our Lady of Consolation comes principally from two authors, Rev. M. Stanislaus Jen, O.C.S.O., who was educated at Our Lady of Consolation and went to Our Lady of Joy in 1940, and Rev. Patrick J. Scanlan who was a monk at Our Lady of Consolation from 1938 until his internment by the Japanese in 1943. See: M. Stanislaus Jen, O.C.S.O., *The History of Our Lady of Consolation*, Hong Kong: n.p., 1978; Patrick J. Scanlan, *Stars in the Sky*, Hong Kong: Trappist Publications, 1984. Additional information about the destruction of Our Lady of Consolation may be found in Rev. M. Stanislaus Jen, O.C.S.O., *The History of Our Lady of Joy (Liesse) Written For Its Golden Jubilee of Foundation*, Hong Kong: Catholic Truth Society, 1978. Also: Postulatio Generalis, O.C.S.O., *Dossier "China" pro Capitulo Generali 1980*, Montecistello, Rome: Stampato Presso Eurstampa, 1980.

2. M. Stanislaus Jen, O.C.S.O., *The History of Our Lady of Consolation, Yang Jia Ping, op. cit.*, 18.

3. Patrick J. Scanlan. *Stars in the Sky, op. cit.*, 295.

4. *China Missionary*, Shanghai, vol. 1, no. 1, March 1948, 108.

5. *Ibid.*, 108–109. Also *cf. China Missionary*, Shanghai, vol. 1, no. 5. October 1948, 626–627.

6. *Ibid.*

7. *Ibid.*

8. *China Missionary*, Shanghai, vol. 1, no. 2, May 1948, 220.

9. *Ibid.*, 221.

10. *Ibid.*

11. *Ibid.*

12. *China Missionary*, Shanghai, vol. 1, no. 3, July 1948, 346–348.

13. Mao Zedong. "On Coalition Government," *Selected Works of Mao Tse-tung*, vol. III. Beijing: Foreign Language Press, 1965, 313.

14. See, for example, Mao Zedong. "On Some Important Problems of the Party's Present Policy," January 18, 1948, *Selected Works of Mao Tse-tung*, vol. IV. Beijing: Foreign Language Press, 1967, 181–189; "Different Tactics For Carrying Out the Land Law In Different Areas," February 3, 1948, *Ibid.*, 193–195; "Correct the 'Left' Errors In Land Reform Propaganda," February 11, 1948, *Ibid.*, 197–199; "Essential Points In Land Reform in the Liberated Areas," February 15, 1948, *Ibid.*, 201–202; "On the Question of the National Bourgeoisie and the Enlightened Gentry," March 1, 1948, *Ibid.*, 207–210; "Speech at a Conference of Cadres in the Shansi-Suiyuan Liberated Area," April 1, 1948, *Ibid.*, 227–239.

15. *The China White Paper, August 1949*, [Originally issued as *United States Relations With China, With Special Reference to the Period 1944–1949*,

(Department of State Publication 3573, Far East Series 30)], Reissued with the Original Letter of Transmittal to President Truman from Secretary of State Dean Acheson and a New Introduction by Lyman Van Slyke. Stanford, CA: Stanford University Press, 1967, 872.

16. Mao Zedong. "Essential Points in Land Reform in the Liberated Areas," *Selected Works of Mao Tse-tung*, vol. IV. Beijing: Foreign Language Press, 1967, 201.

17. *Ibid.*, 202.

18. Mao Zedong. "Speech At A Conference of Cadres in the Shansi-Suiyuan Liberated Area," *Selected Works of Mao Tse-tung*, vol. IV, Beijing: Foreign Language Press, 1967, 229.

19. Mao Zedong. "On The Policy Concerning Industry and Commerce," *Selected Works of Mao Tse-tung*, vol. IV, Beijing: Foreign Language Press, 1967, 204.

20. *China Missionary*, Shanghai, vol. 1, no. 7. December 1948, 835.

TWO

CHAIRMAN MAO ON THE PEOPLE'S DEMOCRATIC DICTATORSHIP

> Religion is a historical phenomenon which exists in human society at a certain stage of its development. It appears, develops, and then dies out.[1]

O f the myriad problems facing China's communist leaders since the establishment of the People's Republic of China (PRC) on October 1, 1949, it is certain that religion, or the religious "problem" as they have continued to regard it, has not been at the top of the list. Yet sizeable resources, human, organizational and otherwise, have been dedicated to policing this otherwise seemingly trivial activity. How can we possibly explain that such resources, which by any rational calculation could have been put to far more important uses, were allocated to control, contain, reshape, and, hopefully, eliminate religion from Chinese society? And why was the Catholic Church singled out for special viciousness and hostility by the communist authorities?

The answer to the first question, I believe, lies in the nature of the sanctioning ideology of the PRC, namely: Marxism-Leninism-Mao Zedong Thought. Unlike many other legitimizing ideologies or "authorizing myths," but like the sanctioning ideologies of other Leninist-communist states, Marxism-Leninism Mao Zedong Thought claims to deal with "truth." That is, this body of ideas does not simply explain and validate why the ruling elite occupies its position as would be the case with a sanctioning ideology such as democratic theory. Marxism-Leninism-Mao Zedong Thought also claims to understand "scientifically" human history, the human condition, and the future of mankind. Moreover, the ruling elite, the members of the Chinese Communist Party (CCP), are said legitimately to occupy their leading positions due to their superior understanding of this "scientific" doctrine.

A sanctioning ideology of this type is by its nature all-encompassing, and its coherence is thus potentially threatened by ideological competition. The governmental institutions which are legitimized by such an ideology, therefore, will make every effort to prevent the randomization of behavior which might lead to the emergence of ideological innovations and critiques. Such a government will also do everything possible to bring under governmental control those institutions such as the social and behavioral sciences, and philosophy and the arts, whose job it is normally to innovate new responses to the empirical world.[2] Religion by its very nature must come into conflict with this type of sanctioning ideology: religious faith because it insists on the truth of the revealed word of God, and religious institutions because they hold, teach, and propagate this truth. While two different versions of the truth need not find themselves locked in deadly conflict, such conflict may be entirely predictable if governmental institutions which wield the power to apply the ultimate sanctions of torture, deprivation and death base their claim to legitimacy on their own notion of truth. The cultural historian Morse Peckham has observed that "Killing is the most effective method of social control," at least as far as the victim is concerned.[3] A dead person, after all, cannot challenge the coherence or validity of the sanctioning ideology. And killing, as we can already see from the examples cited above, along with the application of the other sanctions of force and violence, has been an important strategy in the PRC for maintaining the preeminence of Marxism-Leninism-Mao Zedong Thought against all rivals, real or imagined, actual or potential, and religion prominent among them.

So far as the Catholic Church in particular was concerned, because of its hierarchical organization and the existence of a "head" in Rome, the Church was perceived to be a greater threat than other religious institutions, with the possible exception of Islam which, by virtue of the extremely large number of its adherents, posed a different sort of political problem for the government. Moreover, because the Catholic Church in China, like Catholic churches everywhere, professed obedience to the Holy Father in Rome and accepted the authority of the Holy See, the Church was seen as a paradigm of foreign "imperialist" exploitation of China. Attacks against the Church over the years, therefore, were generally two-dimensional; first, against the beliefs themselves, which were attacked as poisoning the minds of the people; and second, against the foreign connection which was said to represent imperialist meddling in Chinese affairs.

With these few introductory remarks in mind, let us consider the roots of the Chinese communist view of religion, and see how these ideas were played out in the context of the political system of the PRC.

Religion, The "Spiritual Gin"

The basic communist position on religion was formulated by Lenin on the basis of ideas which he had inherited from Marx and Engels. "Religion," wrote Lenin, "is the opium of the people—this dictum of Marx is the cornerstone of the whole Marxist view on religion."[4] According to this view, religion created in the minds of men a false view of the world. It was, wrote Engels, "the fantastic mirror image of human things in the human mind,"[5] and as such it was used by the ruling class to dull the minds of the workers and to divert them from their true historical mission, the march to the communist revolutionary millennium. The English bourgeoisie, said Engels, "had now taken part in keeping down the 'lower orders,' the great producing mass of the nation, and one of the means employed for that purpose was the influence of religion."[6] Lenin expressed the same idea in more blunt language: "Religion," he wrote, "is a kind of spiritual gin in which the slaves of capital drown their human shape and their claims to any decent human life."[7]

As materialists, Marxist-Leninists were implacably hostile to religion, and though the doctrine held that religion, as the product of particular historical conditions, would eventually die out, the Leninists were not content simply to await this eventuality. Religion, taught Lenin, must be fought in the interests of class struggle and revolution. In pursuit of this objective, the Soviet communists waged a relentless struggle against religious belief and religious institutions. Much of the pattern of anti-religious activities in the early years of the U.S.S.R was to be repeated in China many years later. The Soviet government, among other measures, employed anti-religious propaganda; arrested priests and other religious and charged them with a variety of criminal activities; abolished lay religious organizations; nationalized the religious schools and prohibited or severely restricted religious instruction to the young; placed heavy financial pressure on the churches through punitive taxation and/or confiscation of church properties; and established state-sponsored religious organizations under the control of the government. All of this, as we shall see, would become very familiar in the PRC after 1949.

Mao Zedong's views on religion were not different in any substantial way from those of Lenin, though the religious policies of the Chinese communists were employed in a rather different cultural context. There were, for example, no sizeable number of Christians in China as a percentage of the total population. The total number of Catholics in China at the time of the communist victory in 1949 was less than 3.5 million. The most popular religion in China was a combination of Taoism and ancestor worship. This body of beliefs and customs could scarcely be called a creed, as there was no formal church organization and no body of doctrine to which all of the followers subscribed. Yet, these Taoist practices were intimately connected with the rhythm of life—particularly in rural China—and as such, were especially hard to attack and to uproot. In addition, though the Catholic Church had enjoyed a presence in China since the 16th century, the Church was still considered by the communists to be a "foreign" import, and was not viewed as a homegrown institution like the Orthodox Church in the U.S.S.R. When Mao viewed the religious "problem" in China, therefore, he saw two main tasks: First, achieving a cultural transformation in the Chinese countryside in order to remove the influence of religious "superstition," and second, ridding the country of the harmful influence of foreign religious "imperialism."

The society in which China's communist revolution took root was characterized by Mao Zedong as colonial, semi-colonial, and semi-feudal. Since the time of the Opium War in the mid-19th century, with the coming of the western powers and the penetration into China of western capital, China had become, in Mao's view, both semi-colonial and semi-feudal. China had not been completely colonized by the "imperialists," nor had the 3,000-year-old "feudal" system—as characterized by the Marxists—been completely transformed by the inflow of western capital. And with the invasion of China by the Japanese in 1937, China had acquired elements of colonialism as well. Hence, the formula repeated by Mao again and again in several of his major essays: the China of the Maoist revolution was colonial, semi-colonial, and semi-feudal.[8] In this situation, wrote Mao, the Chinese people were victims, among many other things, of the "cultural imperialism" of the West, and especially of the western missionaries:

> ...the imperialist powers have never slackened their efforts to poison the minds of the Chinese people. This is their policy of cultural aggression. And it is carried out through missionary work, through establishing hospitals and schools, publishing newspapers and inducing Chinese students to study abroad. Their aim is to train intellectuals who will serve their interests and dupe the people.[9]

There was in China, said Mao, an imperialist culture, "which is a reflection of imperialist rule, or partial rule, in the political and economic fields. This culture is fostered not only by the cultural organizations run directly by the imperialists in China but by a number of Chinese who have lost all sense of shame. Into this category falls all culture embodying a slave ideology."[10]

Clearly the Christian religion introduced into China by foreign "imperialists" fell into this category of slave ideology, and as such it was to be attacked and destroyed. Yet Mao, like Lenin before him, was not only a revolutionary visionary, but an extremely practical man as well. He understood well the necessity and the value of temporary alliances with those classes and groups which he would eventually seek to attack and destroy.

In a revealing discussion of the rich peasants in China's countryside, Mao had this to say:

> The rich-peasant form of production will remain useful for a definite period. Generally speaking, they might make some contribution to the anti-imperialist struggle of the peasant masses and stay neutral in the agrarian revolutionary struggle against the landlords. Therefore we should not regard the rich peasants as belonging to the same class as landlords and should not *prematurely* adopt a policy of liquidating the rich peasantry.[11] [Emphasis added.]

Rich peasants would be liquidated, there was no mistaking that point, but it should only be done when the time was right. The same sort of temporary alliances could be made with other groups as well. Mao made it clear, however, that forming an alliance of convenience with a particular group or class did not imply an acceptance of the aims, values, or interests of that group. Mao applied the same principle to the churches:

> In the field of political action communists may form an anti-imperialist and anti-feudal united front with some idealists and even religious people, but we can never approve of their idealism or religious doctrines.[12]

Religion was thus viewed as the product of particular historical conditions and a tool of the ruling class which would disappear when the conditions were transformed and the ruling class overthrown. Yet both Lenin and Mao came to recognize, as a practical matter, that old ideas and habits might linger well into the new historical, revolutionary epoch. The demise of religion would thus have to be pressed forward and hastened by the Communist Party as the most advanced representative of the revolutionary forces. But both men also realized that there would be times when, for reasons of expediency, the attack on religion should be slowed down or even stopped. And, as we have noted, there might even be times when temporary alliances could be formed with religious believers.

Religious policy in the PRC has thus shifted over time from harsh to permissive with, however, the principle always in mind that at some point in the future, however distant, religious belief and practice would disappear. Even in more recent times, when, as we shall see below, a new era of religious toleration has been said to reign, the party has not wavered from this principle. A 1984 *Beijing Review* article titled "Religious Policy in Full Force," stated the principle in this way:

> Although Chinese communists are atheists, they advocate freedom of religious belief. This is because they see religion as a historical phenomenon in human society, and believe it develops along the inevitable process of emergence, growth, and dying out.[13]

This formula had been developed at length in a major party theoretical statement on religion published in the Party theoretical journal *Hong Qi* (Red Flag) in 1982:

> Religion is an inevitable phenomenon at a certain stage of human history. This phenomenon has to undergo the stages of emergence, development, and withering away.[14]

And, while it was said that the conditions which gave rise to the development of religion have been eliminated since the communist revolution, "the development of people's ideology always falls behind social existence (therefore) it is inevitable that religion will exist and have an impact on some people for a long time in a socialist society."[15] The article further asserted that, "we communists are atheists and we advocate and will propagate atheism among the masses of the people. However, at the same time, we understand that it is not only ineffective but also harmful to use simple and forceful methods to handle ideological problems of the people and problems concerning the spiritual world of the people, especially the problem of religious belief."[16] This was not to be equated, however, with complete religious freedom. Said the editors of *Hong Qi*, "We must never allow the practice of forcing youngsters below the age of 18 to be converted to some religion or to be sent to some temples to monks or to learn religious scriptures.... Furthermore, we must in no way allow anybody to use religion to oppose the Party's leadership and the socialist system or to use religion to carry out propaganda against Marxism-Leninism-Mao Zedong Thought."[17]

There has not always been a reluctance to use "simple and forceful" methods in dealing with religious believers, as we have already seen and shall see again. Indeed, it is not clear that the spirit of this policy statement has ever been followed completely. Nevertheless, the *Hong Qi* article sums up fairly well the official Chinese communist position on religious belief which has been advocated in one fashion or another since the 1930s.

"Citizens Enjoy Freedom of Religious Belief"

In spite of the very clear position that communists are atheists and, as such, implacably hostile to religion, the Chinese communists have always maintained that they would, nevertheless, protect the rights of religious believers. Long before the communist victory in the Chinese mainland, the Constitution of the Chinese Soviet Republic, adopted in November 1931, provided that, "The Soviet Government of China guarantees true religious freedom to the workers, peasants, and the toiling population."[18] But, in keeping with the general principles described above, the Constitution also provided that, "All Soviet citizens shall enjoy the right to engage in anti-religious propaganda. No religious institution of the imperialists shall be allowed to exist unless it shall comply with Soviet law."[19]

Similar expressions of a policy of freedom of religion, or more specifically freedom of "religious belief," have been included in all of the various constitutional documents adopted since the founding of the PRC. The General Program adopted by the First Plenary Session of the Chinese People's Political Consultative Conference in 1949, the document which served as a state constitution prior to the election of the First National People's Congress and the adoption of the first PRC Constitution in 1954, declared in Article 5 that, among other freedoms, the people of the PRC enjoyed the freedom of "religious belief." But, it was stipulated in Article 7 that, "The People's Republic of China shall suppress all counterrevolutionary activities, [and] severely punish all...counterrevolutionary elements who collaborate with imperialism, commit treason against the fatherland and oppose the cause of people's democracy."[20] This latter was to constitute the most widely used category of charges levelled against Chinese Catholics.

The first Constitution of the PRC, adopted by the First National People's Congress in September 1954, contained similar language. Article 88 stated simply, "Citizens of the People's Republic of China enjoy freedom of religious belief." The Revised Draft Constitution of 1970—the so-called Lin

Biao Constitution because it proclaimed Lin Biao as Mao's anointed successor, a document which was adopted by the Communist Party Central Committee but never enacted into law by the National Congress—declared in its Article 28 that citizens enjoy, "freedom to believe in religion and freedom not to believe in religion and to propagate atheism."[21] The Revised Draft Constitution of 1973, which removed any reference to the now-dead Lin Biao (a document, which like the previous draft, emanated from the Party Central Committee and was never enacted into law), contained identical language about religious belief, disbelief, and the propagation of atheism,[22] as did the PRC Constitutions of 1975,[23] and 1978.[24]

The PRC Constitution currently in force at the time of this writing (1990) was adopted in 1982 by the Fifth National People's Congress. The principles of "religious freedom" are in no way substantially different from those cited above, though the 1982 Constitution does treat the matter in somewhat more detail. Article 36 reads as follows:

> Citizens of the People's Republic of China enjoy freedom of religious belief.
>
> No state organ, public organization, or individual may compel citizens to believe in, or not to believe in, any religion; nor may they discriminate against citizens who believe in, or do not believe in, any religion.
>
> The state protects normal religious activities. No one may make use of religion to disrupt public order, impair the health of citizens, or interfere with the educational system of the state.
>
> Religious bodies and religious affairs are not subject to any foreign domination.[25]

Reference to the right to "propagate atheism" is absent from the 1982 Constitution, but Article 24 contains this language:

> The state advocates the civic virtues of love for the motherland, for the people, for labor, for science, and for socialism; it educates the people in patriotism, collectivism, internationalism, and communism and in dialectical and historical materialism; it combats capitalist, feudalist, and other decadent ideas.[26]

The constitutional position of religion in the PRC thus remains substantially unchanged. Freedom of religious "belief" is protected, though the state pledges to make every effort to see that such "decadent ideas" are eventually eliminated. Likewise, the state promises to protect "normal" religious activities so long as they do not "disrupt" or "interfere with" the more important interests of the state. And, finally, special note is taken of the Roman Catholic Church with the prohibition of "foreign domination" of religious affairs, which describes the official view of the relationship of Chinese Catholics to the Holy See in Rome.

The Chinese government and the CCP have gone to some trouble in this latest constitution to create at least the pretense of religious freedom in the PRC, however limited that notion of freedom might be. But what, after all, does such a concept of religious freedom really mean?

"Adhere to the People's Democratic Dictatorship and Follow the Socialist Road"

Considering the somewhat cavalier disregard with which China's ruling elite have treated their various state constitutions, one might well wonder why they bother to create a constitution at all. Clearly the concept of constitutionalism in the PRC is fundamentally different from that of the western constitutional democracies. In considering the concept of religious freedom, this point must be clearly understood. The Chinese Constitution, in theory as well as in practice, is fundamentally different from, let us say, the Constitution of the United States.

In the United States one constitution has served for 200 years. Important changes have been introduced, to be sure: the granting of federal citizenship in the 14th Amendment and, the income tax and female suffrage, for example; yet the same document has continued to provide fundamental guidelines and serve as the basic law of the American republic over this long period of time. In terms of rights, the most important function of the Constitution is to place limitations on the power of government. The 1st Amendment to the U.S. Constitution begins with the words, "Congress shall make no law..." The concept embedded in this statement is that citizens have rights which exist as a condition of their personhood, rights which may not be violated by the government for any reason. In addition, the government which the U.S. Constitution establishes does not have its own pre-existing agenda, but exists rather to serve the needs and interests of its citizens. This principle is clearly articulated in both the U.S. Declaration of Independence and in the Preamble to the Constitution.

The U.S. Constitution provides both substantive and procedural guarantees which protect individual freedom. If, as Hobbes suggested, liberty consists of "power cut up in pieces," the U.S. Constitution may be considered a model of the division and separation of power to insure that the inalienable rights of its citizens cannot be violated by the state. Perhaps central to this notion is the establishment of an independent judiciary with the power to review and overturn acts both of the legislature and of the executive which threaten to violate these rights.

In the Chinese view of constitutionalism, none of these principles is recognized. First of all, the Constitution of the PRC is not fundamental law, but a programmatic political document. In the section above, we referred to seven different constitutional documents created in a span of less than forty years. Each of these represented a slightly different set of power arrangements and policy decisions agreed upon by the power-holding elite of the CCP. Rights granted in such a constitution are not inalienable and inherent in the person of the citizen, but rather are granted by the state. Neither in theory nor in practice does the citizen of the PRC possess rights which the state may not violate.

Indeed, the Marxist-Leninist concept of "democracy" turns western democratic theory on its head. Power in the Chinese system does not flow from a sovereign people who make a certain grant of power to the state; power flows from the state which grants to the people such freedoms as may be deemed appropriate at any given moment. Nor does the state exist to serve the will of its citizens; the state has its own purpose which is to achieve socialism and communism, and this purpose takes precedence over the exercise of any individual rights. All of the constitutional documents cited above contain some statement as to the purpose of the state in the preamble. The 1982 Constitution describes the purpose in this way:

> The basic task of the nation in the years to come is to concentrate its effort on socialist modernization...adhere to the people's democratic dictatorship and follow the socialist road...[and] step by step to turn China into a socialist country...[27]

And lest there be any doubt about the subordinate nature of the people's rights, Article 51, after the enunciation of the rights of Chinese citizens in the previous eighteen Articles, issues this qualifying statement about the primacy of the interests of the state:

> The exercise by citizens of the People's Republic of China of their freedoms and rights may not infringe upon the interests of the state, of society, and of the collective.[28]

Of course, Marxist-Leninist theory asserts that the Communist Party, as the most advanced element of the proletariat, embodies the will of the "people" and, therefore, legitimately leads the way to the millenium. And because of the "scientific" nature of Marxism-Leninism-Mao Zedong Thought, the question of the purpose of the state is considered to be settled. Those who might disagree, therefore, have no legitimate right to be heard. Mao Zedong discussed this point at some length in his famous 1957 essay, "On The Correct Handling Of Contradictions Among The People."[29] Contradictions, said Mao, were of two types: those "among the people" and those between the people and the "enemy."

Contradictions of the first type were considered "non-antagonistic"; they were disagreements about tactics or details among those who essentially agreed with the aims of the revolution. The second type, contradictions between the people and the "enemy" were to be considered "antagonistic." The "enemy" were defined as "counterrevolutionaries" who disagreed with the basic, settled purposes of the state, however that purpose was defined by the ruling elite at any given moment. Non-antagonistic contradictions could be resolved through gentle persuasion. Antagonistic contradictions could only be resolved by uprooting and suppressing the counterrevolutionary enemy:

> Our state is a people's democratic dictatorship led by the working class and based on a worker-peasant alliance. What is the dictatorship for? Its function is to suppress the reactionary classes and elements and those exploiters in our country who resist the socialist revolution, to suppress those who try to wreck our socialist construction, or in other words, to resolve the internal contradictions between ourselves and the enemy. For instance, to arrest, try, and sentence certain counterrevolutionaries...this comes within the scope of our dictatorship.[30]

None of this was to bode well for China's Catholics. Given the clearly defined hostility toward religion of atheistic Marxism-Leninism-Mao Zedong Thought, the absence of any real guarantees of religious freedom, and the ease with which labels like "counterrevolutionary" could be applied to any activity which violated the vaguely defined but supremely important "interests" of the state, it should have been easy to predict that Leninist-communism and religion would not live peacefully side-by-side. Indeed, it should be clear from a brief review of these principles that those who hoped for some sort of long-term, peaceful co-existence between Chinese Catholics and the "people's democratic dictatorship" were destined to be sadly disappointed. All freedoms in People's China were to be subordinated to the interests of the state, and religious activities by their very nature—upholding and propagating an alternate version of the truth—were especially susceptible to the charge that they operated against these interests. With these principles in mind, then, and with the history of the bloody winter of 1947–48 before them, it might seem surprising that there were those who could still express optimism about the fate of the Catholic missions in China. It was a fragile, even pathetic optimism, to be sure. Yet, in September 1949 *China Missionary*, (now renamed *China Missionary Bulletin* with its editorial offices moved from Shanghai to Hong Kong), wrote:

> Actually, the communists are too busy with the reorganization of the enormous territories they have occupied to bother with such a trifling minority as we Catholics in China.

And they expressed the hope that the missionaries might be "left in comparative peace for a certain period to come."[31]

In view of the historical record, and of the doctrine which drove the revolution, it is difficult to see what might have given cause for even this limited optimism. In any event, as we shall see, the hope for peaceful coexistence between the two sides proved to be without much foundation.

NOTES

1. A Document of the Central Committee of the Communist Party of China, *Chung-fa*, 1982, no. 19, "Central Committee Notice on the Basic Problem of Religion During the Socialist Period in Our Country." *Issues & Studies*. Taipei: Institute of International Relations, August 1983, 72–90, 74.

2. I have attempted to develop this point at much greater length in James T. Myers. "Socialist Spiritual Civilization and Cultural Pollution: The Problem of Meaning," Yu-ming Shaw, ed., *Mainland China: Politics, Economics and Reform*. Boulder, CO: Westview Press, 1986, 277–328.

3. Morse Peckham. *Explanation and Power—The Control of Human Behavior*, New York: The Seabury Press, 1979, 187. For a further development of this idea see James T. Myers. "China: The 'Germs' of Modernization," *Asian Survey*. Berkeley: University of California Press, October 1985.

4. V.I. Lenin. "The Attitude of the Workers Party Toward Religion," *Selected Works*, 12 volumes. New York: International Publishers, 1943, vol. XI, 664.

5. Frederick Engels. "Socialism: Utopian and Scientific," *Marx and Engels, Selected Works*, Two volumes. Moscow: Foreign Languages Publishing House, 1958, vol. II, 87.

6. *Ibid.*, 106.

7. V.I. Lenin. "Socialism and Religion," *Selected Works, op. cit.*, vol. II, 658.

8. See, for example, Mao Zedong. "The Chinese Revolution and the Chinese Communist Party," December 1939 and "On New Democracy," January 1940, *Selected Works of Mao Tse-tung* [Mao Zedong], vol. II. Beijing: Foreign Languages Press, 1965.

9. Mao Zedong. "The Chinese Revolution and the Chinese Communist Party," *loc. cit.*, 312.

10. Mao Zedong. "On New Democracy," *loc. cit.*, 369.

11. Mao Zedong. "The Chinese Revolution and the Chinese Communist Party," *loc. cit.*, 323.

12. Mao Zedong. "On New Democracy," *loc. cit.*, 381.

13. Xi Lin, social ed., "Religious Policy in Full Force," *Beijing Review*, no. 3, January 16, 1984, 4.

14. "Our Party's Basic Policy On Religious Questions During the Period of Socialism," by the Editorial Department of *Hong Qi* [Red Flag], Beijing, no. 12, June 16, 1982, 2–8. In Foreign Broadcast Information Service (hereafter: FBIS), Washington, D.C., Joint Publication Research Service (JPRS) 81504, 11 August 1982, 3. This is essentially the same as the *Chung-fa* document cited in note no. 1 of this chapter.

An excellent analysis of this long article on religious policy may be found in Angelo S. Lazzarotto. "The Chinese Communist Party and Religion," *Missiology: An International Review*. Chicago, vol. XI, no. 3. July 1983, 267–290.

15. *Ibid.*
16. *Ibid.*, 5–6.
17. *Ibid.*, 6.
18. Conrad Brandt, Benjamin Schwartz, and John K. Fairbank. *A Documentary History of Chinese Communism*. Cambridge: Harvard University Press, 1952, 223.
19. *Ibid.*
20. "The Common Programme of the Chinese People's Political Consultative Conference," adopted September 29, 1949. In Michael Lindsay, ed., *The New Constitution of Communist China*. Taipei: Institute of International Relations, 1976, 282–283.
21. Revised Draft of the Constitution of the People's Republic of China, adopted September 6, 1970; Second Plenary Session of the Ninth Central Committee of the Communist Party of China, Michael Lindsay, ed., *The New Constitution of Communist China op. cit.*, 320.
22. Revised Draft of the Constitution of the People's Republic of China, adopted November 12, 1973; First Plenary Session of the Tenth Central Committee of the Communist Party of China, Michael Lindsay, ed., *The New Constitution of Communist China, op. cit.*, 327.
23. The Constitution of the People's Republic of China, adopted January 17, 1975; First Session of the Fourth National People's Congress, Michael Lindsay, ed., *The New Constitution of Communist China, op. cit.*, 336.
24. *The Constitution of the People's Republic of China*, adopted March 5, 1978 by the First Session of the Fifth National People's Congress. Beijing: Foreign Languages Press, 1978, 35.
25. Constitution of the People's Republic of China, adopted by the Fifth Session of the Fifth National People's Congress, December 4, 1982. *Beijing Review*, no. 52, December 27, 1982, 16.
26. *Ibid.*, 15.
27. *Ibid.*, 11.
28. *Ibid.*, 18.
29. Mao Zedong. "On the Correct Handling of Contradictions Among the People," *Selected Readings from the Works of Mao Tse-tung*. Beijing: Foreign Languages Press, 1967, 350–387.
30. *Ibid.*, 353.
32. *China Missionary Bulletin*, Hong Kong, no. 1, September 1949, 3. After a three month hiatus, *China Missionary*, now re-named, began publishing in Hong Kong, and re-numbered its issues beginning with no. 1.

THREE

THE FATE
OF THE MISSIONS

Religious freedom as generally understood no longer exists in China today.... Obstacles that render propagation of the faith difficult are the order of the day.

China Missionary Bulletin, Feb. 1950[1]

The Catholic Church which confronted the new communist government of China in the fall of 1949 was a sizeable and far-flung institution. The official Catholic population of China given in the Catholic census of 1947–48, was 3,274,740, or one Catholic for every 140 Chinese.[2] The small number of Catholics in the Chinese population, however, belied the significant presence of the Church as an institution in Chinese society.

The Church was organized in 144 ecclesiastical districts, consisting of 20 archdioceses, 85 dioceses and 39 apostolic prefectures covering virtually every part of the country. On the eve of the communist victory, there were 5,788 Catholic priests in China, of whom 2,698 were native Chinese. There were, in addition, 7,463 religious in China of whom 5,112 were native religious.[3] In addition to their specifically religious duties, these representatives of the Church engaged in a wide range of social and educational activities.

The bombing and destruction of the war with Japan and the Chinese Civil War had reduced the number of Catholic schools in China from a pre-war figure of 12,739[4] to a post-war figure of 4,446 with a student enrollment of 319,444,[5] still an impressive number in a nation of largely illiterate peasants. The Diocese of Shanghai alone ran 509 schools with an enrollment in excess of 50,000 students, more than 35,000 of whom were non-Catholics.[6] The Church also ran three universities in China: Aurora (Chen Tan) University in Shanghai founded in 1903, Catholic (Fu Jen) University in Beijing founded in 1925, and Tsinku University in Tianjin founded in 1923.[7]

By the end of 1948, the Catholic Church operated 272 orphanages in China which cared for 2,020 boys and 13,676 girls. In 1948 alone, the Holy Childhood Association received 17,357 babies, many of whom were near death when they were left on the sisters' doorsteps. Of that large number of infants received in 1948, the orphanages eventually provided care for fewer than 2,000. Partly because of the extremely high mortality rate among the dying infants left with the Holy Childhood Association, the orphanages were to become a major target in the new government's attempt to embarrass and discredit the Church (discussed in Chapter Five).[8]

The Church also operated 216 hospitals in China, which provided care for more than 81,000 patients during 1948. In addition to the hospitals, the Church ran four leprosariums and 781 dispensaries in China which handled more than 11,000,000 treatments and consultations during the year preceding the communist victory. Nearly 5,000 old people were cared for in more than 150 "old-folks" asylums, while for the young, the church missions operated 103 vocational workshops which trained boys and girls in various trades. The Church also established schools for the blind, deaf and mute in conjunction with the orphanages.[9]

Indeed, so extensive were the Catholic Church establishments in China that the pre-war inventory of the Church's holdings revealed more church buildings existing there (32,930) than in the United States (32,091).[10] This extensive church presence in China presented both opportunities and problems for the new communist government. The opportunities lay in the valuable services and resources provided by the Church which the government of the PRC had neither the funds nor the trained personnel to duplicate. The problems lay in the doctrine which guided the work of the Church and in the fact that the large number of foreign missionaries in China and the foreign connections of the Church constituted a major "imperialist" thorn in the side of the new government.

Victory and Consolidation

On April 5, 1948, the communist armies captured the ancient city of Loyang. Three days later Mao Zedong sent a telegram to the headquarters of the Loyang front in which he directed the victors to pay attention to nine points, the first point beginning with the words, "Be very prudent..."[11] Mao urged the victorious forces to go slow in replacing the "organs of Kuomintang rule," cautioned that only the worst reactionaries should be arrested, and that care should be taken not to "involve too many persons."[12]

Though the great, decisive battles of the Chinese Civil War were yet to come, final victory now appeared all but certain to the communist leader. Mao wanted to enlist the broadest possible base of support among the various groups and classes of the Chinese population for the final drive for victory, and for the period of national consolidation which would follow. In the task of national economic reconstruction, it was especially important to the communists to reassure and seek the support of the bourgeoisie and the middle classes. The "united front" policy, intended to bring together a number of patriotic or "progressive" groups in collaboration with the communists, as set forth by Mao Zedong in his major essays, "The Chinese Revolution and the Chinese Communist Party" (1939) and "On New Democracy" (1940), was to be stressed again on the eve of the communist victory in Mao's essay commemorating the 28th anniversary of the CCP, "On The People's Democratic Dictatorship" (June 30, 1949).[13]

In this essay Mao gave his answer to those who said, "You are dictatorial." "My dear sirs," wrote Mao, "you are right, that is just what we are. All the experience the Chinese people have accumulated through several decades teaches us to enforce the people's democratic dictatorship, that is, to deprive reactionaries of the right to speak and let the people alone have that right."[14] And who were the "people"? "At the present stage in China," said Mao, "they are the working class, the peasantry, the urban petty bourgeoisie, and the national bourgeoisie."[15] As we suggested earlier, the precise attributes of the categories "reactionaries" or "people" were murky at best so that it was not at all clear whose rights, in theory, were actually protected by the people's democratic dictatorship. Nor, as we shall see, was it difficult to assign the labels "reactionary" or "enemy" to those who were or who became impediments to the new regime's plans and programs.

On one count, though, Mao was reasonably clear and straightforward. All united front alliances were considered to be temporary in nature. In defining the "people," after all, Mao added the qualifying phrase, "at the present stage," indicating that this status was likely to change, just as we saw earlier that he cautioned against liquidating rich peasants "prematurely."[16] Policies for dealing with those who were part of the "united front" but who were not devoted followers of the communist revolution were thus extremely flexible, and subject to considerable shifts over time and from place to place depending upon conditions. Mao's admonition to the victorious communist forces in Loyang to "Be very prudent," was, therefore, tempered with the final assertion that, "It would be entirely wrong to apply our policies and tactics for cities under Kuomintang administration to a city under the people's own administration,"[17] a clear indication that the liberal and "prudent" policies might be short-lived indeed.

In 1949, the Catholic missions were spread over all of China. Some were in areas which had been under communist control for years (the old liberated areas), some in areas which had recently fallen to the communist armies (the new liberated areas), and some in areas which fell during the final stages of the civil war as the communist armies rolled south during the spring and summer of 1949. Most of North China was in communist hands by January 1949. On January 22, the nationalist commander of Beijing surrendered and went over to the communist side. Nanjing fell to the communist armies in April, Shanghai in May, and Guangzhou (Canton) in October. From September 21–29, 1949 the communist authorities convened the Chinese People's Political Consultative Conference (CPPCC) in Beijing. The CPPCC was comprised of 662 delegates representing the Communist Party and the various cooperating united front groups. It was to serve as a national legislature until the election of the First National People's Congress (NPC) in 1954. The CPPCC passed an Organic Law for the PRC and adopted a Common Program which was to serve as a constitutional document until the first state constitution was adopted by the NPC in 1954. At the opening session of the CPPCC Mao Zedong had declared, "Ours will no longer be a nation subject to insult and humiliation. We have stood up."[18] On October 1, 1949, Mao delivered the same message to the world as he stood atop the ancient Gate of Heavenly Peace (Tian An Men) and announced the formation of the Central People's Government.

The announcement by Mao of the formation of a central government under communist control did not imply, however, that the political center was overseeing the orderly functioning of its parts. As he spoke, Mao's armies still raced south. Canton would not fall for another two weeks. It would be December before the nationalist government was moved over to Taiwan, and 1950 before Tibet and Hainan Island were conquered. Near chaos was the order of the day in many of the newly liberated areas. One author described the situation in Canton in this way:

> The *sine qua non* for gaining governmental control was the collection of basic information, and in the early months after Liberation this task loomed so large that it almost became an end unto itself. At the time of Liberation there was no adequate list of schools, let alone of teachers, students, and courses. There was no adequate list of business enterprises, let alone data on goods, prices, and personnel. With society in turmoil, accurate data was difficult to obtain, and even if obtained it was soon outdated.[19]

Policies toward the Catholic missions thus varied considerably, depending on local conditions. Few representatives of the Church remained in the old Revolutionary Base areas, such as the area in northern Shaanxi (Shensi) Province around the communist capital at Yan'an. Here, the land reform had long ago been carried out and the activities of the Church effectively proscribed since the middle or late 1930s. Even in the areas conquered in the mid-1940s—the "old" liberated areas—land reform had been underway for several years by 1949. The CCP had promulgated an Agrarian Reform Law in October 1947 which provided for the confiscation of landlord properties without compensation. These policies they put into effect in the areas under their control. Such policies usually brought with them a severe curtailment or prohibition against Church activity in the areas undergoing land reform.

In northern Shanxi (Shansi) Province, for example, William Hinton recorded the coming of the communist revolution to Long Bow Village in the spring and summer of 1948. The Catholic Church was the largest landowner in the village and soon came under attack. First, the priest, a Chinese, was arrested as a collaborator. Then, the Peasants' Association confiscated some 40 acres of church land. In addition, they confiscated from the church, the orphanage, the orphanage hospital, and the "Carry-On Society" (the financial arm of the church), "four milk cows, large stores of wheat and corn, 100 new quilts, 15 sets of priestly vestments, many sets of new children's clothes, two bicycles, glassware, stocks of medicinal drugs, hundreds of candles, bronze crosses, bronze candelabras, 16 bronze lamps, and 2,000 silver dollars."[20] The head of the leading Catholic lay family, a certain Mr. Wang, was attacked as a landlord, though Hinton describes his landholdings as those only of a "middle peasant," and his son was accused of spying for the nationalists. Eventually, the accused son committed suicide by jumping into a well, and another son and the father were both beaten to death. "With the destruction of the Wang family," wrote Hinton, "the Church ceased to exist as an organized institution in Long Bow."[21]

As indicated above, though the communists proclaimed freedom of religion, actual policies toward the missions and religious personnel varied greatly from one location to the next. Nor does this appear to have been entirely a function of the length of time the communists had occupied the area in question. Individual military commanders and local political leaders interpreted the policy of religious freedom in different ways. In some areas the mission personnel were left pretty much to operate as they had in the past, while in other areas movement of the priests and the religious was severely restricted, in some cases amounting to house arrest. In all cases where communist rule was securely established over time, however, the Church could look forward to serious difficulties.

It was generally reported that communist troops behaved in exemplary fashion in their initial encounters with missionaries in newly liberated territories. Communist commanders all seem to have been familiar with the policy of religious freedom, and most took pains to proclaim it. From the Diocese of Kwei-teh in Henan Province came a typical report as communist troops entered the city in October 1948:

> The communist forces entered the city without any fighting at the end of October. They asked for sleeping quarters in the mission for one night. They were polite and correct. Their commander-in-chief told the fathers that "he was not so well," was given medical care and he promised the complete protection of the Church: "Do not be afraid of us. We have changed our policy. Now we proclaim liberty of conscience though our government is atheistic."[22]

A similar report from the Diocese of Pengpu in Anhui Province was even more sanguine:

> With the fall of Chuhsien, railroad town between Pengpu and Pukow, the whole diocese is now under the Red regime. The city was evacuated without fighting. The Fathers there made a visit to the army commander who received them with great courtesy and promised them perfect freedom to go on with their apostolate. On the same day the Red leaders returned the visit.[23]

While a certain degree of freedom continued to exist in many locations, however, most missionaries soon found their movements increasingly confined. It was common, for example, for priests and religious to be prohibited from venturing into the countryside without permission. Some were confined to their quarters. From a parish in Hebei Province came a report that the father had been told, "he could sing, jump, do whatever he wants in his house, but never leave it."[24]

Not all of the missionaries chose to stay under conditions of uncertainty or growing hostility. Bishop Celestine Ibanez of the Diocese of Yenan in Shaanxi Province had been driven from the See city late in 1935 by the communist forces which settled there following the Long March. He had carried on his work from the city of Yulin on the edge of the diocese, but decided to leave the area when the nationalist commander abandoned the garrison there in 1948. As the communists had blockaded the main roads out of Yulin, Bishop Ibanez hired a caravan of camels and struck out westward across the desert toward Ningxia Province. He took with him a group of students and orphans.

The prelate and his charges traveled for three weeks by camel, and then for five more days, by a three-wheeled "Peking" cart. Eventually, the group reached Ningxia where the Bishop engaged an airplane to carry them to the safety of Shanghai, still at that time not yet under communist control.[25]

However cordial the initial contacts between communists and Catholics may have been, storm clouds were on the horizon. The *China Missionary Bulletin* reported that, "From various regions come reports of remarks dropped by individual communists to the effect that the present attitude of toleration does not represent a permanent policy."[26] And if there was any doubt about whether the communists had moderated their previously announced positions about the Church, The Federation of People's Organizations of Shanghai issued the following warning as the communist forces moved toward the city:

> Missionaries, especially those of the Catholic Church, are the forerunners of imperialist invasion. Under the pretext of preaching, they expand their influence to every corner of this vast territory. They build up colleges and universities, establish hospitals and donate large amounts to charity institutions for hidden aims. All these activities, however, are aimed at nourishing a group of pro-imperialistic Chinese compradors, without whose help the imperialists might never be able to infiltrate into the innermost China to strengthen their control. Furthermore, among the missionaries there are also secret agents of the imperialists.[27]

The pressure on the Church, when it did come, was usually applied in several ways.

Church-Operated Schools

The schools operated by the Church were an obvious early target for the new communist government. As important as the educational mission of the schools might be in a poor country hoping to develop, the communists had no intention of giving the missionaries free rein to operate as they had traditionally done, especially in the matter of instruction in moral values. In many cases, the authorities asked the missionaries to continue running the schools, as they were simply not prepared to take over school operations all over China. The typical pattern, however, was for the communist authorities immediately to insist upon securing several places on the school board or other governing body. Typically, an eight-member school committee would be required to include two communist representatives.[28]

Catholic teachers remaining on the faculty of the schools were usually scheduled immediately for indoctrination courses lasting for periods up to two weeks or more. Communist authorities took a direct interest in the schools, visiting them frequently to address the students and to teach them communist songs. It was also a common practice for the communist authorities to insist that the schools, which had always been segregated by sex, should become co-educational.

In those schools where the student body consisted of older pupils, especially in the universities, the new government decreed that substantial responsibility for controlling school affairs should pass to the students. Matters which had formerly been left to the governing boards or to the faculty were henceforth to be decided in some "democratic" fashion by students and school workers, including those who served in a menial capacity, such as janitors. It was reported from Beijing, for example, that in one church-sponsored middle school, "all the teaching brothers but one were ejected by the students from one boys' school and all the sisters were forced to leave their school for girls. Leftist students from Peita (Beida), the National University of Peiping (Beijing), came to direct these two schools."[29]

Disorder and lack of discipline were especially severe in the three Catholic universities. Fu Jen University also reported a substantial decline in enrollment due apparently to the belief that graduates would have little hope of being accepted for positions in the government or in any public organization. At Aurora University in Shanghai, a students' self-governing body was formed. Noting this event, the Shanghai press reported:

> The committee is now working for a reform in the curriculum of the school. Student representatives were sent out to other universities yesterday to collect materials for the purpose. A student on the committee claimed that formerly all notes were taken in French, but in the future the Chinese language will be used. Whether the Catholic fathers will continue to be at the helm of the school will be decided by the student body.[30]

At Tsinku University in Tianjin, it was reported that, "The school has been reorganized according to the communistic pattern: committees of teachers, students, and servants, meet and decide everything."[31]

Having seized control of the schools from the Church authorities, the next step was usually to reform the school curriculum. In most cases, there followed quickly an examination by communist school administrators of all textbooks in use. Books in history, literature, and social sciences came in for particular scrutiny. Books in sciences and mathematics were of less interest to the government. Textbooks and courses of instruction in materialism were introduced at every level of instruction. At Fu Jen University, for example, it was reported that the North China Higher Education Committee had decreed that, "every university, college, and normal school must require all students in all departments to follow courses in historic and dialectic materialism and in the doctrine of New Democracy. Both courses are to be given three hours a week during one semester."[32]

Though instruction in Christian doctrine still tended to be permitted, in many cases communist authorities moved to have the symbols of Christianity removed from the schools. In Nanjing an inspection committee from the Bureau of Education ordered banished from the middle school, which was the object of their scrutiny, "all crucifixes, statues and religious pictures," including a painting of the great Jesuit missionary Father Matteo Ricci who was described by a woman committee member as "the first foreign imperialist to invade China."[33] In some areas, as well, local authorities took a less permissive attitude toward the religious activities of the missionaries. In Jiangxi Province, the teaching of catechism to those under sixteen years of age was prohibited. Local authorities also forbade the teaching of Catholic doctrine on school property, even after school hours, and prohibited the Catholic children from attending Mass.[34]

The missionaries, who stayed on as teachers despite their mounting difficulties, continued to decry the lack of discipline and declining standards. One of the teaching fathers complained that a student caught cheating on an examination threatened to bring him, the teacher, up on charges before a People's Court for "imperialistic" behavior. The dean interceded, however, solving the problem by giving the student a good grade for the test, and no charges were brought against the father.[35] In spite of the problems which they faced, many of those who stayed remained optimistic that their presence might "preserve the good elements from contagion," and that the intellectual and spiritual support which they could offer to the Catholic students would continue to be important.[36]

As the fall semester 1949 registration was recorded, enrollment at Catholic schools throughout China showed a serious decline. The decline can be explained in part as a consequence of the fears of discrimination noted above, but there were also economic reasons for parents to withdraw their children from church-run schools. The new government had already begun to impose heavy taxes throughout the country, and many parents were no longer able to afford even the modest tuition fees charged by most of the schools. Many schools lowered tuition costs which, in turn, necessitated lowering the salaries of teachers and professors, but still the problem remained. At Fu Jen University, the fall registration brought 875 students compared with 2,386 a year earlier. Only about 500 undergraduates enrolled at Aurora University in Shanghai, compared with approximately 3,500 the previous year. Against this trend, Tsinku University showed a slight increase over the 1948 roster.[37]

For most of the schools, the "Catholic" element soon ceased to exist. In some cases, the operation of the schools was taken over directly by the government. Fu Jen University was taken over by the government in October 1950, though a half-dozen priests and a like number of sisters stayed on as faculty members. Those schools not taken over by the government continued to be run by the missionaries for the benefit of the state until such time as the government was prepared to take over their operation. The missionaries in Jiangxi Province summed up the prevailing situation throughout the country:

> The Catholic schools...have ceased to be Catholic schools in everything but name. Forced by the school authorities to include the teaching of materialism and Marxism in the curriculum, the missionaries found themselves unable to continue as instructors in their own institutions. And because of the need of education facilities, they were not permitted by the authorities to discontinue their schools, although they were no more than nominal administrators of these institutions.

> The course of studies of these "Catholic" schools has now been brought in line by the officially appointed directors with the other public schools run by the government. Atheism and materialism are underlying tenets that color the teaching of all subjects. The time before and after classes is taken up with dancing and singing. Catechism classes have been forbidden even after regular school hours.
>
> Catholic books remain the only means now available to propagate the faith to the broad masses of the students....[38]

Though many of the missionaries remained hopeful, even optimistic, the situation in the Catholic schools was only to get worse.

Mission Properties

Most of the missionaries quickly learned that they were in possession of valuable property coveted by the new communist authorities. In some cases the property in question was a mission vehicle or other useful object which the army or the new civilian governors would ask to "borrow." The diligence of the borrowers in returning these borrowed goods varied greatly from place to place. More often, however, the most valuable commodities which the missionaries posessed was space and buildings.

It was not uncommon, especially in the villages and rural areas, that the largest and most substantial structures available to the victorious army, and the officials which accompanied it, were represented by missions, churches, temples, monasteries and the like. Large shelters available to quarter soldiers or officials, or to hold public meetings, were scarce indeed, and the mission churches, rectories, schools, hospitals, convents and orphanages, therefore, provided excellent targets of opportunity for the communist authorities.

It was, in fact, rare that the new government did not take the opportunity to occupy some portion of the mission properties for its own use. The first accounts reaching the outside from the newly liberated areas usually contained reports lamenting the confiscation of mission property:

> ...the authorities asked for permission to occupy the school building till the re-opening of classes....[39]
>
> ...Father C. has had his house and church occupied for the good of the people, with the exception of two rooms for himself and the sisters.[40]

...The Cathedral of Tsitsihar is now used by the communists as a storehouse....

...The church building has been declared the property of the Christians. The other buildings of the mission have been confiscated for public use....

...The bishop's residence is occupied but not the cathedral....[41]

...Bishop Bassi, the fathers and native sisters still reside in the hospital at Loyang. The entire residence and cathedral are occupied by the military. A few days ago, the bishop was told that the general would shortly place the cathedral at his disposition for religious services and might restore some rooms in the fathers' residence to the missionaries.[42]

...In the towns of [x and y], the mission buildings are occupied, except for one room reserved to the priest. The churches are used to store rice, wheat and beans contributed to the government by the people.

...In Nanchang, the Bishop's residence and a secondary school of the mission, have been occupied at least in part. The cathedral was put to use, at least once, for a political meeting....[43]

...In the district of Mienyang, which has the largest proportion of the diocese's Catholic population, the church and parish residence are still left to the pastor, all other buildings have been removed from their administration. The church has at times been appropriated for use as a meeting hall.[44]

...The girls' orphanage was evicted by the authorities after weeks of negotiations and threats. A pitiful procession of children came out of the gates, some blind, others deaf, the older girls leading the younger.[45]

...These last few days a great assembly of the whole *hsien* [district] was held. We have had to say our Masses at 4 A.M. to leave the church free as a meeting place.[46]

...The pastor of a big locality has just recently been notified that the major church is to be converted into a cinema. Of the twenty fathers only one has succeeded so far in remaining at his post up country. All the others have been compelled to abandon their churches and compounds and return to the central mission. Their missions have been taken over for use as military barracks. The only father who remains at his mission lives in a small room in his own compound and soldiers are quartered in the rest of the building.[47]

...the bishop and priests had to evacuate their residence and move to the smaller sisters' compound and the school had to be reorganized elsewhere. The officials declared that the residence "was too big for a few missionaries, who were forbidden to lead such a comfortable capitalistic life or to make imperialistic propaganda as before." The provincial authorities asked lodging space for 20,000 men. The greatest part of the mission's main buildings, including the seminary, the residences for the fathers and the Chinese sisters were occupied. The episcopal residence was occupied and despoiled of all its vessels, both sacred and profane.[48]

...Eight out of nine centrally located churches in this mission district have been seized and occupied by the government. Sixty out of 67 other churches and chapels have also been taken over by civil authorities. Every Catholic school in the diocese, including the seminary, has also been seized.[49]

In many cases, the seizure of church property represented more than merely an inconvenience to the missionaries. Much of the mission property produced revenue for the support of mission activities. The loss of this property, therefore, frequently represented a severe financial blow to the missions as well. Thus, in addition to reports bemoaning the loss of control over mission buildings to the civil authorities, numerous other reports reached Hong Kong of missionaries who had been rendered virtually penniless by the seizure of the property which had supported them.

A prefect apostolic from Shanxi Province wrote, "I am poor, we have nothing any more. They have taken all the furniture from the residence and hospital to another town—left us nothing but one key."[50] From a mission in North China came the message that, ...Father farms for himself a few acres of land that have been left to him. He works the whole day in the field. Like any other peasant he, single-handed, has to repair the straw roof of his hut. He climbs the mountain daily to cut the fuel he needs, yet he is never resentful; he has become a perfect workman."[51]

The seizure or occupation of church properties can thus be seen as one part of a pattern of persecution of the missions which developed rather quickly after the establishment of control by the new civil authorities. In many cases, the taking of church property was simply one aspect of the policy of subjecting the missions to severe economic pressure, which will be discussed in more detail below. One diocese reported, for example, that an edict had been posted on the walls of houses in the city which, "forbid the mission to receive any further revenues from its property. The reason given for this new ruling was that the mission has unjustly occupied the property these many years.

It stated further that the missionaries were worthy of severe punishment in the future. What the punishment for [the Chinese bishop] and his priests would be was not mentioned. It is feared that they may be forcibly expelled from their residences and obliged to leave behind everything they possess, including sacred vessels. At present the priests are permitted to use some small rooms in the compound."[52]

The Chinese government was certainly not unaware of the implications of its economic policies toward the missions. Not only were the missions frequently a ready source of space, food, commodities and other useful items, including tax money, but the economic pressures could be used to strangle the missions slowly—or sometimes not so slowly—and render them incapable of carrying on their work.

Economic Pressures

It is an axiom of politics that the power to tax is the power to destroy. The great American jurist Oliver Wendell Holmes, Jr. asserted that, "The power to tax is not the power to destroy while this Court [the U.S. Supreme Court] sits,"[53] but as we have already noted, no meaningful legal or constitutional guarantees existed to protect the Church against punitive actions by the new civil authorities. What may have begun in many cases as random opportunities for local authorities to "requisition" from the missions that which they wanted or needed, rapidly developed into a clear government policy of bleeding the missions of anything of value, and of using the power of taxation to drive the missions out of business.

Registration of mission property and personnel was an essential first step in the government's effort to establish administrative control in what was still, to some degree in many places, a relatively chaotic situation. A diocese in Hebei Province, for example, reported:

> The missions have been asked to present reports on the properties and the financial situation, on the personnel, etc. Financial accounts eight or ten years old had to be handed over to the authorities.[54]

The acquisition of such information was usually a prelude to the imposition of severe economic sanctions on the missions. In some cases the economic demands were cast as "voluntary" contributions, such as "350 silver dollars as a voluntary contribution to the Public Works Bureau for beautification of the city," and the following month of a further contribution of "200 bags of wheat."[55] One diocese reported that the bishop had been told by the mayor that he must contribute 500,000 JMP [the currency of the new regime] to the "troop-comforting collection." The report reveals that, "after long parleys, the mayor consented to accept half the sum he had named," and gave the bishop, "three days in which to sell furniture and other objects at the mission to raise the needed money."[56]

The most onerous burden, however, was created by the heavy, punitive taxes, both of goods and of property, which in many cases left the missions in poverty:

> ...At present our missions have no income. We had to give out to Christian families all the orphans of our Holy Childhood, keeping only the sick and abnormal ones. The old men formerly supported by the mission have to go begging in the villages.[57]
>
> ...Mission activity in the Yenchow countryside grows more difficult, with the authorities unfriendly and the people uneasy and anxious. Taxes exacted are becoming impossible to pay and normal ministry for souls cannot be carried on.[58]
>
> ...Almost every mission has had several exactions of rice. In some cases, the missionaries were jailed when they could not pay the quantity required. At Susung, the priest, deprived of rice to pay his teachers, had to close the school.[59]
>
> ...One mission society was asked to pay 300,000,000 JMP, the equivalent of US $150,000. This mission's properties consist of church, two orphanages, seminary, scholasticate, residence, hospital.[60]
>
> ...The mission is able to realize practically no revenue from its fields and was forced to sell 100 *tan* of rice in order to pay the taxes.... Taxes are so heavy that the mission reaps no profit from its land.[61]
>
> ...Soon after the occupation the situation began to worsen on account of the heavy taxation imposed on the already over-taxed people. The mission was ordered to pay 5,000 *tan* of rice.[62]
>
> ...Difficulties for the church and its activities are growing. The religious superior had to undergo a public trial and was heavily fined for alleged misappropriation of rice fields which belonged to the Holy Childhood and provided for its maintenance.[63]
>
> ...A new local ordinance has made all Mass wine taxable. Even though the Mass wine in many cases had been imported a long time ago, the priests were ordered to declare the amount on hand, so that it could be taxed.[64]
>
> ...The mission has no finances with which to support the orphans.

The few handmade articles which the children produce and which were formerly sold to townspeople now have no market.[65]

...Increased tax rates on the mission orphanage used up finances otherwise earmarked for the support of the children. To prevent their being taken away and forced into various communist youth programs, all of the older girls were married off or sent to live among Catholic families.

...So gigantic have been the difficulties of taxation that the priests after paying their taxes have been without funds with which to buy food and clothing for themselves. They have had to beg wheat door-to-door in an effort to fill the amount required by the government to cover certain tax items. Missionaries were informed that if they were unable to pay their taxes, their house furnishings would be confiscated.

...Thoughtful Catholics bring the priests their food each day.[66]

...750 tons of rice has been levied against the properties of this mission—churches, schools, and seminaries. Special pressure was brought on the mission for the payment of this assessment, which the Ordinary of the diocese finds impossible to meet. Night and day he was visited by the officials and questioned; then he was called to the local government offices and made to answer the questions all over again. The mission has been threatened with reprisals if it fails to meet these obligations.[67]

The problem of taxation of agricultural lands used by the missions to finance their activities became moot in February 1950 when the Central People's Government issued a "directive for dealing with agricultural lands in the suburbs of the cities and in the old liberated areas." Article 6 of this directive provided that, "All land for financing schools, land belonging to clans, and land devoted to ancestral shrines, temples, churches and public organizations should come under state ownership and should be properly distributed."[68] The land reform, which dealt with the remaining rural church properties, would become national policy a few months later.

One additional method used for extracting a financial toll from the missions involved fining the missionaries—especially medical personnel—for alleged misconduct:

Father Zotti, judged guilty of having operated badly and having caused the death of a woman in childbirth, was condemned to a year in prison and a year of house arrest. Actually the operation was well done, but the woman was beyond saving. Moreover, the court decided that the mission must pay the husband 1,600 pounds of wheat....[69]

...Three doctors and sisters have been brought before the People's Court. One of the doctors was compelled to "confess" that he had taken up the work of a doctor in order to extract money from the people. The court insisted that the sisters make similar confessions. They positively refused and a fine of JMP 5,700,000 was imposed on them.[70]

...The mission has suffered its greatest blow through the hospital. Some months ago one of the patients underwent a surgical operation, but her life could not be saved. The case came before the court. The hospital was held responsible, fined 6,000,000 JMP and forced to reorganize according to government wishes.[71]

It is interesting to note that in the midst of the pressures and harassment visited upon the missions, and at a time when many feared the return of full-scale religious persecution, many of the missions reported a tremendous increase in religious fervor and religious activities among their Catholics. Attendance at Mass increased, especially on feast days, as did the numbers of those receiving Communion. Indeed, such claims abound in the mission reports of the end of 1949 and the beginning of 1950. Perhaps an increase in religious fervor should have been anticipated as a response to religious persecution; it surely appears to have been one indicator of the response by Chinese Catholics to the much more severe forms of persecution which were yet to come.

And perhaps we should also have anticipated that the unwelcome persecution which many would suffer would be regarded by Catholics as an opportunity to demonstrate their steadfastness in the Faith. As a missionary in Hunan Province wrote to his brothers in Hong Kong, "Everyone is in good spirits and eager to suffer something for Our Lord."[72]

Indeed, they would not be disappointed by the opportunities for suffering which the government would provide them in the years ahead.

NOTES

1. "Editors' Notes," *China Missionary Bulletin* (hereafter CMB), Hong Kong, vol. II, no. 2, February 1950, 144.
2. CMB, Hong Kong, vol. I, no. 3, November 1949, 203.
3. *Ibid.*
4. Bishop F.X. Ford. "Mission Buildings in China," CMB, no. 2, October 1949, 104.
5. CMB, no. 3, November 1949, 203.
6. *China Missionary*, Shanghai, no. 2, February 1949, 217.
7. See Jessie Gregory Lutz. *China and the Christian Colleges, 1850–1950*, Ithaca, NY: Cornell University Press, 1971, *passim*.
8. "Catholic Social Work in China," CMB, September 1954, 655.
9. *Ibid.*, 656.
10. CMB, *op. cit.*, October 1949, 104.
11. Mao Zedong. "Telegram to the Headquarters of the Loyang Front After the Recapture of the City," *Selected Works of Mao Tse-tung*, vol. IV, Beijing: Foreign Language Press, 1967, 247–249.
12. *Ibid.*
13. Mao Zedong. "On the People's Democratic Dictatorship," In Commemoration of the Twenty-eighth Anniversary of the communist party of China, June 30, 1949, *Selected Works of Mao Tse-tung*, vol. IV, Beijing: Foreign Languages Press, 1967, 411–424.
14. *Ibid.*, 417.
15. *Ibid.*
16. See Chapter Two, footnote 11.
17. "Telegram to the Headquarters of the Loyang Front After the Recapture of the City," *loc. cit.*, 249.
18. Mao Zedong, "The Chinese People Have Stood Up!" *Selected Works of Mao Tse-tung*, vol. V, Beijing: Foreign Languages Press, 1977, 17.
19. Ezra Vogel. *Canton Under Communism: Programs and Politics in a Provincial Capital, 1949–1968*, Cambridge: Harvard University Press, 1969, 72.
20. William Hinton. *Fanshen: Documentary of Revolution in a Chinese Village*, New York: Vintage Books, 1968, 143–144.
21. *Ibid.*, 144–145.
22. CMB, no. 2, 1949, 221.
23. CMB, no. 3, 1949, 331.
24. CMB, no. 4., 1949, 448.
25. CMB, no. 3, 1949, 326–327.
26. *Ibid.*, 325.
27. CMB, May 1954, 414.
28. See, for example, CMB, no. 1, 1949, 75; CMB, no. 2, 1949, 213.
29. CMB, no. 5, 1949, 571–572.

30. *Ta Kung Pao*, Shanghai, June 3, 1949. In CMB, no. 7, 1949, 69.
31. *Ibid.*
32. CMB, no. 9, 1949, 293.
33. CMB, no. 1, 1950, 94.
34. CMB, no. 2, 1950, 200.
35. CMB, no. 3, 1959, 259.
36. *Ibid.*
37. CMB, no. 10, 1950, 952–953.
38. CMB, no. 8, 1950, 785.
39. CMB, no. 4, 1949, 455.
40. CMB, no. 7, 1949, 455.
41. CMB, no. 7, 1949, 70.
42. CMB, no. 8, 1949, 189.
43. *Ibid.*, 190.
44. CMB, no. 9, 1949, 304.
45. CMB, no. 1, 1950, 97.
46. CMB, no. 8, 1949, 185.
47. CMB, no. 2, 1950, 198–199.
48. CMB, no. 3, 1950, 297–298.
49. CMB, no. 10, 1959, 954.
50. CMB, no. 3, 1950, 296.
51. CMB, no. 2, 1949, 81.
52. CMB, no. 3, 1950, 294.
53. *Panhandle Oil Co.* v. *Knox*, 277 U.S. 223, 1928.
54. CMB, no. 6, 1949, 697.
55. CMB, no. 7, 1949, 73.
56. CMB, no. 1, 1950, 105.
57. CMB, no. 5, 1949, 569.
58. CMB, no. 8, 1949, 182.
59. *Ibid.*, 185.
60. CMB, no. 9, 1949, 300.
61. CMB, no. 3, 1950, 309.
62. CMB, no. 6, 1950, 588.
63. *Ibid.*, 589.
64. CMB, no. 8, 1950, 774–775.
65. *Ibid.*, 779.
66. *Ibid.*, 780.
67. CMB, no. 9, 1950, 875.
68. CMB, no. 4, 1950, 390–391.
69. CMB, no. 8, 1949, 189.
70. CMB, no. 2, 1950, 194.
71. CMB, no. 4, 1950, 410.
72. CMB, no. 1, 1950, 103.

FOUR

THE EARLY CAMPAIGNS

> A revolution is not a dinner party, or writing an essay, or painting a
> picture, or doing embroidery; it cannot be so refined, so leisurely
> and gentle, so temperate, kind, courteous, restrained and magnan-
> imous. A revolution is an insurrection, an act of violence by which
> one class overthrows another.
>
> Mao Zedong[1]

The year 1950 was both a year of continuing consolidation for
the new government, as well as a year in which aggressive new
campaigns were undertaken. The Marriage Law was promulgated on May 1, marking the beginning of the government's
attempt to revolutionize domestic social arrangements in the
PRC. A Trade Union Law was put into place on June 29, and on
June 30, the Agrarian Reform Law—about which we will have
more to say below—became effective. On October 25, Chinese
"volunteers" entered the Korean War and the government began
a massive nationwide campaign to "Resist America—Aid Korea."
1950 is also the year in which we meet two Chinese whose lives
might serve as metaphors for the fate of the Church under communist rule in China. The first, Dominic Tang, became Bishop
of Canton (Guangzhou) in southern China at a time when the
new communist authorities were consolidating their control over
that area. The second, Wang Xiaoling, a young woman from
Shanghai, entered the Roman Catholic Church at about the same
time in that eastern stronghold of Chinese Catholicism.

The Bishop and the Teenager

Dominic Tang Yi-ming [Deng Yi-ming] was born in Hong Kong in 1908. He entered the Society of Jesus in 1930 and continued his education in the Portuguese colony of Macau and in Europe. He returned to China to study theology at Shanghai, and was ordained in that city in 1941. When the communist armies completed their victorious push south to Canton, Father Tang was serving as a missionary in a district outside Macau. It was 1950 when he was called by Pope Pius XII to replace the retiring french Bishop of Canton, Monsignor Deswaziere, as apostolic administrator of the Canton Diocese.[2]

Archbishop Tang:

One day about November 1950 I received a large registered letter from Nanjing.... It was from the apostolic internuncio, Archbishop Antonio Riberi, who was then in Nanjing. At the top of the letter in large print were the words "SECRETUM SANCTI OFFICII" (Secret of the Holy Office). It read, "Pope Pius XII has decided to appoint Dominic Tang as apostolic administrator of the Archdiocese of Canton with the rights and duties of a residential bishop. I (Riberi) hope you will comply with the desire of the Pope and generously accept the office, especially in the present special circumstances when the communists have occupied China."

...At that time I was the vicar forane of Chungshan, parish priest of Shekki town, headmaster of Po Ling Primary School and the person in charge of the Pui Ki Kindergarten. I gave the parish of Shekki to Father Matthias Tse Hau-pei (who died later in a labor camp in Qinghai Province). Mr. Tse Yu-choh became headmaster of Po Ling Primary School. (He later died in prison by swallowing chopsticks).

...I arrived in Canton on December 30, 1950. About a month after my arrival in Canton, Monsignor Deswaziere gave me the Bull of Appointment.

...On February 1, 1951, I held the ceremony of installation in the chapel of the Bishop's House. The ceremony included the oath and profession of faith, etc. On the same day I took charge of the Archdiocese of Canton.

...Originally, we wanted to have the consecration ceremony in Shanghai because there were a number of bishops there, including Bishop Ignatius Kung [or, Gong] Pinmei, Bishop Simon Zhu Kaimin, and Bishop James E. Walsh. However, we feared that the communist government would prevent me from returning to Canton after that.

...On February 15, 1951, the border of Guangdong Province was closed by the government. People going to Hong Kong and Macau had to apply for permits. We were afraid that the communist government would detain or expel Monsignor Deswaziere. The priests in Canton urged me to be consecrated as quickly as possible. Whereupon preparations for the ceremony were made and the celebration was advanced from the 19th to the 13th of February.

...On that day, the consecration ceremony was held in the chapel on the first floor of the Archbishop's residence. Monsignor Deswaziere was the chief celebrant.

...On Sunday, February 19, 1951, we had a solemn High Mass at 9:00 A.M. in the Cathedral of Shek Shat. After Mass the Bishop went out to meet the faithful; Catholics had come from different parishes of Canton city to congratulate the new Bishop.

...On February 20, 1951 I sent formal letters to notify the People's Governments of Guangdong Province and Canton City of this appointment.[3]

Wang Xiaoling was born and raised in Shanghai. She was fourteen years old when the communists came into power. Though her family was not Catholic, Xiaoling attended Catholic schools from the age of six.[4]

Wang Xiaoling:

Immediately after the Liberation, our family remained comfortable. Every Sunday my mother took us, as usual, to the cinema or a concert or else to visit friends or relatives. Business was fairly good and people's way of life was stable. But their outlook was beginning to change—they were apprehensive, alert, suspicious, and uneasy. Relatives from my mother's native place brought news from the countryside; landlords were being "struggled," land was being redistributed.

...In 1950, there seemed to be little change in the Catholic Church of Shanghai, on the surface, at least, with all the church bells still ringing. All kinds of liturgical celebrations and ceremonies took place as usual. Activities in the Church flourished even more: various devotional practices, choir-practices, catechetical and spiritual talks took place more frequently. Meanwhile, foreign priests were replaced in all the parishes and Chinese priests took up the position of parish priest and important posts such as rectors of major and minor seminaries. In particular, Bishop Gong Pinmei became the bulwark of the Church in Shanghai, and took charge of church affairs.

At that time the Catholic schools were all nationalized. The remaining Chinese priests and sisters became heads or assistant heads, but government-appointed personnel were in important top posts. In political study classes, "Evolution: From Ape to Man" was a common topic. "Religion is the Opium of the People" was another. So in the schools a struggle was beginning between two groups: some students followed the teachers of politics and the communist youth organizations while the Catholics supported the priests and nuns as before.

...At that time I did not actually realize that an attack on the Church was impending. When my sister, her friend Xiaobai and I attended the religious instruction classes, we eagerly desired to be baptized, enter the Church, and become God's children, free from the sin in which mankind was entangled, and ready to advance toward the state of radiant glory.

One day Sister called us to her office and said, "I thank God because He has chosen you for baptism. But I must tell you frankly that the Church is now facing persecution and is beginning gradually to meet trials. I hope you will consider this carefully... Tell me afterwards what you have decided." We walked away from her office. We did think it over again, pondering on how we could follow the faith we wished to embrace, never anticipating that we, who had never done evil, would one day have to suffer. We spoke to our parents quite frankly.

...My parents were upright people who loved us and always granted our requests. In fact, they themselves were also naturally inclined to religious belief, so they agreed without the slightest hesitation.

It was May 13, 1950, the day of Our Lady's apparition in Fatima, when my younger sister, Xiaobai and I, just like the three eye-witnesses of Our Lady's apparition, were entrusted to her care, and entered the Church as God's daughters.

The 14th was a beautiful morning in May. Again each one wore a white dress, a wreath of flowers on her head, and a white veil. In front of the altar, we received for the first time the Body of Christ. No matter how high price the price to be paid, I would forever seek eternal life, supreme truth, goodness and beauty.[5]

Both Bishop Tang and Wang Xiaoling would have ample time to reflect on just how high a price they would be asked to pay for their steadfastness and devotion to the Catholic faith.

Marriage and the Family

As already mentioned, spring and summer 1950 brought the passage of two important new laws in the PRC. On May 1 the new Marriage Law was promulgated, and on June 30 the Agrarian Reform Law took effect. It would be difficult to overestimate the importance which the new government attached to these two laws, and to the huge national mass campaigns which were organized to implement them. These two initiatives were not intended simply to change the legal or regulatory environment in certain areas; they were intended to alter radically traditional patterns of behavior, and to transform in a fundamental, revolutionary way the very structure of Chinese society.

It is interesting to note that the adoption of a new Marriage Law preceded the promulgation of the Agrarian Reform Law. Perhaps the timing of these two acts offers some additional insight into the importance attached by the communist authorities to the social revolution which the Marriage Law was intended to spearhead. As one sympathetic observer noted, "In one step immemorial feudal customs were made illegal."[6] Since time out of mind, the Chinese family had been the foundation of Chinese society; now, nothing less than the complete transformation of Chinese family life was the objective of this new law.

In its legal aspect, the law sought primarily to insure the equality of the sexes, and in order to do so, it outlawed a number of practices and traditions deeply embedded in Chinese culture. In Article 1 the new law declared:

> The arbitrary and compulsory feudal marriage system, which is based on the superiority of man over woman and which ignores the children's interests, shall be abolished.
>
> The New Democratic marriage system, which is based on free choice of partners, on monogamy, on equal rights for both sexes, and on protection of the lawful interests of women and children, shall be put into effect.

Article 2 banned "bigamy, concubinage, child betrothal, interference with the remarriage of widows, and the exaction of money or gifts in connection with marriage."[7] The remaining sections of the law dealt with the marriage contract, rights and duties of husband and wife, relations betwen parents and children, divorce, maintenance and education of children after divorce, property and maintenance after divorce, and "bylaws."

Most of the provisions of the Marriage Law sound quite modern and Western, aiming as they did to liberate women from the control first of their fathers and later of their husbands, or in the case of widows, of their husband's male relatives. Yet, modern and desirable as many of the provisions might have been from a Western point of view, they were aimed at the nexus of relations which formed the very heart of the Chinese family system. They sought to bring about, that is, not merely the evolutionary shift toward a more "modern" view of equality of the sexes, but rather the immediate, revolutionary transformation of the patterns of relationships and loyalties which formed the very bedrock of Chinese society. Indeed, the desire to "sweep away" the old ways in one bold thrust appears to have characterized much of the thinking of the leaders of New China during this early period. In this regard, the Marriage Law, it seems, represented not so much impatience with the old ways, but rather the confidence that "feudalism" in family relations could be more or less quickly overcome. Over the years, however, the cultural and historical patterns of social interaction which the Marriage Law sought to eradicate would prove more durable than many would have imagined at the time.

In the early 1950s, however, all change seemed possible to the leaders of New China, and quickly too. There is no reason to doubt that these same leaders regarded the twin thrusts of Marriage Law and Agrarian Reform (combined with education of the young and re-education of the no-longer-young) as among the principal policies which would usher in a new era in China. And this new era would be characterized by the more or less rapid transformation of Chinese society according to the Maoist revolutionary vision.

Agrarian Reform

If the Marriage Law was intended to alter traditional patterns of domestic relations, the Agrarian Reform Law attacked entrenched patterns of social and economic relations in the countryside where nearly 90 percent of the Chinese lived and worked.[8] The aim of the land reform was to give land to the landless by redistributing the landholdings of those who had too much and were, therefore, considered to be "exploiters." In the case of the worst of the exploiters, those defined as "landlords" (as distinguished from "rich peasants" who were to be spared liquidation temporarily), they were to be struggled against and liquidated, thus involving the peasants in a form of class warfare.[9]

The land reform began peacefully enough in the summer of 1950 but soon evolved into the sort of mass revolutionary terror that the Party leaders had initially said they wished to avoid.[10] The violence of the land reform melded with that of the campaign against counterrevolutionaries which began in 1951, and both eventually claimed millions of victims through execution, confinement in labor camps, and suicide.[11] Nor was the violence of the land reform movement simply the result of local leaders becoming overzealous. As one scholar observed:

> For all its local upheaval, the process of land reform never quite eluded central direction and control. Its violence was, with local variations, choreographed by the cadres, and the cadres, with local exceptions, responded to direction from the center.[12]

And though the party hoped to avoid disruption in agricultural production to the greatest extent possible, the revolutionary aims of the land reform required the toleration or instigation of class warfare and violence. Long before, Mao Zedong had written this dictum:

> To put it bluntly, it is necessary to create terror for awhile in every rural area, or otherwise it would be impossible to suppress the activities of the counterrevolutionaries in the countryside or overthrow the authority of the gentry.[13]

Socially, then, the most important result of the land reform movement was the elimination of the gentry class in the rural areas. Since imperial times the rural gentry had provided a link between local society and the central government. This group had traditionally provided leadership in the countryside by virtue of its social status, education, and access to those in positions of power.[14] Into the power vacuum created by the destruction of the rural gentry moved the Communist Party. In addition to its social objectives, therefore, the land reform movement also provided the party with a political opportunity and a strategy for consolidating its power in the countryside.

While it was no doubt hoped by many that the distribution of land to landless peasants was the final and ultimate objective of the land reform program, the leaders of the Communist Party had longer-range objectives. Indeed, it soon became clear that the private ownership of land by the peasants was not the objective of the agrarian reform movement at all. Redistribution of land was but the first step toward the ultimate goal of collectivization of agriculture. The push toward collectivization would begin with the creation of peasants' mutual-aid teams and culminate with the organization of the vast agricultural communes.

For Catholics in the countryside, the land reform movement proved to be a difficult trial. The beginning of land reform almost always brought with it a prohibition against organized religious activities. All churches in the rural areas were closed during the land reform, and most never re-opened. The government made no secret of this policy the *Xinhua* (New China) *News Agency* announced:

> ...in areas where the land reform is going on, church activities may upset the government's work. Therefore it is better to stop all church activities in such areas (including services and Bible classes) before the land reform is completed.[15]

Moreover, church lands were among those designated to be "requisitioned" by the government. Article 3 of the Law specified that, "The rural land belonging to ancestral shrines, temples, monasteries churches, schools, and organizations... shall be requisitioned."[16] Though the Law specifically stipulated that "appropriate measures" should be devised to make it possible for schools, orphanages and the like to "solve the financial problems" facing them as a result of the confiscation of church lands, the land reform effectively sounded the death knell for such institutions. The twin burdens of taxation and confiscation of land would soon make it impossible for the Church to carry on its educational and welfare activities in the countryside. Indeed, as the months passed it became more and more difficult for the priests and religious to survive at all. One diocese in Central China reported:

> Only two mission-sponsored schools in country places remain open; all others have come under communist control. The last surviving Catholic hospital in the diocese's outlying districts has been taxed to a point where it can no longer operate.[17]

Another diocese in Sichuan wrote:

> The old cliché about death and taxes being among life's inflexible certainties is being brought home more and more to missionaries of this diocese. Taxes have reduced them to a state bordering on pauperism. Many priests now live with Christian and pagan families who graciously supply them with free food and lodging.[18]

Still, Catholic priests and religious, including many of the foreign missionaries struggled to persevere. For the foreign missionaries especially, the situation would become even more tenuous with the outbreak of the Korean War.

Resist America—Aid Korea

On June 25, 1950, North Korean forces invaded the South across the 38th parallel. Two days later, the United States interposed the Seventh Fleet in the Taiwan Straits between Taiwan and mainland China, thus preventing a communist attack on the island stronghold to which Generalissimo Chiang Kai-shek and the Nationalist armies had retreated in 1949. On October 25, PRC "volunteers" entered combat against American and United Nations forces on the Korean peninsula.

China's entry into the Korean War was accompanied by a massive nationwide campaign to "Resist America" and "Aid Korea." So violent were the emotions unleashed during this campaign that the possibility of any future foreign missionary activity in China was cast seriously in doubt. Indeed, one author observed of China's entry into the war, "[it] brought any speculation concerning a possible future role of the missionary in China completely to an end."[19] Supported and encouraged by the government, the Resist America—Aid Korea campaign unleashed a nationwide wave of xenophobia. Anti-Americanism became the *sine qua non* of Chinese patriotism. Everywhere churches and religious institutions were forced to sever their connections with foreign, especially American, sources of support. Foreign missionaries, and their Chinese counterparts as well, were pressured to sign statements and to participate in movements denouncing American aggression in Korea lest they be accused of collusion with the imperialists.

Archbishop Tang:
> Religious people, especially the Catholics and Protestants, were summoned for meetings as frequent as once or twice a week. Sometimes it was necessary to join their parades, with all walks of life in the city represented. The parade usually started at 8 A.M. and lasted until 4 or 5 P.M....
>
> The government sometimes sent fundraising collection teams from door to door. The Catholics, in order to avoid trouble and not to appear unpatriotic, donated the following items:

1) Fifty cotton-padded garments for the volunteers, each costing fifteen *yuan*....

2) Each priest donated five *yuan*, and I had to give a double sum, i.e., ten *yuan*.

3) A second donation of the same amount as the last time.

Concerning the parades, I did not join in, but neither did I stop others from going. Sometimes I even lent my own white shirt to the priests. (It was necessary to put on white shirts and blue trousers for the processions.)

Once three young girls of about sixteen or seventeen, whom I did not know, came suddenly to the parlor of the bishop's house (the 2nd floor of the Carmelite monastery) to interview me. They asked this one question, "Bishop, is the Korean War just or unjust?" I answered, "I do not know whether it is just or not. You are students, and you should work hard at your studies." They left our place. Later, people discovered that these three girls had been sent to test my attitude toward the "Resist America-Help Korea" movement [sic].

When I was arrested later, the cadres asked me, "Why did you not encourage people to join the army? Instead, you told them to study and held them back. You opposed the 'Resist America-Help Korea' movement. It is lucky for you that you got no American money. That would have made things worse."[20]

For Catholics, the Resist America—Aid Korea campaign posed special difficulties. Like the Protestant churches, many Catholic activites in China depended upon foreign financial support. In addition, however, the Catholic Church suffered from the special stigma of its foreign connection with Rome. In an atmosphere which was increasingly anti-religious and anti-foreign, prospects for any sort of accommodation between the new government of the PRC and the Holy See in Rome became less and less likely. Barely eight months after the entrance of China into the Korean War, the Papal Internuncio in China, Archbishop Antonio Riberi, would be placed under house arrest in Nanjing.

Increasingly, reports reached Hong Kong of Catholic missionaries being charged with "counterrevolutionary" activities, or with "imperialist" crimes. Priests were no longer merely cultural imperialists or poisoners of Chinese minds. More and more, they were accused of being American or imperialist spies as well. One diocese sent this report:

A two-day police investigation was undertaken at [the] mission. Guards were posted and the premises, not excluding the chimney, eaves, wood piles and rice bins, were minutely searched. On the following day the pastor learned the reason for the fine-toothed combing. Someone had filed a report with the police that the mission was concealing a radio transmitter, hand weapons, shells, unregistered radios and conducting anti-Red activities.[21]

In another case, a priest was expelled after thirty years of missionary work in China. The *Mission Bulletin* reported:

He was accused of being a spy, and held in custody for almost a year and a half before being sent out of the country. The accusation was brought against him by one individual. The fact that he posessed a typewriter seemed to confirm the charge for the officials.[22]

Expulsion of Catholic missionaries was also becoming increasingly common. These expulsions would reach a flood in 1952.

The anti-foreign atmosphere of the "Resist America—Aid Korea" campaign also made it easier for the authorities to justify squeezing and pressuring the missions through the already-established methods of taxes and confiscations. Confiscations steadily reduced churchholdings, and increasingly the confiscations came to be churches themselves rather than auxillary buildings. Every issue of the *Mission Bulletin* was now filled with reports such as:

There is hardly a church in the diocese which has not been taken over by the Reds.

The cathedral as a place of worship was closed down by the authorities on December 10. Mass, confession, benediction, baptisms, and public devotions are now forbidden.... The cathedral is now being used as a public meeting hall and for theatricals....

Recently two churches were requisitioned as meeting halls. Pictures of the new "national heroes" were placed over those of the saints....

The latest tax levy on mission churches and compounds was computed according to the solidity of the buildings.[23]

On December 29, 1950, the 65th session of the Cabinet passed an ordinance decreeing the "Registration of the cultural, educational and relief organs and religious organizations which receive foreign assistance or are engaged in financial transactions with foreign countries."[24] The registration of church properties still in the hands of church authorities, including most of the properties in the cities, was a prelude to the heavy taxation of those properties. In many cases, the immediate tax burden was sufficiently heavy that the dioceses were rendered virtually penniless, and properties such as the bishop's house, the Catholic Center, seminaries and the like had to be abandoned by the missionaries and let out to tenants so that rental income could be generated to pay the ongoing taxes.[25]

It was also in the context of the anti-foreign, anti-imperialist atmosphere of China's entry into the Korean War that the government began to bring strong pressure to bear on all of the Christian churches, both Protestant and Catholic, to sever all of their foreign institutional connections. Failure to do so would soon be offered as *prima facie* evidence of an unpatriotic, or pro-American, or imperialist stance. For patriotic Catholics this posed an especially painful dilemma.

Origin of the Three Autonomies

In the first two weeks of May 1950, a group of approximately twenty Protestant church leaders held a series of three meetings in Beijing with Premier Zhou En-lai. The meetings produced a "Manifesto" approved by Premier Zhou and authored by Wu Yao-zong of the Chinese YMCA, a long-time communist who was destined to become one of the principal leaders of the Protestant Three Self Movement.[26]

The thrust of the manifesto was to assert the anti-imperialist patriotism of the various Christian groups and to affirm their support for the notion that the Protestant churches should be independent of foreign imperialist connections in terms of administration, finances and propagation of the faith. The title given to the movement, in its fully developed form, was *San Zi Yun Dong*, translated by Protestant groups as the Three Self Movement and by Catholics as the Three (or, sometimes, Triple) Autonomies, that is, autonomy of administration, autonomy of finances and autonomy of propagation of the faith.

There were no Catholic representatives at these first meetings with Zhou En-lai, and indeed there was not yet officially created any organizational form through which the Three Self Movement might operate, but the idea of such autonomy for the Christian churches had been much discussed, and many expressions of support for the Manifesto had been publicized nationwide by the time a similar movement toward "autonomy" was launched in the Catholic Church. Though the government's motives in pressing the autonomy movement were quite clear, as we shall see, the individual motives of those who organized and supported the movement pose much more complex and difficult questions.

There can be little doubt that the government's principal objective in pushing the autonomy movement was to weaken, penetrate, and control the religious institutions and their activities. Autonomy meant that the foreign missionaries would be expelled or encouraged in a variety of ways to depart China on their own, and that the churches would be cut off from the foreign sources of financial support without which many of their activities would be unsupportable. Such independent or autonomous religious institutions would presumably be more susceptible to state control. That penetration and control was precisely the aim of the communist authorities would become unmistakably clear with the establishment of a cabinet level Bureau of Religious Affairs in 1951, and with the creation of the Chinese Catholic Patriotic Association (CCPA) in 1957 to replace the *San Zi Yun Dong* organization.[27]

The individuals promoting and supporting the autonomy movement exhibited a complex variety of motives. Some, to be sure, were agents of the Communist Party, as opponents of the movement charged. Others harbored deep-seated resentments against the foreign domination of the various Christian denominations. Many apparently believed that support of the movement was an honest way of demonstrating patriotism and love of country. Finally, there were those who believed that supporting the autonomy movement was the only way to insure the survival of the churches at all. This was the faint hope of some that it might be better to have a church controlled by the government than to have no church at all.

The autonomy movement in the Catholic Church began with the publication on November 30, 1950 of a "Manifesto on Independence and Reform."[28] [See Chapter Four, Appendix 1.] Father Wang Liang-zuo of Guang Yuan in northern Sichuan Province was credited as author of the manifesto, which was said to have issued from a meeting of more than 500 Catholics called to support the "complete severing of all relations with Imperialism and for the establishment of a self-governing, self-supporting and self-propagating new church."[28] The manifesto began with this assertion:

> Since Catholicism came to China, imperialists have tried by all possible methods to use the church as a forerunner of aggression.... American imperialists have been particularly condemnable; they have used money and various little kindnesses to bribe the Chinese. Their obvious purpose was to use the church in China as a means of long-term aggression.[29]

The publication of the manifesto was followed by reports from various parts of China of "reform meetings" usually attended by several hundred Catholics for the purpose of "propagating the patriotic movement."[30] A little more than one month following the publication of the manifesto, a second "manifesto" was published in Sichuan Province. [See Chapter Four, Appendix 2.] This second, so-called Chungking [Chongqing] Manifesto, was said to have been writen by the Vicar General, Father Shi Ming-liang, following a reform meeting of nearly seven hundred local Catholics. The tone of the Chungking manifesto is fairly well summed-up in its last paragraph:

> Faithful of Chungking and other places! We must increase our vigilance, heighten the learning (of politics), lay bare the facts of how imperialism has used the Catholic Church for the secret invasion of China. We have to liquidate those elements in the church who are ready to serve imperialism, in order to delete all trace of imperialism.[31]

Of the Chungking manifesto, the *Mission Bulletin* observed that it "does not look too innocent, and what is more, it does not appear to be a document written by a Catholic, be he good or bad. The style of the manifesto contains all of the usual clichés of communist documents; there is hardly a word in it which would prove that the writer knew the Church from the inside."[32] Even allowing for the admitted bias of the *Mission Bulletin* in the matter of an "independent" Catholic Church, their description of the Chungking manifesto appears to be an appropriate one. The use of the term "liquidate" in connection with those who "serve imperialism" hinted of even bigger trouble ahead, especially in view of the rather precise meaning applied to the term "liquidate" by the communist authorities.

The beginning of the *San Zi Yun Dong* was accompanied by a sizeable nationwide campaign to publicize the movement and lend it support. Indeed, perhaps support is too weak a term, as it was already clear at the time—and would become even clearer as government pressure on behalf of the movement mounted—that the communist authorities were the chief authors and sponsors of the movement. Articles in support of the movement began to appear almost daily in the news organ of the Communist Party, the *People's Daily* [*Renmin Ribao*], and in the releases of the official government *Xinhua* [*New China*] News Agency. These articles bore titles such as "Government Administration Council Decision to Stamp Out American Imperialistic Cultural Aggression Warmly Supported by Shanghai Religious and Relief Circles,"[33] "Exposure of American Churches' Aggression Against China,"[34] and also "80,000 Christians Sign Reform Statement in Determination to Sever Relations with Imperialism."[35]

All over the country, meetings were called by the authorities for the purpose of promoting the *San Zi Yun Dong*. Leaders of the various religions and Christian denominations would be recruited to address the meeting in support of China's efforts in Korea, against American imperialism, and in favor of independence for the religious institutions. In the case of the Catholic representatives, special emphasis was placed promoting the notion that Catholics should sever their relationship with the Holy See. The results of these meetings were not always pleasing to the officials who organized them. On more than one occasion priests brought in to speak for the local Catholic community displeased the authorities by rising in defense of the universal church rather than promoting the movement toward independence. One particularly clear defense of the traditional Catholic position was offered by Father Joseph Li Wei-ch'wan [Li Wei-quan] at a December 1950 meeting in Western China. [See Chapter Four, Appendix 3.] About the relationship of China's Catholics with the Holy See, Father Li gave this explanation:

> We do not look on the pope as a political leader but as our leader in faith and morals for he is the head of the church and the vicar of

> Jesus Christ. We have no political relations with him, no relations at all except in those things which concern our supernatural faith.[36]

Despite the clarity of Father Li's defense of the position of the Catholic Church, the official press announced the following day that he had spoken in support of "independence."[37]

At the same time there began again, for the first time since the establishment of the communist government, what would become a drumbeat of charges of espionage against representatives of the Catholic Church. The *People's Daily* editorialized:

> For a long time imperialist elements have controlled the higher organs of Catholicism in Rome and America and have fostered in China the notorious reactionary conspirators [Nanjing Archbishop, later Cardinal Paul] Yupin [Yubin] and his like in their control of Chinese Catholic affairs.[38]

The editorial also charged that Chinese Catholic students were gathered into the espionage organization of Archbishop Yupin "to send them to the United States for espionage training." The espionage charges would become even more frantic and widespread as the government launched a massive campaign to eliminate "counterrevolutionaries" later in 1951.

The *San Zi Yun Dong* posed serious problems for all of the Christian churches, most especially in the area of finances, but also as a result of the loss suffered by the departure of the foreign missionaries. For the Catholic Church, however, there was an additional, probably insurmountable problem. Independence of administration and of propagation of the faith meant separation from the Holy See and from the Pope as the Vicar of Christ and Shepherd of the Universal Church. An "independent" Chinese national Catholic Church would be a church not in union with Rome, and thus not in union with the body of Catholic faithful around the world. That this was precisely what the government had in mind would become clear soon enough.

For the faithful, most of whom were also patriotic Chinese, the independence movement would pose an especially painful dilemma. Those who stood clearly and steadfastly for the universal church, symbolized by Bishops Tang of Guangzhou and Kung of Shanghai, would endure decades of suffering for their faithfulness to Rome. For those faithful leaders of the Church who came to symbolize the resistance to the *San Zi Yun Dong*, the implications of the movement were unmistakably clear, as was their response. Bishop Tang wrote:

> They urged me to give in to the People's Government and launch the "Three-Self" Reform like the Protestants and so on. I felt very sad and reproached them saying, "We must stand in the church's position to face the other side (the communist government). We should not stand in the other side's position to face the church!"[39]

The choices for Chinese Catholics would not become any easier as the pressure to participate in the *San Zi Yun Dong* became more intense during the year 1951. The *San Zi Yun Dong* would also usher in a period of nearly four decades of uncertainty about the nature of the Catholic Church in China, or as some saw it, the Chinese Catholic Church, about its relationship with Rome, and about the relationship of the Vatican with the government of the People's Republic of China. Most of those who remained faithful to Rome would eventually be removed from the public stage. They would be imprisoned, confined to labor camps, or killed. For those who survived, however, their re-emergence into public life in the late 1970s and early 1980s raised once again most of the unsettled questions remaining from the early 1950s.

APPENDIX ONE
"Manifesto on Independence and Reform"
Father Wang Liang-zuo
November 30, 1950
(*China Missionary Bulletin*, February 1951)

Fellow Catholics throughout the country:

Since Catholicism came to China, imperialists have tried by all possible methods to use the church as a forerunner of aggression. France, for instance, declared a war of aggression on China on the pretext of the unexplained death of a French priest. When the war was over, the French forced the article guaranteeing "the right to preach in China" into the Peace Treaty [Treaty of Tientsin (Tianjin) June 1858, ed.], thus betraying their intention of carrying on aggression against the Chinese. American imperialists have been particularly condemnable; they have used money and various kindnesses to bribe the Chinese. Their obvious purpose was to use the church in China as a means of long-term aggression.

Today a new China has arisen; independent, democratic, and free. Imperialists are hostile to the Chinese people; they are set on expanding their war of aggression. In spite of the repeated warnings by peace-loving Chinese, they have carried the flame of war to the borders of our north-eastern provinces. They have bombed unarmed cities and innocent civilians. Speaking as patriotic citizens, therefore, we have decided to break off all relations with imperialist countries and rid ourselves of all pro-American attachments, as well as of sentiments of fear and inferiority. We are determined to build up a new church which practices self-government, self-support and self-propagation. We will not allow the Holy Church to be soiled by imperialist filth.

Dear Fellow Catholics: in order to shatter the imperialist conspiracy of aggression, we should support the Anti-American, Aid-Korea and Home-Defense movement with even greater activities, strengthen the world's democratic "peace-camp," and fight for the reconstruction of new China.

We have convened a meeting on the 30th of November, at which local authorities were invited to be present. All Catholics expressed their wholehearted support for this movement, and we ask you to respond to our call with action, so as to ensure the success of this movement, and make known the experience of your own conscience.

APPENDIX TWO
"The Chungking Manifesto"
Father Shi Ming-liang
(*China Missionary Bulletin*, February 1951)

During the last hundred years' history of our country, the invasion of imperialism, by a series of unequal treaties, placed an iron chain around the neck of the Chinese people, and degraded China to the weak state of semi-colonialism and semi-feudalism. Imperialism used religion as a tool of this invasion, and in order to realize the secret aim of invasion, abused the privilege of propagating the faith freely in China, and under the cover of hospitals and schools founded by the Church, espionage and destructive activity was carried on [and] exercised in the interior of China. At the same time, with small gifts and services, the simple people were enticed to enter into their service.

At present the whole population of China has risen up against imperialism. We Catholics too have become conscious that the Church, when used for the aims of imperialism, not only hinders the realization of independence, democracy, peace and union of China, but in the face of the proven fact that missionaries have worked as spies in Shih Chia Chuang [Shijiazhuang] and elsewhere, we now know that the originally Immaculate Church is steeped in murderous blood. We Catholics have decided, for love of our country, to stand united and firm in the viewpoint of the People, so support the Common Program, to realize self-government, self-support, and self-propagation of the Chinese Catholic Church, in order to strengthen the lasting peace of the world, and to fight for an independent, democratic, unified strong New China.

Faithful of Chungking [Chongqing] and other places! We must increase our vigilance, heighten the new learning [of politics], lay bare the facts of how imperialism has used the Catholic Church for the secret invasion of China. We have to liquidate those elements in the Church who are ready to serve imperialism, in order to delete all trace of imperialism. We must strive valiantly to realize this aim of renewal in the shortest period of time.

APPENDIX THREE
Speech of Father Li Wei-ch'wan [Li Weiquan]
  December 27, 1950
  (*China Missionary Bulletin*, March 1951)

1) The end of every religion is the attainment of beatitude in the other life. No one can attain this end unless he lives well in this life, for this life is a preparation for that which is to come. No Christian can live a good life unless he is a good citizen and a patriot. Therefore we Christians should be first-rate patriots and it is our duty to defend our country. We are, then, against every imperialism in so far as it is inhuman, or unjust, or injurious to our country.

2) The Church and the Faith have no connection with imperialism. Not all foreigners are imperialists. We do not put our trust in men but in Jesus Christ whose word has come to us. Further we believe in Jesus Christ not because he was an historic Jew but because he is the Son of God and God himself. This indeed is foolishness and a stumbling block to those who do not believe, but to us who believe, He is the Way, the Truth and the Life. We put no trust in the words of missionaries unless they preach the Gospel of Jesus Christ.

3) We do not look on the Pope as a political leader but as our leader in faith and morals, for he is the head of the Church and the Vicar of Jesus Christ. We have no political relations with him, no relations at all except in those things which concern our supernatural faith.

4) On religious independence we have our own views:

a. I am a missionary and these two seminarians [at the meeting] will one day be missionaries. We know from history that in every part of the world, the foundations of the faith were laid by foreigners; then it was built up and completed by native priests. This is true of Italy, England, Germany and all of the other countries of Europe. This is what is now happening in China, Japan, India and in many other nations of Asia and Africa.

Twenty-six years ago there were no Chinese among the rulers of the Church in China. Now almost a quarter of the hierarchy is composed of Chinese bishops. It is the wish of the Holy

Roman Church that the native clergy should flourish and increase and that it should last. The transference of the local Archepiscopal See to Chinese clergy is merely a matter of time. It will come about as soon as there are enough Chinese priests to run the archdiocese.

b. The number of our Christians is still very small. The educational and cultural institutions of the Church and its works of charity are maintained by the subscriptions of foreign benefactors. These are nearly all poor humble folk whom no one could call capitalists or imperialists. When the day comes on which all Chinese are Christians, then all our works will stand on their own feet and there will be no more need for foreign alms. Then we will gladly come to the aid of foreigners in their similar needs, in the same spirit of the love of Christ.

c. On many points the Protestants hold the same faith as we do. But the ideals and the spirit of their faith are very different. We have our own ideas and our own explanation of the threefold independence which they put forward, and we act according to those ideas and that explanation.

NOTES

1. Mao Zedong, "Report on an Investigation of the Peasant Movement in Hunan," March 1927, *Selected Works of Mao Tse-tung*, vol. 1, Beijing: Foreign Languages Press, 1965, 28.

2. Information on Archbishop Dominic Tang comes primarily from two sources: first, a series of personal interviews and visits over a period of five years, including one long tape-recorded interview at his residence at Wah Yan College in Hong Kong conducted on July 10, 1984. A shortened version of this interview was published in James T. Myers, "Catholics and Cultural Revoltuion," *America*, New York, vol. 152, no. 21, June 1, 1985. The second source is Archbishop Tang's memoirs published in Hong Kong but still largely unavailable to a more general audience, *How Inscrutable His Ways: Memoirs 1951–1981*. Hong Kong: Aidan Publicities and Printing, 1987. [Hereafter cited as *Tang: Memoirs*.] Sections of the *Memoirs* are used with the kind permission of the Archbishop.

3. *Tang: Memoirs*, 9–19.

4. Information about Wang Xiaoling comes from personal conversations with her, and from her memoirs which, like Archbishop Tang's, have received only very limited circulation. Wang Xiaoling, *Many Waters: Experiences of a Chinese Woman Prisoner of Conscience*. Hong Kong: Caritas Printing Training Center, 1988. "Wang Xiaoling" is the pen name of Catherine Ho used to protect her identity when she was living in Hong Kong. [Hereafter cited as *Xiaoling: Memoirs*.] Selections from *Many Waters* are used with the kind permission of Catherine Ho.

5. *Xiaoling: Memoirs*, 13–19.

6. Felix Greene, *China: The Country Americans are not Allowed to Know*. New York: Ballentine Books, 1961, 396.

7. *The Marriage Law* [Promulgated by the Central Peoples Government on May 1, 1950], in Theodore H.E. Chen, ed., *The Chinese Communist Regime: Documents and Commentary*. New York: Frederick A. Praeger, 1967, 270–274.

8. The Chinese State Statistical Bureau calculated the urban population of the People's Republic of China at 10.6 per cent at year end 1949. See: Judith Bannister, *China's Changing Population*. Stanford, CA: Stanford University Press, 1987, 329.

9. For the text of the *Agrarian Reform Law of the People's Republic of China* (Promulgated by the Central People's Government on June 30, 1950) see: Theodore H.E. Chen. *The Chinese Communist Regime, op. cit.*, 196–203.

10. On the land reform see: A. Doak Barnett. *Communist China: The Early Years, 1949–55*, New York: Frederick A. Praeger, 196, 172, *ff*; Maurice

Meisner. *Mao's China: A History of the People's Republic*, New York: The Free Press, 1977, 100, *ff*; H.F. Schurmann. *Ideology and Organization in Communist China*, Berkeley, CA: University of California Press, 1966, 434, *ff*; Richard L. Walker. *China Under Communism: The First Five Years*, New Haven: Yale University Press, 1955, 88, *ff*; Jan S. Prybyla. *The Political Economy of Communist China*, Scranton, PA: International Textbook Co., 1970, 33–52.

11. Precise figures are probably impossible to obtain. Some sense of orders of magnitude may be gauged, however, by Chinese figures which placed the rural population at about 500 million and the "landlords" at 4 percent of that number. Meisner asserts that the "great majority of the 20,000,000 people classified as members of landlord families were provided with small plots of land," rather than being executed or confined in labor camps. Even if the great majority were to be placed at 90 percent, that would still leave 2 million who were harshly dealt with. See Maurice Meisner, *Mao's China, op. cit.*, 108. Walker cites a figure of 24,000,000 confined in forced labor camps by 1954. See Richard L. Walker, *China Under Communism, op. cit.*, 222.

12. Jan S. Prybyla, *The Political Economy of Communist China, op. cit.*, 52.

13. Mao Zedong, "Report on an Investigation of the Peasant Movement in Hunan," *Selected Works of Mao Tse-tung*, vol. 1, *op. cit.*, 29.

14. See Chung-li Chang. *The Chinese Gentry: Studies on Their Role in Nineteenth-Century Chinese Society*, Seattle: University of Washington Press, 1955; also Kung-chuan Hsiao, *Rural China: Imperial Control in the Nineteenth Century*, Seattle: University of Washington Press, 1960.

15. "What One Should Know About the Question of Catholic and Protestant Religions, *New China News Agency* (NCNA), Beijing, November 23, 1950. *Cf.*, "Gleaning Communist Policy," CMB, no. 1, January 1951, 50–51.

16. Theodore H.E. Chen, *The Chinese Communist Regime, op. cit.*, 196.

17. CMB, no. 1, January 1951, 75.

18. *Ibid.*, 76–77.

19. Richard C. Bush, Jr. *Religion in Communist China*, Nashville, TN: Abingdon Press, 1970, 42.

20. *Tang: Memoirs*, 29–31.

21. CMB, no. 2, February 1951, 181.

22. CMB, no. 3, March 1951, 264.

23. CMB, no. 4, April 1951, 364–365.

24. *Ta Kung Pao*, Hong Kong, December 30, 1950; *cf.*, CMB, no. 2, February 1951, 158.

25. See, for example, *Tang: Memoirs*, 20–25.

26. For the origins of the Protestant Three Self Movement, see Richard C. Bush, Jr., *Religion in Communist China, op. cit.*, 177 *ff*. On Wu Yaozong see Eric O. Hanson, *Catholic Politics in China and Korea*, New

York: Orbis Books, 1980, 74–75; also *ibid.*, chapter VI, endnote 9.

27. *Cf.* L. Ladany. *The Catholic Church in China.* New York: Freedom House, 1987, 15–16. Also *cf. China News Analysis* (Hereafter CNA), no. 186, Hong Kong, June 28, 1957.

28. "Welcome to the Patriotic Movement of Catholics," *Renmin Ribao (People's Daily)*, editorial, Beijing, January 8, 1951. *Cf. Xinhua* (New China News Agency)—English, January 8, 1951, in *Survey of the China Mainland Press* (Hereafter SCMP), US Consulate General, Hong Kong, no. 44, January 9, 1951. Also *cf.* CMB, no. 2, February 1951, 148–150.

29. *Xinhua*, Beijing, December 13, 1950. *Cf.* CMB no. 2. 2, Feb. 1951, 149–150.

30. *Renmin Ribao* editorial, Beijing, January 8, 1951.

31. CMB No. 2, February 1951, 150.

32. *Ibid.*, 151.

33. *Xinhua*, Shanghai, January 4, 1951, in SCMP no. 42, January 5–6, 1951, 8.

34. *Xinhua*, Beijing, December 15, 1950, in SCMP no. 46, January 11, 1951, 14.

35. *Xinhua*, Shanghai, January 14, 1951, in SCMP no. 48, January 14–15, 1951, 14.

36. CMB, no. 3, March 1951, 273–274.

37. *Ibid.*, 274.

38. *Renmin Ribao* editorial, Beijing, January 8, 1951.

39. *Tang: Memoirs*, 64.

FIVE

THE SUPPRESSION OF COUNTER-REVOLUTIONARIES

> Please make certain that you strike surely, accurately and relentlessly in suppressing the counterrevolutionaries.... To strike relentlessly means resolutely to kill all such reactionary elements as deserve the death penalty.
>
> Mao Zedong[1]

The year 1951 was marked by a relentless series of assaults by the government against the Catholic Church in China. Pressures continued to build behind the government-sponsored drive for Catholic "independence." The Papal Internuncio was placed under house arrest and then expelled. A campaign to defame and discredit Catholic-run orphanages was begun nationwide. The government launched an attack to eliminate the Legion of Mary in China. Departures and expulsions of Catholic missionaries continued. Finally, a number of priests and bishops were charged and convicted of counterrevolutionary crimes. Indeed, the notion that the Catholic Church provided safe haven for counterrevolutionary elements and represented one of the principal institutions fostering pro-imperialist, anti-government activity henceforth became the standard justification for virtually all attacks against the Church.

Defining Counterrevolutionary Crimes

On February 20, 1951, the Central People's Government Council promulgated the "Regulations for the Suppression of

Counterrevolutionaries."[2] [See Chapter Five, Appendix 1.] This suppression campaign launched what can only fairly be described as an open reign of terror throughout most of China in 1951. The human toll of this terror can only be estimated but it was surely enormous, probably in the millions.[3]

The problem of calculating the number of executions resulting from the campaign to suppress counterrevolutionaries is complicated by the fact that the land reform movement was still under way in the countryside and most observers agree that the body count in the countryside was even higher than that in the cities.[4] Some idea of the scale of the terror can be estimated, however, from the reports of those who attempted to piece together local government statistics on the suppression of counterrevolutionary activities. One scholar studying Canton, for example, reported more than 28,000 executions in Guangdong Province in a period of ten months between August 1950 and October 1951.[5]

All over China the press reported mass trials followed by mass executions. In many cases radio broadcasts of the trials and executions were used, including broadcasts over public loudspeakers, in order to give the widest possible publicity to the campaign. The high visibility given to the suppression campaign was at least partly to gain the widest possible public support, but the use of terror in this way was also intended as a warning to those Chinese citizens not wholly committed to the aims of the communist revolution. Regarding the campaign in the city of Canton [Guangzhou], it was reported:

> In Canton alone, for example, an estimated 70,000 representatives from various groups in the city were organized to attend mass rallies; 170,000 were mobilized to attend exhibitions; and 1,130,000 heard the proceedings of the large accusation meetings on the radio.[6]

What, precisely, were the crimes of which the victims of this campaign were guilty in the view of the government? The "Regulations" prohibited a number of very specific acts such as, "Pointing out bombing targets for enemy planes or vessels," or, "Dropping poison, disseminating disease germs, and other means of causing serious disasters among men, livestock or agricultural products." The "Regulations," however, also cast a broader net of more vague offences. There was, in fact, no attempt made to define the term "counterrevolutionary activities" which appears over and over in the "Regulations" in contexts such as, "Those who use feudalistic sects and societies to carry on counterrevolutionary activities shall be sentenced to death or life imprisonment," or, "Engaging in counterrevolutionary propaganda or manufacturing and spreading rumors," the penalty for the more serious cases of which was death. Other proscribed acts were sufficiently broad and vague that it was clear that the authorities could use the counterrevolutionary charge to cover an almost limitless range of activities. In addition, the "Regulations" also retroactively prescribed penalties, including the death penalty, for acts committed "before liberation [1949]."

As we have indicated, the Chinese authorities were not operating according to a Western concept of law and legality. It was probably considered unnecessary and superfluous, therefore, to define precisely the concept of "counterrevolutionary activities." Such activities were by definition any which impeded or retarded the progress of the Chinese revolution toward the communist millenium. As we suggested in Chapter Two, the goals of the revolution, as determined by the most advanced element in the society, the communist vanguard, were not open for debate. It was a settled matter that China had been set on the road to socialism and communism, and anything less than complete enthusiasm for the goals of the revolution, therefore, left one vulnerable to the charge of "counterrevolutionary activity."

Were the traditional secret societies which became a prime target of the campaign actually counterrevolutionary? By this definition there is no doubt that they were. Indeed, by their very existence they represented a counterrevolutionary force in Chinese society. The position of the Catholic Church in China was somewhat analogous to that of the secret societies insofar as the very existence of the Church represented a counterrevolutionary force in Chinese society. It was probably logically impossible to be both a faithful Catholic and, at the same time, to be totally committed to the goals of the communist revolution.

In addition, it cannot be disputed that a sizeable majority of the Catholic hierarchy in China was more than a little hostile to the Chinese communist movement. This is not to say that the entire Catholic leadership was sympathetic to the

Kuomintang (KMT) of Generalissimo Chiang Kai-shek, though some prominent church leaders such as Archbishop Yupin did have close connections to the KMT. Even the vast majority of those who considered themselves non-political, however, feared the communists and opposed what they stood for insofar as the communists were atheists and materialists. In fact, the very non-political stance of many missionaries could itself be regarded as a form of counterrevolutionary activity in that it did nothing to advance the revolutionary cause.

Nor can there be any doubt that the Catholic Church represented an obstacle to the realization of certain revolutionary plans, directives or programs. The official Church hierarchy, and many of its most prominent representatives, opposed the *San Zi Yun Dong* and all that it implied for the Church; prominent bishops opposed the government's assault on the Legion of Mary and ordered their faithful Catholics not to obey the government directive to register as counterrevolutionaries because of their association with the Legion. In addition, there were probably some missionaries who were engaged in activities which were clearly anti-communist, though evidence presented in the cases of espionage prosecuted by the government was usually flimsy and frequently appeared fabricated.

The Catholic Church, therefore, though its representatives may have seen themselves entirely innocent of any wrongdoing, and though these representatives may not have been guilty of any activity which could be considered illegal under a Western concept of law, still represented an important obstacle to the implementation of the communist revolutionary program.

On the other hand, viewed from another perspective, this hostility toward the Church might well appear to have been self-destructive or wasteful. Catholics, after all, were an insignificant minority; why not leave them alone? In fact, an enormous amount of systemic energy went into the government's effort to penetrate, control and eliminate organized religion in the PRC. Catholics, especially the educated and trained missionaries, could have been extremely useful in a poor and backward "developing" nation. Why not co-opt these patriotic and well-meaning elements and utilize their talents? Professor Eric Hanson suggests that the new communist regime most feared the social power of the Church as a transnational actor.[7] This is certainly a plausible assertion, but it seems the threat posed by the Church involved more than this as well.

The Roman Catholic Church, after all, was not the Rotary International, or the Lions Club, or even the YMCA, other transnational actors not without social power. The Church and its various agencies—for example, the Legion of Mary which soon became one of the principal targets of police repression—was dangerous, not because it harbored KMT spies (despite the flurry of such charges leveled at the Church during the suppression campaign), but because it held, taught, proselytized and defended an alternate version of the truth. That it was a transnational actor as well simply made it a more difficult problem for the regime than the other organized religions which, from the government's point of view, could be more easily controlled.[8]

The Church Under Fire

In the first ten months of 1951, the Papal Internuncio, Archbishop Antonio Riberi, and nine other foreign bishops were expelled from China. Nineteen foreign and Chinese bishops were arrested and remained in prison, and five others were under house arrest. Approximately 300 native and foreign priests were being held in jail or labor camps, in addition to the more than 1,000 priests, brothers and sisters who had already been expelled from China, many after spending months in jail under extremely harsh conditions.[9] Two celebrated "espionage" cases were prosecuted in 1951, the description of which may serve as examples of the many such charges of criminal counterrevolutionary activity leveled against Catholic missioners.

On March 7, 1951, three French Jesuits were arrested in Tianjin and charged with espionage. They were Father Alfred Bonningue, former Rector of Tsinku University, Father Henry Pollet, Dean of Sciences at the University, and Father Louis Wattine, Dean of Economics. Aproximately one month later, the official Chinese press began a campaign of publicity against the three priests. In an editorial, the *People's Daily* charged that the French priests had been "serving the interests of American imperialism by sabotaging the liberation enterprise of the Chinese people."[10] More specifically, they were accused of having "sabotaged the Resist U.S.-Aid Korea movement by alleging the 'appearance' of 'Virgin Mary' before American forces of aggression in Korea; and sabotaged the Catholic reformation movement by branding patriotic Catholics as 'renegades' and as the 'devil.'" "Is this not proof enough," asked the editorial, "that they are closely connected with American imperialism?"

The *People's Daily* also sought to refute the assertion that the Catholic Church as a religious institution was above politics and beyond nationalism:

> No man of any sense can possibly consider the kind of espionage activities undertaken by Bonningue and company as 'above politics.' They have collected secret information, sabotaged agrarian reform, sabotaged the Marriage Law, slandered the People's Government, acted as the accomplices of American imperialism, and carried out sabotage activities in general whenever possible.[11]

The editorial closed with a call to all "patriotic" Catholics throughout the country to, "wake up and keep resolutely united so as to smash American imperialism's vicious plot to make use of the Catholic Church for espionage activities."

Three days following the publication of the editorial attacking the three French Jesuits, another *People's Daily* editorial appeared, praising the formation of the Tianjin Catholic Church Reform Promotion Association which had been inaugurated on April 7. It was clear that the government had launched an all-out push for the establishment of an "independent" or "patriotic" Catholic Church in Tianjin. The Catholic churches of Tianjin, said the editorial, "were originally manipulated by imperialist elements and their running dogs who are mortal enemies of the reform movement, and originally the Catholics were not highly awakened." Now, however, "with the arrest of American spy Al Bonningue, which exposed the imperialists' lies 'above nation, above politics,' and 'never having any connection with imperialism,' the reform movement has been further developed."[12]

And, lest the message of the editorial should somehow have escaped the reader, the official Communist Party press organ added this call:

All propaganda agencies and people's bodies should support the patriotic movement of Catholics and help them in their struggle against imperialists.[13]

An even more celebrated case involved Maryknoll Bishop Francis X. Ford. Bishop Ford was one of the early Maryknoll missionaries in the Far East having arrived in China in 1918, one year after his ordination. He was consecrated Bishop of Meihsien [Meixian], Guangdong Province, in 1935. On April 14, 1951, Bishop Ford and his secretary, Sister Joan Marie Ryan, were arrested at the Bishop's residence. The Bishop had been under house arrest since the previous December 27.[14] An April 23rd *Xinhua* news release charged that Bishop Ford had:

...used the occasion of prayer meetings to disseminate rumors, to slander openly the people's government, and to distribute large quantities of booklets published in Hong Kong such as the 'Truth Series.' Bishop Ford had also drawn up a 'plan' to sabotage the Catholic movement for independence, self-support and independent propagation of the faith.[15]

A much longer article describing in detail the charges against Bishop Ford was also released by *Xinhua* on the same day. It was clear that the government wished to justify its attack on Bishop Ford and to solidify public support behind the prosecution. The long article was authored by the top *Xinhua* representative in South China.[16] The article detailed the various "espionage" activities of the Bishop who was described as, "long an American espionage agent in China." The Bishop's mission, said the *Xinhua* correspondent, "[had] been engaged in espionage activities for the American government ever since the day of its establishment." In addition to gathering information for the United States, Bishop Ford was said to have colluded with the KMT, harbored in his mission members of a pro-KMT "Black Legion" together with various other KMT spies and a local "despot landlord." Further, said the report:

Ford consistently engaged in rumor-mongering in the Church and spoke to slander and insult the People's Government. He spread all sorts of rumors...and gave away the 'America Today' and other reactionary pamphlets. Much perturbed by the spreading independence and reformation movement of Chinese Catholics, Ford resorted to scheming for ways and means to sabotage the movement.[17]

Most of the specific counterrevolutionary activities of which Bishop Ford was accused occurred before 1949, the majority taking place during World War II. It has been asserted by some writers that Bishop Ford was in fact involved in gathering information which was useful to the U.S. Army and the Chinese government during the war against Japan. These assertions are strongly refuted by others, including Archibiship Dominic Tang, who knew Bishop Ford personally.[18] There seems little doubt, however, that Bishop Ford, as did many other faithful bishops and priests, opposed the *San Zi Yun Dong*, and the various other efforts of the communist authorities to penetrate and control the Catholic Church. For all of these reasons, Bishop Ford was, by definition, a counterrevolutionary.

On the 200-mile journey from Meihsien to Canton, the Bishop and the Sister were bound like common criminals and paraded through the streets. They were publicly abused and humiliated. The Bishop was brutalized and tortured. He died in a prison hospital on February 21, 1952, less than a year after his arrest.

In the month before the arrest of Bishop Ford, Archbishop Antonio Riberi, the Papal Internuncio, had come under violent press attack from the Chinese government as a result of his having circulated at the end of March 1951, a letter, in Latin, to his fellow bishops warning of the schismatic nature of the *San Zi Yun Dong*. The Archbishop's letter had followed the publication of a highly-publicized "Manifesto" in favor of "independence" signed by some 700 Nanjing Catholics including Father Li Wei-guang, the Nanjing vicar-general. Archbishop Riberi had remained in his post as Papal Internuncio in the former nationalist capital at Nanjing despite the fact that the nationalist government had retreated from the Chinese mainland to Taiwan in 1949. His letter to the bishops made it clear that the Nanjing Manifesto had been drawn up without his knowledge or permission, and that he strongly disagreed with the manifesto's declaration of support for the *San Zi Yun Dong*.

Monsignor Riberi suffered from many of the same liabilities which afflicted other prominent Catholic "enemies" of the communist regime. He was clearly not pro-communist in his political sympathies; he opposed the creation of the *San Zi Yun Dong*;

and he sponsored the establishment of the Legion of Mary (*see below*) in China. The fact that he was still the accredited papal representative to the nationalist government of Generalissimo Chiang Kai-shek also did little to help his cause with the Beijing authorities.

The press campaign against Archbishop Riberi began in April with a *People's Daily* article entitled "Irrevocable Proof of Vatican's Support for Imperialists to Intervene in Internal Affairs of Various Countries."[19] The article reprinted portions of a 1947 order signed by Monsignor Riberi addressed to all organizations, officers, and members of the Catholic Church in China. The thrust of the order was that Catholics should refrain from participating in three pro-communist organizations: the Women's International Democratic Federation, the World Federation of Trade Unions, and the World Federation of Democratic Youths. The Archbishop's order claimed that the organizations, "are ideologically occupied with the propagation of the communist faith and the spread of communism throughout the world. Consequently it behooves all Catholic organizations to avoid cooperating with the above-mentioned organizations as well as to avoid giving sanctuary to their enterprises."[20]

The *People's Daily* then editorialized: "Now let us ask":

(1) If the Vatican is not concerned with political issues, why should it keep watch over these three international democratic organizations.

(2) The Vatican claims that it opposes these three organizations because of their sympathy for communism. Granted that this is true, but what has it to do with the Vatican? Is this not irrevocable proof that the Vatican hates communism and is the mortal enemy of communism?

(3) What right does the Vatican have to order about the Catholics of all nations? Don't the Catholics enjoy any political freedom, or do they have to listen to the Vatican even in such activities as the reviewing of Boy Scouts? Is it not irrevocable proof of the Vatican's attempt to make use of religion as a means of interfering with the internal affairs of various nations?

Therefore, it behooves all patriotic Catholics to refuse to believe the myth that the Vatican is completely unrelated with the imperialists and that it is not concerned with the internal affairs of all countries. Only complete independence shall assure us of a bright future.[21]

On April 19, 1951, *Xinhua* announced the convening four days earlier of the inaugural meeting of the Beijing Catholics' Committee for World Peace and Against American Aggression. The meeting, among other things, called for all Catholics to, "carry out the independence movement and sever all relations with imperialism, accepting no filthy money from imperialists," to "popularize and intensify the independence movement," and to criticize those Catholics with "incorrect thoughts."[22] This meeting coincided with other similar meetings and rallies held in various parts of the country, the purpose of which was to push forward the independence movement of the Protestant and Catholic churches.[23] In Beijing, for example, a huge meeting of Protestant leaders was convened to hear Vice Premier Guo Mo-ruo.[24] The opening of the meeting was accompanied by a *People's Daily* editorial entitled, "Sever Completely Relations Between Christian Churches and Imperialism."[25] The meeting of Protestant leaders created a "Preparatory Committee of Chinese Christians Committee Against American Imperialism, for Aiding Korea, and for Church Reform," chaired by Wu Yaozong, and released a statement signed by Wu and 152 other Protestant leaders.[26]

It was against this background that the attacks on the Papal Internuncio were launched.

On May 23, 1951, the *People's Daily* published a facsimile of Archbishop Riberi's letter in Latin to the bishops. The accompanying *People's Daily* "Comment" was titled, "The Chinese People Cannot Tolerate It."[27] The Archbishop was described in the "Comment" as a "running dog of American imperialism and a citizen of Monaco." The *People's Daily* quoted Monsignor Riberi's assertion, "I do not agree [with the Nanjing 'Manifesto']," and then asked:

> What does he mean by "I do not agree"? It means that he does not agree with the opposition to the imperialist use of Roman Catholics for aggression on China, does not agree with the Resist U.S.—Aid Korea campaign, does not agree with...the banning of interference on the part of the Vatican in the domestic affairs of China, does not agree that the Roman Catholics of China should carry out self-government, self-propagation and self-financing. In a word, Riberi does not agree with the patriotic movement of Roman Catholics in China.[28]

The Archbishop's letter, said the *People's Daily*, "is ironclad proof of imperialist use of Vatican interference with the domestic affairs of China." And, the "Comment" concluded, "Such things cannot be tolerated at all. All patriotic and anti-imperialist Roman Catholics and Catholic priests should arise and clear away the imperialists and their running dogs."

Events then began to unfold rapidly. Around the country groups were organized to demand Archbishop Riberi's expulsion from China. On May 30, *Xinhua* reported the demand of the Beijing "Catholic Committee for World Peace and Against American Aggression" for the government to deport Monsignor Riberi.[29] The same day, *Xinhua* reported that a meeting of Catholics at Aurora University in Shanghai had concluded that Archbishop Riberi, "must not be allowed to continue his criminal activities in China."[30] On June 3, *Xinhua* headlined, "Shanghai Public Demands Deportation of Anthony Riberi."[31] The same day it was reported that, "more than 500 Roman Catholics in Chungking [Chongqing] held a demonstration in the morning of June 3 to protest against Anthony Riberi's action in interfering with the internal affairs of the Chinese people and in undermining the movement for the reform of the Church."[32] The following day, *Xinhua* published "Deportation of Riberi Demanded by Patriotic Catholics and Christians of Nanking [Nanjing]."[33]

The attacks continued, and on June 26, 1951, Archbishop Riberi was confined to his residence in Nanjing, under house arrest.

On June 8, at the height of the attacks on the Papal Internuncio, the Catholic Central Bureau of Shanghai, the central organization of the Catholic Church in China, had been ordered by the government to suspend its activities and to submit all of its publications to the authorities for "investigation."[34]

And the economic pressures continued.

Archbishop Tang:
> Owing to the very heavy property tax, we could not make ends meet. So we decided to let all our rentable houses in order to get money to pay taxes and support the priests. Some people advised me not to leave the bishop's residence as that might affect the ideas of the Catholics, who would think that even the bishop had no place to live in. But I said, "I had to do this to pay the taxes and support the

priests." At first we moved to St. Francis' Minor Seminary. It was very
good there; there were many rooms, a parlour, a garden, etc. It was
quite comfortable. But because of the poor economic situation, we
decided to move again, to the Carmelite convent. This was the
residence of the parish priest of the cathedral. It was a small place.
The priests were then living together and were more united. The
Catholics sympathized with us. At that time, many old pieces of
furniture were piled up in the small courtyard of the convent. There
was nowhere to put them. Father Narbais chopped up some odd
pieces of furniture for firewood. (We had no money to buy firewood.)
It was a great loss; but we could not help it. I dressed in short-sleeved
shirt and trousers and worked in the garden. Some Catholics found
it hard to look at us; for they had great sympathy with us.

The assault against the Church now proceeded on all fronts.
Attacks against mission works of mercy, especially against the
orphanages (*see below*) had begun earlier in the year and
reached a peak during the spring and summer of 1951. The
Legion of Mary came under attack during the summer, and a
drive was begun to identify, register and roundup its members.
On July 25, security police in Beijing sealed two-thirds of the
city's Catholic churches and arrested an undetermined number of
Chinese and foreign priests.[35] On September 4, the Chinese press
announced that the Nanjing Military Control Commission of
the Chinese People's Liberation Army had ordered the permanent deportation of Archbishop Riberi. The order was carried
out immediately.[36] The Papal Internuncio reached Shanghai on
September 5, 1951 under armed guard, and after being subjected to a search of his person, was loaded aboard a third-class
"hard seat" train for the fifty-hour trip to Canton where he
would cross the border to the British colony of Hong Kong.
Two days later on September 7, four department heads of the
Catholic Central Bureau were arrested in Shanghai. Those
arrested included Reverend Francis X. Legrand, director of the
cultural department, Reverend Matthew Chen, the archbishop's private secretary, Reverend Joseph Sheng, director of
Catholic Lay Action and Reverend W. Aedan McGrath, envoy
of the Legion of Mary, about whom, more later.[37] All the while,
the arrests of Catholic prelates and of other religious, both
foreigners and native Chinese, continued, as did the steady
stream of expelled foreign missionaries crossing the Lowu
Bridge from China to Hong Kong.

The Orphanages

An important part of the campaign to discredit the Church in China came in the form of attacks on missionary works of mercy, especially the orphanages and homes for foundlings.

At the time of the communist takeover of China, the Catholic Church operated at least one institution for the care of orphans or foundlings in 102 of the 144 ecclesastical districts. Some of the sees operated as many as ten such institutions, the oldest of which dated back to 1868.[38] During the year 1948, Catholic orphanages were caring for approximately 16,000 homeless children, in addition to nursing many thousands of others who eventually died from disease, exposure or starvation suffered before they came under the care of the sisters. Indeed, it was probably because of the deaths of the large numbers of sick and dying children taken in by the sisters that the orphanages offered such an attractive target of opportunity to the communist authorities.

On February 28, 1951, the communist press in both Canton and Hong Kong launched an attack on the Canadian Sisters of the Congregation of the Immaculate Conception, accusing them of criminal negligence in their operation of the Holy Infant Foundling Home in Canton.[39] The Congregation of the Immaculate Conception had established its first mission in Canton in 1909. The sisters there ran two schools and a leprosarium in addition to the orphanage which they founded in 1932. The press attack claimed that 94 percent of the babies received at the orphanage during the previous year had died as a result of neglect by the sisters. Shortly after the initial attack on the Canton nuns, a similar campaign was begun against two institutions in Nanjing—the Sacred Heart Orphanage operated by the Franciscan Missionaries of Mary, and the Mercy Home, formerly under the direction of the Sister Servants of the Holy Ghost—both of which were charged with "indescribable inhuman treatment of orphans."[40] Similar charges were soon to be leveled at orphanages across the country, including well-publicized cases in Nanchang, Wuhan, and Shanghai. In all, a total of 37 orphanages were confiscated by the government in 1951.[41]

About the campaign against the orphanages, the *China Missionary Bulletin* had this to say:

> It is patently incompatible for the government to allow these institutes to continue giving concrete evidence of Christian charity, while the authorities at the same time are promoting a 'hatred' campaign against these 'imperialists'.... Nor is it sufficient merely to close down these charitable institutions; they must be reviled and turned into objects of hatred.[42]

The process of turning the orphanages into "objects of hatred" everywhere followed essentially the pattern of Canton. A relentless attack against the sisters was mounted in order to inflame public opinion. Editorials appeared almost daily decrying the "brutality" of the conditions under which the children of the orphanage were forced to live. Following an intense press attack of nearly two weeks' duration, the Canadian sisters were arrested on March 11, 1951. The following day the communist authorities assumed control of the orphanage. Conducted tours were arranged for the people of Canton, especially the school children, to display the "horrors" of the orphanage, most especially the "death pit," the common grave for babies in the Catholic portion of the cemetery. And the press attacks continued. *Xinhua* declared, "The death pits where thousands of little bodies were dumped in the past still serve as grim, mute evidence of the atrocious conduct of the imperialist agents wrapped in the sheepskin of false charity," and called for a complete break with "the imperialists." Of the orphans, they said, "the poor, starved mites have begun to feel the warmth of human society for the first time in their lives," since the orphanage was taken over by the People's Relief Administration.[43]

On March 12, the day after the arrest of the Canadian nuns in Canton, a press attack was begun against the two orphanages in Nanjing. The two were the Sacred Heart Orphanage operated by the Franciscan Sisters of Mary and the Mercy Baby Home. The Sister Servants of the Holy Spirit had already been evicted from the Mercy Baby Home the previous December, yet they, too, came in for a share of abuse for the "inhuman" treatment of the children in these institutions.

By mid-April, the attacks on the orphanages had reached a frenzy in several parts of the country. On April 12, Bishop John O'Shea, C.M. of the Kanchow [Ganzhou] Diocese in Jiangxi Province was accused of "atrocities" in the operation of the

Catholic orphanage in that city.[44] On April 15 two Franciscan Missionaries of Mary were brought before a public accusation meeting in connection with their work at the Catholic orphanage outside the city of Chungking [Chongqing]. On April 17, the Chinese press reported calls for the expulsion of the seven nuns remaining at the Sacred Heart Orphanage in Nanjing, the director and one other nun having already been deported on March 26; and on April 27 *Xinhua* reported that 30,000 "irate" citizens at a public accusation meeting had demanded punishment for the nuns. On April 18, a second orphanage in Guangdong Province (the province in which Canton is located), this one also operated by the Franciscan Missionaries of Mary, was accused of "killing babies."[45] Meanwhile, the Hong Kong press reported on April 4 that life imprisonment had been demanded for the five Canadian Sisters of the Immaculate Conception who were already in custody in Canton.

In all cases the campaign to arouse public sentiment against the missionaries followed the same pattern. Bodies were exhumed, and grisly displays of bones were prepared for public viewing. It was alleged that animal bones were sometimes represented as human, but given the condition in which many of the children arrived at the orphanages, and the high mortality of these abandoned infants, there was usually no shortage of human bones in the orphanage graveyards. A study prepared by the United Nations Relief and Rehabilitation Administration prior to the communist takeover of China observed:

> Mortality rate of these children of all ages picked up in the streets, where they had been discarded when the mothers despaired of being able to cure them, was over 90 percent. Tuberculosis, meningitis, and tetanus were prevalent in the new babies; advanced beri-beri was present in almost 100 percent of the cases.[46]

There was no way for the ordinary Chinese to be privy to this sort of information, however, nor would they have known much about the details of the operation of the orphanages. The skillfully conducted government campaign to discredit the missionaries, therefore, appears to have met with substantial success.

Archbishop Tang:
> The sisters of the orphanage were falsely accused of being murderers of infants. The communist government used the mass media,

including all the large radio stations of the whole country and newspapers everywhere, to portray the Catholic sisters, who were usually well-loved and respected by the Chinese, as "imperialistic murderers who wear the cloak of religion." They arrested five Canadian sisters...took over all the property of the orphanage and called for a public trial in the Chung Shan Memorial Hall, the biggest conference hall in the city. They forced all organizations and groups, schools and residents to send representatives to participate in the trial. They even arranged all the accusations beforehand and broadcast the public trial on the radio to the whole city.

After the trial, the five sisters were immediately put in a big lorry and escorted around the city under guard with a few police cars in front and behind them. They were treated like extremely vicious criminals being dragged out in public as punishment. The sisters were not allowed to put on their religious habits, only Chinese-style black shirts and trousers. On the way some people deliberately threw stones and rubbish at them. Sister Germaine Gravel was so wounded that her face was covered with blood.[47]

Eventually the Canadian sisters, and all of the other foreign nuns operating orphanages in China, including those initially sentenced to prison, were expelled from the country.

The Legion of Mary

Wang Xiaoling:
It was an autumn morning in 1951. The headlines of the newspaper read: "The Military Control Commission of the Chinese Liberation Army orders the eradication of the reactionary group, the Legion of Mary." "All who belong to this reactionary group must go to their residential area office to register their resignation from the Legion of Mary," said the report. In our school, nearly every Catholic was an active or auxillary member of the Legion of Mary. This unexpected announcement came as a shock, and immediately the atmosphere became extremely tense.[48]

The Legion of Mary was introduced in China in the late 1930s on a small, local scale by an Irish priest, Father W. Aedan McGrath, in the Hanyang Diocese of Hubei Province. Father McGrath's bishop had recently visited Ireland where he had met Frank Duff, the Legion's founder, and he advised Father McGrath to organize such a group in his local parish. Under Father McGrath's direction, the local organization of the Legion grew to five Praesidia [the name used by the Legion for a group of members], including groups of men, women, girls and boys.

The Legion operated according to strict rules laid down in its "Handbook" which described the Legion's function as, "the sanctification of its members by prayer and active cooperation, under ecclesiastical guidance, in Mary's and the Church's work of crushing the head of the serpent and advancing the reign of Christ."[49] Father McGrath assigned his legionnaires a variety of responsibilities, the first of which was to check on attendance at Mass and at the Sacraments by his parishioners. Legionnaires also visited the local prison on a weekly basis to preach to the prisoners and to distribute Catholic literature. Father McGrath also turned the problem of attending to dying beggars over to his legionnaires as well. He wrote:

> Formerly people used to call me to the roadside to attend one of those unfortunates. There I would have to make my way through an unruly crowd and then set about washing him, instructing him and baptizing him under most distressing conditions. I dreaded those calls. The legionnaires now looked after these cases. It was hard on them to have to bring out their own basins and towels and wash a beggar before a laughing crowd. It was not easy to instruct a dying, and in most cases an ignorant man. But they did this with the best will in the world—once they had conquered their first repugnance. Later on they suggested and actually did build a house which they called 'St. Joseph's home for dying beggars.' They used to carry the dying beggars to this home. There they washed them so that they were ready for the last sacraments. The chief mourners at the funeral were Legionnaires. Thus these poor outcasts of society, 'the least of God's little ones,' received more respectful burial than many of the wealthy.[50]

In 1948, Archbishop Riberi invited Father McGrath, who had returned to Ireland, to assist him in establishing the Legion of Mary all over China. The Legion grew rapidly under Father McGrath's direction, establishing organizations in Tianjin, Beijing, Shanghai, Hankou, Guilin, Guangzhou and many other places. Following the communist takeover in 1949, the work of the Legion became increasingly important in the face of growing persecution of the Church. As the movements and activities of the native and foreign religious came to be restricted, and especially as the missionaries began to leave or to be expelled from China, it fell to the legionnaires to do the catechetical work, the visiting of the sick, and various other ministerial tasks formerly performed by priests and nuns. In many places the

Legion became especially important in holding the Catholic community together. As Archbishop Tang observed, "the Legion of Mary was very suitable for meeting the need of spreading the faith in the circumstances of the time."[51]

It was for these reasons, and especially for the Legion's influence among young Catholics, that the Legion became the target of perhaps the most vicious and unrelenting attack mounted by the government against the Catholic Church.

On June 24, 1951, *Xinhua* announced that the Public Security Bureau of the Tianjin Municipal People's Government had "unearthed a counterrevolutionary secret league," headed by a Catholic father of Dutch nationality, Reverend Henri Hermans.[52] *Xinhua* asserted that the Legion of Mary was a "reactionary organization" which "made a speciality of undermining public security and threatening patriotic Catholics by terroristic tactics." It was claimed that the Tianjin authorities "broke the organization on the eve of the culprits' attempted throwing of sharp knives at patriotic Catholics." Police were said to have seized as evidence copies of "threatening letters" and "three sharp knives."[53] An editorial appearing in the *People's Daily* on the same day claimed that the activities of the Legion of Mary were evidence that "imperialist elements have lost control over the thought of a large number of Patriotic Catholics and are desperately adopting terroristic and murderous tactics in their attempt to obstruct the progress of the patriotic reform movement."[54]

The press attacks continued until July 13 at which time the Tianjin Military Control Commission announced the "prohibition of the imperialist controlled reactionary secret organization, the 'Legion of Mary.'"[55] The *People's Daily*, in reporting the Tianjin ban on the Legion declared: "The whole aim of the 'Legion of Mary' was to be hostile to the whole nation, to the People's Government and the PLA, to the Communist Party, that is, to overthrow the people's democratic state power of New China." The *People's Daily* "Commentator" claimed that the aim of the Legion was not to plant "the banner of the kingdom of God," but to plant the "banner of imperialism," and to that end the Legion "paid particular attention to absorbing as members, Kuomintang secret agents, refugee landlords, despots, bandits and vagabonds."

Furthermore, said the "commentator," "the skeleton members of the 'Legion of Mary' in many places were secret service agents of the Kuomintang...or spies of imperialist states."[56]

Over the next several months the campaign against the Legion and its leaders intensified. The Legion was banned in Beijing, Nanjing, Taiyuan, Changsha, Shijiazhuang and Shanghai. In some places during this period, such as Canton, the Legion ceased to function of its own accord.[57] The battle against the Legion in Shanghai was especially intense.

On October 8, 1951, the Shanghai Military Control Commission issued an order banning the Legion of Mary and at the same time promulgated "Measures for Registration of Members of the 'Legion of Mary' and Withdrawal from the Organization."[58] The Legion was accused of engaging in activities such as, "colluding with the armed forces of bandit Chiang [Kai-shek], collecting intelligence, concealing radio stations and arms, printing and distributing reactionary materials, disseminating rumors, undermining the Resist U.S.—Aid Korea campaign and the Catholics' independence and reform movement."[59] The decree warned that, "those who should dare to resist the government laws, prevent others from withdrawal from the Legion and registration, or who continue to carry on counterrevolutionary activities of the Legion of Mary, shall upon discovery, be severely punished."

The pressure on the legionnaires, especially the youngest of the members, was intense. Their priests had ordered them not to register as counterrevolutionaries and they found themselves pulled and tugged in both directions by conflicting pressure from their families, classmates and government officials.

Wang Xiaoling:
My poor father was so worried, he tried to admonish, to persuade, to scold, and to reproach me. Often, he just could not work off his sorrow and anger, and he would pass out....

Mother was afraid that our young hearts could not stand the double pressure from outside and from within the home.... All of us lived from day to day in constant fear and anxiety.... In addition, all the time we were despised and harassed at school.... Gradually, some legionnaires in our praesidium began to give in to their weakness. All this was bringing a not-yet sixteen-year-old to the breaking point....

However, even after a certain period of time only a few legion-naires had registered their resignation. Probably by then, the government was also becoming aware that the Catholics could not be easily subdued....

That was the first time I witnessed in person self-sacrifice in the Legion of Mary. I can never forget how much many brothers and sisters suffered in conscience after they registered and how every-body suffered pressures of all kinds. Apparently the communists had given in, yet in reality they were planning to retaliate and there were signs that a new phase of persecution was on the way. On the other hand, after this first trial, several dioceses were busy strengthening themselves in spirit, like a petrel before a tempest, flying high and strong in the sky.[60]

Though the Shanghai authorities were not yet prepared to launch a full-scale assault on on the city's very strong and well-organized Catholic community, the leaders of the Legion of Mary were all placed under arrest immediately following the ban on the Legion's activities. The *Shanghai News* announced on October 9 that the local Public Security Bureau had been or-dered to arrest Fathers William Aedan McGrath, Gustave Prevost, and Edouard Gabriel Quint, "three imperialist ele-ments who organized the reactionary organization 'Legion of Mary' and directed its counterrevolutionary activities."[61] Fa-ther McGrath was arrested near midnight in his room at the residence of the Fathers of St. Columban in Shanghai where he was recovering from an illness. As the police entered his room, Father McGrath immediately knelt to receive the general abso-lution and blessing of his superior Father McElroy. Father McElroy barely had time to shove a few spare clothes into Father McGrath's arms before he was dragged away by the authorities.[62]

The announcement of the arrests, accompanied by a photo-graph of Father McGrath in the clutches of two officers of the Public Security Bureau, declared that the "three men have been placed under arrest and are under investigation and trial by the Public Security Bureau. Severe punishment will be meted out to them by the local Military Control Commission in accordance with the law."[63] Indeed, Father Aedan McGrath would spend the next three and one-half years in prison, most of it in Shanghai's Ward Road Prison, and most of it in solitary confinement.

The Legion of Mary had not been destroyed by the arrests of its leaders, but it had suffered a serious blow. The price of membership in the Legion and participation in its activities had been raised considerably. The battle between the Catholic faithful and the communist authorities was not over yet, but by the fall of 1951 it seemed clear that the momentum was on the side of the government.

Catholic Martyrs

As we have noted, the assault on the Catholic Church had already produced a sizeable number of martyrs by the time the communist authorities launched their campaign to suppress counterrevolutionaries. The year 1951, however, produced two martyrs who were to become widely recognized symbols of the resistance of the Church in China to communist persecution.

In the summer of 1951, Father John Tung Shih-chih, a Chinese priest who worked with Father Francis X. Legrand at the Catholic Central Bureau in Shanghai, volunteered to go to Sichuan Province to investigate reports that some local Catholics were cooperating with the *San Zi Yun Dong*. On June 2, while he was in Chungking [Chongqing], Father Tung was appointed to be one of the speakers at a mass demonstration which the local communist authorities had organized to agitate for the expulsion of Archbishop Riberi from China, and in favor of the *San Zi Yun Dong*. Instead, Father Tung used the occasion to reaffirm his Catholic faith and his loyalty to the universal Church.[64] (See Chapter Five, Appendix 2.)

He began by asserting that the *San Zi Yun Dong* was being pushed as a purely "patriotic" movement by persons who "do not believe in the existence of God, nor in the existence of the soul, who do not recognize the Pope as being the representative of Christ, and who do not recognize the Catholic hierarchy." The same people, said Father Tung, who profess to believe in the freedom of religious belief, have evolved the movement which today invites Catholics to attack Archbishop Riberi, the representative of the Pope in China. Tomorrow, said Father Tung, "we perhaps shall be asked to attack the Pope himself, who is Christ's representative. Why, the day after tomorrow, should we not be asked to attack Our Lord and God Jesus Christ Himself?"

Father Tung imagined how wonderful it would be if church and state could cooperate. But, on the contrary, he observed, "the more the [*San Zi Yun Dong*] movement progresses the more one is apart from the other.... Very soon the last thread to which we can attach our hope will itself be broken." Unable to remedy the situation, he said, "I have nothing better to offer than my soul to one of the two parties and my body to the other, in the hope of promoting their mutual understanding."

Father Tung concluded his argument in this way:

> I am a Catholic Chinese. I love my country but I also love my church. I categorically disapprove of anything that is in opposition to the laws of my country and to the laws of my church, and before all I strongly refuse anything that could breed discord. But if the church and the government cannot achieve an accord, all Chinese Catholics, sooner or later, will have only to die. Why not then immediately offer my life to hasten the mutual understanding of both parties?

Father Tung was arrested the following day and nothing more was heard of him. His speech was widely circulated and it was assumed that he had died in prison. At least one writer, however, cites "reliable reports" that Father John Tung was seen alive in a remote labor camp in 1965.[65]

A perhaps even more celebrated case of Catholic martyrdom involved the famous educator Father Beda Chang, S.J. [Zhang Boda]. Beda Chang was unquestionably one of the most celebrated and influential Catholic teachers and writers in China. Father Chang, who had earned his doctorate in literature at the Sorbonne, was rector of St. Ignatius College, dean of the Arts Faculty, professor of literature at Aurora University, and director of the Shanghai Catholic Bureau Sinologique.[66]

Father Chang was arrested in Shanghai during the first week of August 1951, along with two other Chinese educators, Father Yao of Gonzaga College and Brother Alexander of St. Francis College. Unlike the arrests of the Catholic Central Bureau priests, these arrests were not publicized at the time by the communist authorities. The local authorities apparently realized that it was not going to be easy to subdue the Shanghai

Catholics. What they most needed was the willing cooperation of the Catholic Bishop, Ignatius Kung Pin-mei—which he would continue to refuse to provide—or that of other prominent members of the local church. It is assumed that because of Father Chang's eminence in the Shanghai Catholic community, the communists hoped to enlist his cooperation in organizing and promoting the government-sponsored *San Zi Yun Dong*.

Like his bishop, however, Father Beda Chang also refused to cooperate, and for this refusal he died a martyr's death in prison at the hands of his captors on November 11, 1951. Father Chang's relatives were allowed to claim the body of the 46-year-old Jesuit. The *China Missionary Bulletin* reported that Father Chang, who had been in perfect health at the time of his arrest, after three months in a communist jail "was unrecognizable even to his own brother, a physician."[67] The *Bulletin* gave this description:

> Black and wasted, the lifeless body lay unclothed on the prison musty floor where he had been found in sudden death, so the prison guards said.[68]

According to the official accounts, Father Chang succumbed either to a "brain tumor" or to "encephalitis."[69]

Fearing that Father Chang might become a symbol of Catholic martyrdom, the authorities prohibited a funeral procession in his honor and permitted only two priests and his immediate family to accompany him to his grave outside the city. No tombstone was permitted at the grave. Still, more than 200 priests, wearing the red vestments symbolic of martyrdom, privately celebrated a solemn requiem Mass for the repose of Father Beda Chang's soul, and Shanghai's churches were filled as public requiem Masses were celebrated all over the city.[70]

Wang Xiaoling:

> Christ the King Church was not usually filled to capacity but on this occasion it was packed; even the parking area in front of the church was full of people. They raised their heads or stood on tiptoe, both inside and outside the church, to participate in the sacrifice of the Mass.
>
> The Mass hymns which were sung in Latin were very suitable; in addition, some sung in Shanghainese... aroused in the congregation a strong sense of solidarity and they sang with deep feeling. Many, their

eyes filled with tears, expressed their feelings, not only of sorrow and anger but also of unwavering love and renewed courage....

We had just received Holy Communion, but alas! Suddenly outside the church door, the siren could be heard and people began to be disturbed.

"It seems they are pushing the gate of the church compound," people whispered to one another. Then the congregation began to show signs of uneasiness and moved about restlessly....

"The Liberation Army has broken through the gate and is rushing in!" Just at that moment, the Liberation Army marched in, two by two, and stopped by the church door.

The Mass was already over, but Father Vincent Zhu continued with the Benediction of the Blessed Sacrament; apart from a few people who left, all continued to pray....

The choir members left their places to maintain order, so that after the Benediction of the Blessed Sacrament, the people could safely leave the church. The enemy was there, in a menacing mood, but did nothing and the people returned home chanting and singing hymns.

The Catholic body was still very strongly united so the communists had to think hard about more devious measures; God permitted them time and time again to try the Chinese Catholic Church.[71]

Part of that "trial" included a public vilification of Father Beda Chang who was characterized in the communist press as a "running dog" of the imperialists, and a counterrevolutionary "criminal." Indeed, said the *Liberation Daily*, "the criminal Chang died of encephalitis before the court could deal out punishment to him," and they gave this assessment of the outpouring of public sympathy for the dead priest:

> Imperialists and their running dogs are taking another view. They would have it that this criminal counterrevolutionary is a "Saint." Such an attitude not only shows their utter stupidity and shameless-ness, but evokes the wrath of Catholics and non-Catholics alike. We ask the government to deal severely with the Legion of Mary's plot to aggravate the relations between the people and the government.[72]

The struggle to subdue the church in Shanghai would continue for several more years, as would the battle against the Legion of Mary. By the end of 1951, however, the battle lines had been fairly clearly drawn, and the government's war of attrition against the Catholic Church continued to extract a very heavy toll.

By the end of 1951, the Church in China was described by the *Missionary Bulletin* as a church "in chains."[73]

APPENDIX ONE
Regulations for the Suppression of Counterrevolutionaries
Promulgated by the
Central People's Government Council
February 20, 1951
(*Current Background*, No. 101, July 24, 1951)

In accordance with Article 7 of the Common Program, the following measures are hereby adopted to punish the counterrevolutionary criminals, suppress counterrevolutionary activities, and to consolidate the People's Democratic Dictatorship. Those who aim at overthrowing the people's democratic power and ruining people's democratic enterprises, and various counterrevolutionary criminals shall be punished according to these measures:

1. Those who rebel against the motherland in collusion with foreign imperialism shall be sentenced to death or life imprisonment.

2. The leading elements who instigate, induce, or bribe public officials, armed troops, or people's militia to revolt or who lead the bands in revolt, shall be sentenced to death or life imprisonment. Others who participate in instigating, inducing, bribing, or revolting, shall be sentenced to a maximum of ten years in prison. Heavier punishment shall be meted out in more serious cases.

3. Chief plotters and directors of armed mass revolt shall be sentenced to death. A minimum penalty of five years in prison shall be meted out to other active participants.

4. Those who engage in one of the following acts shall be sentenced to death:

    a. Spying or stealing state secrets or furnishing intelligence to internal and external enemies;

    b. Pointing out bombing targets for enemy planes or vessels; or

    c. Supplying arms and ammunition and other war supplies to internal or external enemies.

A minimum of five years' imprisonment shall be meted out in less serious cases.

5. Those who participate in the following counterrevolutionary or espionage activities shall be sentenced to death or life imprisonment:

a. Receiving assignment from internal or external enemies to carry on underground activities;

b. Participating in organizing counterrevolutionary or espionage activities after liberation;

c. Having organized or led counterrevolutionaries, secret services, or espionage activities and other crimes before liberation, with no intention of redeeming themselves with meritorious services after liberation;

d. Having participated in counterrevolutionary activities, secret services, or espionage activities before liberation and continuing same after liberation;

e. Continued participation in counterrevolutionary activities after surrendering to and registering with the people's government; or

f. Continuing to associate with counterrevolutionaries, secret service agents, and spies after having been educated and released by the people's government.

A minimum of five years' imprisonment shall be meted out to less serious offenders.

6. Those who use feudalistic sects and societies to carry on counterrevolutionary activities shall be sentenced to death or life imprisonment. A minimum of three years' imprisonment shall be meted out to less serious offenders.

7. Death or life imprisonment shall be the penalty for the following kinds of sabotage or killing:

a. Looting or sabotaging military establishments, factories, mines, forests, farms, dams, transportation, banks, warehouses, danger-precaution equipment, and other important public or private properties;

b. Dropping poison, disseminating disease germs, and other means of causing serious disasters among men, livestock, or agricultural products;

c. Disturbing markets or dislocating currency systems under instructions from internal or external enemies;

d. Attacking, killing, or injuring public officials or the people; or *e.* Forging public documents and testimonials by false representation of military organs and democratic parties in order to carry on counterrevolutionary activities.

A minimum of five years' imprisonment shall be meted out in less serious cases.

8. Those who commit, with counterrevolutionary intent, one of the following provocative and delusory acts shall be sentenced to a minimum of three years in prison:

a. Inciting the masses to resist and sabotaging the execution of the decrees of the people's government concerning the collection of grain or taxes, labor service, military service and other decrees;

b. Undermining the unity of the various national minorities, democratic classes, democratic parties, and the unity between the people's organizations and the government; or

c. Engaging in counterrevolutionary propaganda or manufacturing and spreading rumors.

Death or life imprisonment shall be the penalty in more serious cases.

9. Those who cross the national boundary secretly with counterrevolutionary intent shall be sentenced to death or life imprisonment. Less serious offenders shall be sentenced to a minimum of five years in prison.

10. Plotters who agitate for jailbreaks or staging a riot shall be sentenced to death or life imprisonment. A minimum of three years' imprisonment shall be meted out to active participants.

11. Those who shelter or protect the counterrevolutionaries shall be sentenced to a minimum of ten years in prison. Life imprisonment or death shall be the penalty in more serious cases.

12. The following shall be mitigating circumstances which may be claimed by those punishable under these measures:

a. Voluntary surrender to the people's government and sincere repentance;

b. Sincere repentance and redeeming of guilt with meritorious deeds before or after the discovery or prosecution;

c. Participation in counterrevolutionary activities not voluntarily, but under pressure and deception; or *d.* Having engaged in less serious counterrevolutionary acts before liberation but having since repented and severed all relationships with counterrevolutionary organizations.

13. Those who commit more than one crime shall receive the maximum total penalty as the final punishment.

14. Those who commit counterrevolutionary crimes not listed in these measures shall receive similar penalties.

Those found guilty under these measures may be deprived of their political rights, and all or part of their properties may be confiscated.

These measures shall apply to counterrevolutionary crimes committed before the adoption of same.

Any person shall have the right to inform the government of the counterrevolutionary case, but they should not report falsely because of personal grudges.

In time of military control, counterrevolutionary cases shall be prosecuted by the court martial organized by the local military headquarters, the Military Council, or the Bandit Extermination Command.

These regulations shall become effective on the day of promulgation.

APPENDIX TWO
Father John Tung's Speech
June 2, 1951
(CMB, October 1951)

In the Name of the Father, and of the Son, and of the Holy Ghost. Amen. Most Sacred Heart of Jesus have mercy on us. Mary conceived without sin, Meadiatrix of all graces, pray for us. Holy Apostles Peter and Paul, pray for us.

Authorities of the government, dignitaries of the church, Christians who are loyal to your faith, and gentlemen. The subject of this speech will be: the sacrifice that I make of myself to the two supreme powers (my religion and the state).

Some persons who do not believe in the existence of God, nor in the existence of the soul, who do not recognize the Pope as being the representative of Christ, who do not recognize the Catholic hierarchy, present the Triple Autonomy Movement as a purely patriotic movement. These same persons recognize the liberty to adhere to the Catholic faith; they admit that purely spiritual relations may exist between the faithful and the Pope. But a movement which is evolved outside the hierarchy today invites us to attack the representative of the Pope, H.E. Monsignor Riberi. Tomorrow we perhaps shall be asked to attack the Pope himself, who is Christ's representative. Why, the day after tomorrow should we not be asked to attack Our Lord and God Jesus Christ Himself? We may always, in the course of an attack, make distinctions. But in reality, God is "one," and the Pope's representative is "one," and the Pope himself is "one." No distinction, no division is admissible. Such a development, the Triple Independence, would take from me all possibility of remaining a Catholic. A patriotic movement of such a nature is in fact incompatible with the Catholic Church.

Gentlemen, I have only one soul and I cannot divide it. I have a body which can be divided. It is best, it seems, to offer my whole soul to God and to the Holy Church; and my body to my country. If she is pleased with it, I do not refuse it to her. Good materialists, who deny the existence of the soul, cannot but be satisfied with the offering of my body only. I believe that if the state and the church could collaborate, the movement for a Triple Autonomy, conformable to Catholic principles, would be recognized as a patriotic movement. If it were so, how much good would result both for the state and for the church!

But on the contrary, the more the movement progresses the farther one is from the other. We have reached a point where almost any backward step is impossible. Very soon, the last thread to which we can attach our hope will be broken. How miserable I feel, unable to do anything, but as I am unable to remedy this situation, I have nothing better than to offer my soul to one party and my body to the other, in the hope of promoting their mutual understanding. I have nothing else to do as long as that understanding is not realized. I have no regrets. I only beseech God to have pity on the weakness of my nature and to give me the supernatural courage, and I will remain unshakable till death.

I beseech the authorities to accept my sacrifice and not to show me any sort of indulgence. And above all, if it happens that I weaken, I beseech them not to tolerate this weakness. Are not the weak the scourge of society? Therefore, to prevent myself against all weakness, and in the event that I should lose control of my actions and speak words of weakness, I take this opportunity, while I am perfectly lucid, to solemnly declare that I disavow them and declare them right now null and void.

I am aware that the [civil] authorities have many times clearly explained that their intention is not to use force, but only to stimulate us; which makes it a duty for me to speak in complete frankness and never to say what I do not want to say. [The authorities wish that] I sign a declaration only if I sincerely approve of it, and if I do not approve, not to sign it hypocritically. Have not the authorities manifestedly given us freedom of speech as well as freedom of being silent? Why shouldn't we believe their declarations?

Suppose that under the effect of I know not what fear, I go against my conscience, talk contrary to my own opinions, sign what I disapprove of, then I deliberately deceive the authorities; and if I say in secret that I made a mistake because I was forced, I equally deceive the hierarchy. Would not such conduct sow discord between the government and the church? If I strangle the voice of my conscience, deny my God, leave the church and cheat the government, I am nothing more than an opportunist and a coward. I would then be only one of those persons in whom nobody can have confidence, whose life has no value for anyone. Who then would want to have me, who would want to help me? I would only be a miserable outcast deserving of all punishment from the authorities in this world and eternal punishment in the next from divine justice.

It is true that I am a Catholic. But this does not prevent me from having a very great admiration for the communists. They believe neither in God nor in the soul, still less in Heaven or Hell. It is my conviction that they are mistaken. However, they have more than one quality which compels admiration, shakes my own indolence and brings me to recall vividly the millions of martyrs of our church during the course of 2,000 years. These martyrs are the ones who urge me to beseech God day and night, to forgive my numerous sins and grant me the unparalleled gift of martyrdom.

The first admirable quality of the communists is that they are capable of facing death. They never betray their cause and deceive others by giving some excuse, as General Li Ling did to rationalize his capitulation: "If I did not fight to death, it is because I was preserving myself for future deeds." Should I a Catholic be cowardly, or attached to life, and use the pretext of preserving myself for future service to the church? A Christian who betrays his God, also betrays his church and his country. The communists are wont to say: "For one who falls, 10,000 will rise." How could a Catholic forget: "the blood of martyrs is the seed of Christians."

The second admirable quality of the communists is, they show no fear when accused of crimes and condemned to death: "The people's eyes," they say, "see clearly and are not mistaken." This is the reason they face death with such pride. Now, how could a Christian fear to be falsely accused and abused; how could he fear that this unjust death is without value or meaning? How could he forget that our "Supreme Judge is the omnipotent God, full of wisdom and kindness, justice and equity?"

The communists also possess a third quality. When they are right but fail to convince others, they maintain their own faith intact. If it happens that they are beaten in an argument or discussion, they do not abandon their belief, quit or doubt the party. How could a Christian forget his faith which has been given him by God? How could he feel the entire church is defeated because he himself has been defeated? If he did that, he would soon falsify the church doctrine and weaken its discipline, betray his God and his soul. If I betray my God and my soul, who could then guarantee that I would not betray my motherland and my people? This is why I refuse to be shaken in my faith and be an instrument by which other Christians' faith should be shaken. This is why I refuse to abase my priesthood by misleading the faithful.

The communists whom I admire, have a true consideration of the Catholic Church which I love, and endeavor to win the support of the Christians. I confess that I feel much honored by it. Why then should I not redouble my forces to be an unshakable Christian in answer to the noble intention of the government? I will not "exhibit a sheep's head and sell dog meat."

I do not content myself with admiring the unshakable courage of the communists, and thank them for their noble intention of trying to win the Christians. I still have a great desire. It is to offer them the Catholic Church which is so dear to me, in order to bring them to God and make them our brothers in faith. Do not say I am a fool who prattles crazy things, and do not believe that I lack sincerity! I dare say that the communists, who have a high ideal, would make good Catholics completely devoted to their faith and would surpass a thousand times a Catholic such as I am, when the day dawns that they really know the Catholic Church. I also ask God that in the Communist Party there may be found many Sauls who become Pauls, who will far surpass the poor priest that I am. It is my most fervent prayer. To this end, I spare myself no sacrifice, praying with hope that the earthly life which I offer today might bring the conversion of future generations.

This is my way of seeing things. The composition of this speech is faulty; please excuse a man who could not put the required care into it. Moreover, because I did not obtain ecclesiastical approval, my speech evidently cannot represent the church's opinion. The speech is also without the approbation of the civil authorities. It is only the expression of what seems to be an ideal, but it is perhaps nothing but a beautiful personal dream.

I am a Catholic Chinese. I love my country but I also love my church. I categorically disapprove of anything that is in opposition to the laws of my country or to the laws of my church, and before all, I strongly refuse anything that could breed discord. But if the church and the government cannot achieve an accord, all Chinese Catholics, sooner or later, will have only to die. Why not then immediately offer my life to hasten the mutual understanding of both parties? If my offering is not accepted, the only reason is that understanding is not wanted, that peace is rejected. I hardly believe that the government will permit itself to be drawn irrevocably into demanding the death of 3,700,000 Chinese Catholics.

If a member of the Catholic hierarchy does not accept my prayer, or considers me as one out of order who mixes in things not of his concern, this person may punish me with suspension, but no one can forbid me to have recourse to higher authority, to the Pope himself if need be. But if in this desperate situation we both still have the courage to look for a solution, reconciliation can be attained. May I be pardoned for all the shortcomings of this speech.

In the name of the Father, and of the Son, and of the Holy Ghost. Amen.

NOTES

1. Mao Zedong. "Strike Surely, Accurately and Relentlessly in Suppressing Counter-Revolutionaries," (December 1950–September 1951), *Selected Works of Mao Tse-tung*, vol. V, Beijing: Foreign Languages Press, 1977, 53.
2. See Theodore H.E.Chen. *The Chinese Communist Regime: Documents and Commentary op. cit.*, 293–296.
3. Estimates of the number of executions attributable to the campaign for the suppression of counterrevolutionaries vary greatly. Some writers cite figures without making any attempt to reveal the basis of their calculations. A. Doak Barnett writes, "The hundreds of thousands of 'undesirable elements' publicly executed during the 'Agrarian Reform' program of 1950–52 and the Campaign Against 'Counterrevolutionaries' in 1951 do not represent a large proportion of the Chinese population...." See *Communist China the Early Years, 1949–55, op. cit.*, 46. John K. Fairbank writes that, "Execution of such enemies...were in the hundreds of thousands, some say many millions." See *The United States and China*, 3d ed., Cambridge: Harvard University Press, 1971, 341. Ross Terrill writes, "Hundreds of thousands were either executed or put in labor camps." See *Mao*, New York: Harper & Row, 1980, 214. Craig Dietrich cites the report of 28,000 executions during a ten month period in Guangdong Province [see note 5 below] but not its source. He writes, "In the end, between a half million and a million executions took place throughout the country." See *People's China: A Brief History*, New York: Oxford University Press, 1986, 72. Maurice Meisner attempts to extrapolate total numbers from partial government statistics. He writes, "Using the government's figure of 800,000 counterrevolutionary trials during the first half of 1951, there were some 135,000 official executions during that 6-month period alone. The real figure is no doubt greater, and...the estimate of many relatively impartial observers that there were 2,000,000 people executed during the first three years of the People's Republic is probably as accurate a guess as one can make on the basis of scanty information." See *Mao's China: A History of the People's Republic, op. cit.*, 81. Richard L. Walker has probably attempted the most comprehensive analysis of the various official government statistics. He cites estimates from the "conservative" low estimate of Father Ladany of one million for the toll of the suppression campaign, to a high American Federation of Labor figure of fourteen million deaths from all campaigns between 1948 and 1952. See *China Under Communism, op. cit.*, 93, 219.
4. See Richard L. Walker. *China Under Communism, op. cit.*, chap. 9.
5. Ezra Vogel. *Canton Under Communism, op. cit.*, 64.

6. *Ibid.*
7. Eric O. Hanson. *Catholic Politics in China and Korea*, Maryknoll, NY: Orbis Books, 1980.
8. For another discussion of this point see James T. Myers. "The Catholic church in Mainland China: A Look Back Over Forty Years," *Issues & Studies*, Taipei: Institute of International Relations, vol. 24, no. 2, (February 1988).
9. CMB, no. 10, December 1951, 819.
10. "American Imperialism Shall not be Allowed to Make Use of the Catholic Church for Aggression Against China." *Renmin Ribao* editorial, Beijing, April 6, 1951. In SCMP, no. 93, April 10–12, 1951, 11–12.
11. *Ibid.*, 12.
12. "Achievements of Catholic Reform Movement in Tianjin," *Renmin Ribao* editorial, Beijing, April 9, 1951. In SCMP no. 93, April 10–12, 1951, 12–14.
13. *Ibid.*, 13.
14. *Xinhua*, Guangzhou, April 23, 1951. In SCMP no. 98, April 24–25, 1951, 19–20. Also *cf.* CMB, no. 6, 1951, 534.
15. *Ibid.*, SCMP, no. 98, April 24–25, 1951, 20.
16. Wang Kuang. "Espionage Activities of American Catholic Mission in Meihsien [Meixian]; American Imperialist Attempt to Make Use of Religious Institutions for Aggression Against China," *Xinhua*, Guangzhou, April 23, 1951. In SCMP, no. 98, April 24–25, 1951, 20–22.
17. *Ibid.*, 22.
18. See Eric O. Hanson. *Catholic Politics in China and Korea, op. cit.*, 36 for a discussion or Bishop Ford's alleged involvement with the U.S. Army. Archbishop Tang's position has been expressed in private conversation, and also in correspondence by the author with Fr. Bernard J. Shields, S.J. in Hong Kong.
19. Tse Ming [Ze Ming]. "Irrevocable Proof of Vatican's Support for Imperialists to Intervene in Internal Affairs of Various Countries," *Renmin Ribao*, Beijing, April 4, 1951; *Xinhua*, Beijing, April 5, 1951. In SCMP, no. 92, April 6–9, 1951, 19–20.
20. *Ibid.*, 20.
21. *Ibid.*
22. "Peking [Beijing] Catholics Form Resist-U.S. and Aid-Korea Committee," *Xunhua*, Beijing, April 19, 1951. In SCMP, no. 96, April 17, 1951, 12.
23. See, for example, "Chungking [Chongqing] Christians and Catholics Hold Joint Accusation Meetings Against Imperialists, *Xinhua*, Chongqing, April 23, 1951. In SCMP no. 98, April 24–25, 1951, 13–14; "Over 200,000 Catholics in Peking [Beijing] and Tientsin [Tianjin] Hold Demonstrations For Peace," *Xinhua*, Beijing, April

23, 1951. In SCMP, no. 98, April 24–25, 1951, 16–17.

24. "Crimes of Imperialist Elements Denounced by Representatives to the National Conference of Christian Leaders and Associations," *Xinhua*, Beijing, April 22, 1951. In SCMP no. 98, April 24–25, 1951, 10–12.

25. "Sever Completely Relations Between Christian Churches and Imperialism," *Renmin Ribao* editorial, Beijing, April 17, 1951, 9–12.

26. "Joint Statement of Representatives of Chinese Churches and Christian Associations," *Xinhua*, Beijing, April 24, 1951. In SCMP, no. 99, April 26–27, 1951, 13–15.

27. "The Chinese People Cannot Tolerate It," *Renmin Ribao*, Beijing, May 23, 1951; *Xinhua*, Beijing, May 23, 1951.

28. *Ibid.*

29. "Peking [Beijing] Catholics' Committee Against U.S. and for Aid to Korea Condemns Riberi in Statement," *Xinhua*, Beijing, May 30, 1951.

30. "Catholics in Aurora University, Shanghai, Discuss Anthony Riberi Incident of Nanking [Nanjing]," *Xinhua*, Shanghai, May 30, 1951.

31. "Shanghai Public Demands Deportation of Anthony Riberi," *Xinhua*, Shanghai, June 3, 1951.

32. "Chungking [Chongqing] Catholics Demonstrate Against Riberi," *Xinhua*, Chongqing, June 6, 1951.

33. "Deportation of Riberi Demanded by Patriotic Catholics and Christians of Nanking [Nanjing]," *Xinhua*, Nanjing, June 4, 1951.

34. CMB, 1951, no. 7, 623.

35. CMB, no. 10, December 1951, 821.

36. See CMB, 1951, no. 8, 710–711.

37. *Ibid.*, 712–713. Also *cf.*, "A Church in Chains," CMB no. 10, December 1951, 821.

38. CMB, no. 6, June–July 1952, 447.

39. CMB, no. 5, May 1951, 377–380.

40. CMB, no. 5, May 1951, 378.

41. Rev. H. Madigan, "Catholic Orphanages in Communist China, CMB, no. 6, June–July 1951, 449.

42. CMB, no. 5, May 1951, 378.

43. *Xinhua*, Canton, April 6, 1951. In SCMP, no. 92, April 6–9, 1951, 21–22.

44. CMB, no. 6, June–July, 1951, 528.

45. *Ibid.*, 528–529.

46. Rev. H. Madigan, "Catholic Orphanages in China," CMB, no. 6, June–July 1952, 449.

47. *Tang: Memoirs*, 33–34.

48. *Xiaoling: Memoirs*, 20,

49. Father W. Aedan McGrath, "The Legion of Mary," CMB, no. 4, August 1948, 417.

50. *Ibid.*, 419.
51. *Tang: Memoirs*, 47.
52. *Xinhua*, Tianjin, June 24, 1951.
53. *Ibid.*
54. "Smash the Fresh Plot of the Imperialists to Undermine Catholic Reform Movement, *Renmin Ribao* - Editorial, Beijing; *Xinhua*, Beijing, June 24, 1951.
55. "Tianjin Dissolves Legion of Mary," *Xinhua*, Tianjin, July 14, 1951.
56. "Protect Legitimate Freedom of Belief, Suppress the Counter-Revolutionary 'Legion of Mary,'" *Renmin Ribao* "Commentary," Beijing; *Xinhua*, Beijing, July 14, 1951.
57. *Tang: Memoirs*, 48.
58. "Shanghai Military Control Commission Bans Reactionary Organization 'Legion of Mary,'" *Xinhua*, Shanghai, October 10, 1951.
59. *Ibid.*
60. *Xiaoling: Memoirs*, 23–24.
61. *Shanghai News*, October 9, 1951.
62. CMB, no. 8, 1951, 713.
63. *Ibid.* Also see Father Boniface, "The Scapegoat Legion of Mary," (Part One), CMB no. 10, December 1951, 826–831.
64. See CMB, no. 8, October 1951, 679–681 or CMB, September 1954, 606–608 for the text of Father Tung's speech.
65. Richard C. Bush, Jr., *Religion in Communist China, op. cit.*, 112–113. Bush does not cite the source of the "reliable reports."
66. See "A Martyr Dies," CMB, no. 1, January 1952, 16–18; also, *cf.* Richard C. Bush, Jr., *Religion in Communist China, op. cit.*, 113–114, and Eric O. Hanson, *Catholic Politics in China and Korea, op. cit.*, 75–76.
67. "A Martyr Dies," CMB, no. 1, January 1952, 16.
68. *Ibid.*
69. *Ibid.* See also *Jiefang Ribao* [*Liberation Daily*], Shanghai, November 17, 1951.
70. See *Xiaoling: Memoirs*, 25–29. Also *cf.*, Richard C. Bush, Jr., *Religion in Communist China, op. cit.*, 113–114, and Eric O. Hanson, *Catholic Politics in China and Korea, op. cit.*, 75–76, and "A Martyr Dies," CMB, no. 1, January 1951, 16–17.
71. *Xiaoling: Memoirs*, 27–28.
72. *Jiefang Ribao*, Shanghai, November 17, 1951. *Cf.* "A Martyr Dies," CMB, no. 1, January 1952, 17–18.
73. CMB, no. 10, December 1951, 819 *ff.*

SIX

TRIUMPH OF THE TRUE BELIEVERS

The true believer is emboldened to attempt the unprecedented and the impossible not only because his doctrine gives him a sense of omnipotence but also because it gives him unqualified confidence in the future.

Eric Hoffer[1]

In March of 1952, the *China Missionary Bulletin* reported the death the previous August of Father Vincent She, O.C.S.O. Father She had been one of the Trappists taken prisoner at Yang Jia Ping in 1947. He had escaped death at that time and made his way to Beijing where he joined the remnants of the Trappist community. From there he had moved to the Chengdu Diocese in Sichuan Province to assist in re-establishing the scattered Trappist community and to become its sub-prior.

Father She was arrested in February 1951 along with two other Trappists and accused of dispensing poisonous medicine and of directing the Legion of Mary. He was subjected to several public trials and repeatedly beaten. On August 8, 1951, his fellow priests were called to claim his body at the jail. The *Missionary Bulletin* described the scene as his brothers prepared Father She for burial:

> As they removed the filthy, vermin-ridden clothes, his confreres knew that another name would be added to the roll of martyrs. The emaciated body, the stench of putrefication, the ulcerated sores, and the welts on breast and back proved beyond a doubt that Father She had died of neglect and violence.[2]

A similar, and increasingly familiar, story was told by Sister Mary Rudolf, one of three nuns subjected to mass trials and mob violence before being deported from Manchuria. The sisters had been forced to stand immobile for eleven hours while a frenzied mob hurled insults at them and spat in their faces, all the while demanding that the nuns be put on the funeral pyre which had been prepared for them. The sisters' tale was a harrowing one, but one which they survived. Sister Mary reported on the mission catechist who did not survive:

> Strung up by the thumbs and tortured, because he insisted he would return to the church if released, the valiant catechist defied all attempts of his tormentors to make him apostatize. His aged father, a faithful Catholic of seventy years, stood there watching his son suffering and encouraged him to persevere saying:
>
> "Try to bear the pain just a little longer and then you will be in eternity."
>
> Those were the last words this unknown martyr heard before he succumbed to the protracted torture.[3]

In December 1951, the Hong Kong *Shui Pao*, citing official government statistics, reported that 250,000 persons throughout Guangdong Province had been executed in the second half of the year. In addition, there were reported to be 5,000 more persons under suspended sentence of death, 500,000 people in various prisons in the province, and an additional 200,000 under public surveillance or performing compulsory labor.[4]

In the summer of 1952, Mao Zedong wrote the following notation on a document drafted by the United Front Work Department of the CCP Central Committee:

> With the overthrow of the landlord class and the bureaucrat-capitalist class, the contradiction between the working class and the national bourgeoisie has become the principal contradiction in China....[5]

Throughout 1951, the year of revolutionary terror, the government had moved in a massive way against those it considered enemies or potential enemies of the regime. And we have seen how many Catholics, both religious and laypersons, became victims of this revolutionary terror. In this sense, therefore, the revolution had already turned against the large numbers of those who could have been most useful in national reconstruction, and who were eager and willing to participate in this effort. Now, however, Chairman Mao was indicating that a new stage in the revolution had begun. The Communist Party now officially declared its intention to discard onto the rubbish heap of history its non-communist middle-class allies. The "national bourgeoisie" were, after all, along with workers, peasants and "petit" bourgeoisie, represented by one of the four small stars on China's national flag.

Given the early atmosphere of "united front," the assurances from the beginning that non-communist elements and minority parties would have a political future in the new order, given the rhetoric of "New Democracy" which embraced almost all (if not quite precisely all) those willing to participate in national reconstruction, how can one understand this massive resort to force and to individual and collective brutality, not against the class enemies of the communists, but against those, such as the "national bourgeoisie," the Chinese middle class, and other patriotic and well-meaning Chinese, including the vast majority of Chinese Catholics, who wished to participate in the revitalization of their nation?

The answer, I believe, lies in the hubris of the true believer; the arrogance of the victorious movement, the sense of "omnipotence," to use Eric Hoffer's term, which led the CCP to believe that it required no assistance from its "united front" citizens, many of whom were in fact best equipped to help it most. It would be a very long time before we would see clearly the full effect of this assault against the non-communist "united front" groups—the technically skilled, businessmen and merchants, intellectuals, religious believers, and many others—but in the end the effects would be devastating for China.

It was the pride and arrogance of the true believer which caused the communists to conclude that their revolution did not require the participation of the educated and technically competent, or even of those patriotic Chinese citizens who held and practiced faiths other than Marxism. It was this pride which persuaded the communists to drive away or discard the heirs of a hundred years of Chinese modernization (of which Taiwan and Hong Kong, Vancouver and San Francisco then became the beneficiaries), and it was this pride which convinced them to disregard or deny the enormous reservoir of patriotic goodwill represented by the believers in those faiths which they regarded as "superstition." It is entirely possible that this good-will could have been molded into a significant force for modernization in China if only the communists had not been driven by the requirements of their own doctrine to attempt to destroy it.

Indeed, this doctrine itself, Marxism-Leninism-Mao Zedong Thought, I shall argue, was to assume much of the character and trappings of a religion in the years before Mao Zedong's death in 1976, and the guardians of the doctrine, the Communist Party elite, were to spare no effort to eliminate all rivals for the hearts and minds of the Chinese people.

Enter the Prophet

> The east is red
> The sun rises
> On the horizon of China
> Appears the great hero Mao Zedong...
> He is the great savior of the people
>
> Popular revolutionary song, circa 1949

In contrast to his historical counterpart George Washington, the "indispensable man" of the American Revolution, much greater claims were made for Mao Zedong than simply those of a great historical figure around whom his countrymen could rally. Mao also assumed the role of charismatic prophet-leader of his revolutionary movement.

The term "charisma" has been given a wide variety of definitions, but central always has been the charismatic leader's ability to reduce stress, anxiety or cognitive tension associated with cultural disintegration. It is the function of the charismatic leader to resolve discontinuities and to explain the world and its meaning in a new and more satisfactory way. If we pursue the religious analogy, the purest form of charismatic leadership being found in religious movements, Mao's role was that of prophet of the Chinese Revolution, agent of the birth of New China, possessor of revealed truth.[6]

Religions, whether political religions or not, require prophets. Not only does the prophet appear as the founder of the religion, but as David Apter suggests, if political religion is to serve the needs of individuals, prophets must, "interpret immortality, identity, and purpose through their own personal gifts of grace… [and] light a tinder of hope in the ordinary day-to-day level of human demands."[7] In the effort to elevate Mao to the status of prophet, a considerable personality cult developed through which a Mao of superhuman proportions emerged.[8]

Mao's image would eventually adorn every home, every office, every school, public office and factory. In many homes his image came to occupy the central place on the family altar and replaced the ancestor tablets as the principal object of worship. Mao was compared to the life-giving forces of nature, especially the sun, and his "Thought" was cited as authority for everything from surgery to nightsoil collecting. The *People's Daily* described Mao's role as prophet in this way:

> Today in the era of Mao Zedong heaven is here on earth. Chairman Mao is a great prophet. Each prophecy of Chairman Mao has become a reality. It was so in the past; it is so today.[9]

Also:

> Comrade Mao Zedong is always able to see the essence of things and future development, and able to point to the sun that is about to emerge from behind the clouds, to point to the coming of the dawn in the night, and to point to the correct direction in a maze of complex surroundings.[10]

Prophets, of course, are essentially teachers for those who follow them. In his role as prophet, Mao attempted to control the meaning of the "Word," the rhetoric of the communist revolution. Mao and his lieutenants sought to create a new explanatory system which redefined the meaning of life for the Chinese people. They sought to link human actions to a new "invisible world"[11] of power and meaning. The Chinese Revolution, and, consequently, life and meaning for the Chinese people, was for the communist true believers linked to the Marxist engine of history, with Chairman Mao the prophet-teacher correctly forecasting and explaining the inevitible progress of the communist movement toward the Marxist millennium.

In this setting, then, it can be no surprise that the images of the Chinese Revolution and especially of the Mao cult took on a religious or pseudo-religious character. Indeed, the literature of Mao's revolution, created by both participants and observers alike, abounds with religious imagery.[12] Mao himself appears to have understood well the power of such a religious call. As he told Andre Malraux in 1966:

> Revolution is a drama of passion; we did not win the people over by appealing to reason, but by developing hope, trust and fraternity. In the face of famine, the will to equality takes on a religious force.[13]

Nor can it be a suprise that in this setting Mao's political rivals and the ideological rivals of his movement were regarded as dangerous enemies or even as "devils."

It may well be that there are more complex social and psychological motives which explain the extent and viciousness of the violence and brutality inflicted by China's new communist rulers on those who refused to accept their revolutionary creed. But surely it is the single-minded passion of the religious zealot—the communist "true believer"—which in large measure explains the special measure of contempt and hatred reserved for those followers of various religious faiths who, even in the face of the ultimate human sanctions of torture, deprivation, and death, refused to apostatize, to renounce their God and embrace the dogma of their captors. Accounts of the communists' attempts to force the "conversion" of Catholics, especially of priests and other religious, are legion,[14] but perhaps two will suffice as examples.

"The Imperialist 'Devil'" [15]

Seventy-year-old Father Florent Ver Eecke was arrested in March 1951 in the province of Suiyuan [since 1954 merged into Inner Mongolia Autonomous Region]. As none of the local people could be persuaded to make a charge against the old Belgian priest, the authorities imposed a fine of 270,000 pounds of millet on the Church property. This amount was equivalent to the total revenue from three or four years of good harvests. Unable to pay, the priest was arrested and put into prison.

Handcuffed for ten days and nights, Father Ver Eecke was kept in a 20x20-foot room with more than 60 other prisoners. For more than three months there was no room for the prisoners to lie down. They got what sleep they could by reclining against fellow prisoners for short naps. They received four bowls of millet and four cups of water a day for nourishment with a small amount of vegetables provided once each week.

Each cell was provided with five pounds of coal per week in a country where the winter temperatures reach 40 below zero. The cell was also infested with lice and other vermin and the prisoners had no opportunity to wash themselves during the ten months of Father Ver Eecke's imprisonment.

Despite the terrible conditions of his confinement, the old priest persisted in his pastoral work. He baptized the dying, and explained Christian doctrine to those about to be executed. He heard the confession of Catholic prisoners and made a practice of saying his own prayers aloud for all to hear. It was this latter practice which especially infuriated his captors. They insisted that he stop, but the priest refused. The soldiers brought in a Protestant minister and tortured him in front of Father Ver Eecke. "Now do you dare to continue your foolish prayers?" they asked. "I dare," answered the priest. "If you do," they threatened, "we shall decapitate you." "You can cut off my head," said Father Ver Eecke, "or pull out my heart, but so long as I have breath in my body I shall continue to pray."

Despite the efforts of his jailors, Father Ver Eecke never waivered in his steadfastness. When he was manacled, all of his necessary functions were performed for him by a Catholic fellow prisoner who had been imprisoned as a lay leader of the Legion of Mary. When Father Ver Eecke was finally released to stand trial on the single charge that he had organized and directed the "counterrevolutionary" Legion of Mary, he was crippled by malnutrition and the injuries he had received in prison. He was unable to stand on his own and had to be supported for several hours by fellow priests who were on trial at the same time. Following the trial, the priests were marched through the streets for another two hours. Father Ver Eecke, barely conscious and still unable to stand, was supported by two of his confreres as the guards alternately pushed and dragged him through the streets. The *China Missionary Bulletin* described the scene in this way:

> Seeing the seventy-year-old man, with long hair and white beard, dressed in unkempt and filthy prison clothes—crippled, emaciated, sick and fainting, as he was carried and pulled through the lines of scoffing soldiers—was too much for the decent folk of the city. Not only Christians but many non-Catholic women and children cried

as he passed. Nor could the communist commands of "No pity for the imperialist devils" stop them from weeping and showing their disapproval of the inhuman treatment meted out to a man they knew to be good.[16]

Father Ver Eecke and seven of his confreres were eventually sentenced to expulsion from China and made their way to Hong Kong where he told the story of his captivity and trial.

"The Fool for Christ and the Leper in Ropes"[17]

Father Robert Juigner of the Chengdu Diocese in Sichuan Province was arrested at the beginning of 1952. He was placed in prison where he was forced to follow a rigid program of indoctrination in communist doctrine. Each day the prisoners arose at dawn to perform a "meditation" on communism before breakfast. This was followed with four hours of lectures each day and two hours of classes in which the principal activity was self-criticism and confession of faults.

Father Juigner's progress toward "conversion" was unsatisfactory to his jailers, however, who punished him by placing him in handcuffs day and night. With this punishment came the threat to keep him in prison until he became a "good communist." The missionary's answer was: "Twenty or thirty years—it is all the same to me. But if you are keeping me here until I become a communist, you might as well execute me now for I will never become a 'convert.' "

For his outspokenness Father Juigner was confined in a cell with eighty other prisoners. The cell, which usually held fifty or sixty men, was so crowded that, as with Father Ver Eecke's confinement, the prisoners had to sleep by leaning against each other. When the shackles and other punishment failed to result in Father Juigner's "conversion," a leper covered with sores was thrown into the cell with him. The terrified Chinese prisoners begged for the leper to be removed, which he was, only to be thrown back into the cell with his arms tied behind his back with ropes. Father Jiugner, it was reported, moved to the leper's side, fed him, helped him in other important ways, consoled him and slept under the same blanket with him.

After three months of intensive indoctrination, Father Juigner's jailors gave up. He was bound and escorted by guards to the border where he was expelled from the country.

Clearly, by the middle of 1952 the Chinese revolution had executed a subtle but important shift in course. When Mao announced in 1949 that China had "stood up," he was appealing to strong and deep-seated feelings of Chinese nationalism. In these early days of Mao's New Democracy, the revolution recruited and embraced the united front groups—patriotic civil servants, technicians, merchants, intellectuals, and others— almost all of whom wanted to participate in the revolution for the sake of China, not necessarily for socialism and communism. By early 1952, however, Mao and his party had begun to turn against their former allies in a systematic way in order to pursue the Maoist utopian goals which would eventually thrust the nation into chaos and bring it near to destruction.

"Three-Anti" and "Five-Anti"

A second, related trend which became discernible during 1952 was the increasing centralization and tightening of political control by communist authorities over those non-communist individuals and private activities which had continued to operate with some degree of autonomy during the early period of "New Democracy."

China's entry into the Korean War had permitted the government not only to draw upon a substantial reservoir of nationalistic support and to characterize their opponents as "traitors," but the war had also been used to justify expanded police powers, surveillance of the population and the apprehension and elimination of "counterrevolutionaries." At the same time, as we have seen, the regime had continued to consolidate its control over colleges and universities, hospitals, orphanages and the like, and to arrest and/or expel many of those charged with operating these institutions. For those (mostly Chinese) who remained behind, especially the teachers and professors, they were already required to write detailed life histories including their "confessions" for past erroneous attitudes.

In the countryside, the end of 1951 had seen the establishment of mutual aid teams made up of five to ten households. Land, animals, and tools were still privately owned, but the peasants were under strong government pressure to cooperate with the movement. The year 1952 brought the beginning of Stalinist central economic planning with the development of the first Five-Year Plan to be implemented in January of 1953. By 1953 the government also moved to transform the mutual aid teams to producers' cooperatives comprised of 20–25 households which shared land and tools, and for which each household was paid in proportion to its contribution to the group. This move was, in turn, preliminary to Mao's later push ahead to advanced producers' cooperatives which effectively resulted in the complete collectivization of agriculture. All property, tools, animals, and equipment were collectively owned and peasants were paid according to work points.

All of these new policies contributed significantly to the centralization of political control in the PRC and the penetration by the Communist Party into nearly every aspect of daily Chinese life.

Two of the more important drives of the year 1952 were the Three-Anti [*San-Fan*] and Five-Anti [*Wu-Fan*] campaigns, the former aimed at party cadres and civil servants and the latter at merchants and businessmen. It is probably not too strong to suggest that these campaigns marked the beginning of the systematic elimination of the Chinese middle class.

The Three-Anti movement began in the fall of 1951 in Manchuria where the Party secretary launched a drive against "corruption, decay, and bureaucratism."[18] By December 1951, the National Committee of the CPPCC, under Mao Zedong's guidance, had extended the campaign to the entire country. Officially, the three "evils"or "poisons" to be attacked were corruption, waste, and excessive bureaucracy. This initial campaign was aimed at both party cadres and civil servants, many of whom, at this time, were still hold-overs from the old nationalist regime.

The campaign was conducted amid a considerable fanfare of publicity. A stream of reports was published in the press lauding the successful effort to root out corruption and waste in the Party and government. Statistics on the success of the campaign were publicized as were the numerous People's Courts which punished the wrongdoers. It soon became clear, however, that the campaign would not be limited only to the task of party consolidation and the rooting-out of the three "poisons," but would be aimed at the more general problem of "bourgeois" or "rightist" attitudes and thinking. In this sense, the Three-Anti campaign appears to have been a preliminary to the Five-Anti campaign which followed close on its heels, and which represented a direct assault by the Party against China's bourgeoisie.

The Five-Anti campaign, aimed primarily at merchants, industrialists and businessmen, attacked the "poisons" of bribery, tax evasion, fraud, theft of government property and theft of state economic secrets. The aim of the campaign was not only to terrorize the Chinese bourgeoisie and whip them into line, but also to set the stage for the move toward a centrally planned economy.

A large number of prominent industrialists were executed and tens of thousands were imprisoned. Many who were targets of the drive took their own lives. It was reported in the city of Shanghai that there were approximately one hundred suicides per day at the height of the campaign in 1952.[19] Perhaps equally important to the government was the financial windfall yielded by the campaign. Estimates place the net income to the central government from fines, confiscated property, back taxes and the like, at upwards of US $1 billion or more, a not insignificant amount when one considers that total national revenues for the year were probably in the range of US $10 billion.[20]

The Catholic Church was not directly caught up in the Three-Anti and Five-Anti campaigns, though, as we shall see, Catholics were not unaffected by the general atmosphere created by the continuous "struggle" against suspected or accused offenders. Nor did Catholics escape the tightening noose of central control.

Archbishop Tang:

Although the Three-Anti and Five-Anti campaigns were not aimed directly against the church, the tension, the fear and the political atmosphere spread all over Canton city. All the classrooms and halls of the primary and secondary schools in the city were occupied as accusation and "struggle" centers, day and night. Capitalists, great and small, were the targets to be "struggled against." Suicides were talked about all the time. The screams of accused capitalists and the shouts of working teams [communist teams investigating the capitalists] mingled together, disturbing the ordinary life of the people very much....

> Once [another priest] and I were standing at the window of the Bishop's House facing the classrooms of Ming Tak Primary School. In front of the Bishop's house capitalists were being "struggled against." Watching the accusation meetings...[the priest] said, "The business of the capitalists is legal. They pay the taxes as stipulated. But now the government has confiscated their property and 'struggles' against them. It is not fair." I said, "Yes, it is not fair." This became the [basis of the] charge that I had opposed the Three-Anti and Five-Anti campaigns.[21]

Thought Reform

In line with the tightening of political and ideological control in China throughout 1952, the party launched an "Ideological Reform Study Movement" in the fall of 1951. Relying principally on the familiar technique of criticism and self-criticism, this movement was aimed primarily at intellectuals, professors and other academicians. Some of China's best known academics became victims of this "thought reform" [si xiang gai zao] effort including her most famous philosopher, Fung Yu-lan, who wrote a lengthy self-criticism repudiating all of his previous work and confessing his "bourgeois" and "feudal" errors in thinking.[22]

It was important for the communists to bring intellectuals into line, especially the most famous and influential scholars. If the government was to be able to establish beyond any doubt the "truth" of Marxism-Leninism-Mao Zedong Thought, these influential teachers and scholars would have to admit that they had failed to see the "truth" until they had been exposed to communist ideology. Attacks on the academics were relentless, and the Chinese press was filled with the "confessions" and self-criticisms of these unfortunates on a daily basis during the last months of 1951 and first months of 1952. One of the more brief examples of these self-criticisms, this by Chin Yueh-lin, Dean of the College of Arts and Chairman of the Department of Philosophy at Tsinghua [Qing Hua] University, is reproduced in Appendix One of this chapter.

Artists and writers likewise came under strong pressure to use their art in the service of the revolution. Many intellectuals who could not be made to see the light through criticism and self-criticism were sent to the countryside for "reformation through productive labor" [*lao gai*]. Some, of course, including many Catholic priests, underwent the process of "brainwashing" [a term also used by the Chinese: "*xi nao*"] while confined in prison. Indeed, some of the most terrifying stories of prison mistreatment involved Catholic priests who resisted the efforts of their jailers to force them to "confess," engage in self-criticism, or "reform" their thoughts. The techniques of brainwashing used in the Chinese prisons would also become known to the world through the experiences of repatriated American prisoners of the Korean War. Usually these techniques involved some type of physical abuse, intense psychological abuse, especially through interruption of the normal sleep cycle, and relentless interrogation and ideological indoctrination.

Father Fortunatus Tiberi[23]

Father Tiberi was arrested in North China on September 30, 1951. At the time of his arrest he was teaching mathematics at a Catholic school in Beijing. Father Tiberi underwent a month-long course of indoctrination but still did not see the error of his ways.

Determined to make him "confess," his captors placed him in a darkened cell on October 22 where he was fed a cup of water twice daily and three small slices of bread. He was made to "hunker" on his haunches Chinese-style and was kicked by his guards whenever he lost his balance and fell. He was forced to run up and down stairs until he dropped from exhaustion. After ten days of this treatment, the priest offered to confess. He had not been accused of any specific wrongdoing, and when his captors heard his confession they only laughed. They wanted him honestly to accuse himself of all of his real crimes. Father Tiberi's failure to do so brought on another series of interrogations.

From about November 2 to November 28 he was subjected to almost continuous questioning. During this period he later could not recall having been allowed to sleep at all. A group of seven officials questioned him as a team for two or three sessions each day. On November 8 his arms were shackled behind his back. He remained handcuffed until December 21. At several points Father Tiberi became delirious. By November 24 the priest gave up hope. Nothing he said would satisfy his captors and he refused to answer further questions. For punishment he was forced to stand for 108 consecutive hours as his guards took turns punching and jabbing him to keep him awake. Father Tiberi beat his head against the walls and begged his captors to shoot him. They refused, however, claiming that it was "too cheap a price to pay."

On December 2 Father Tiberi was returned to his cell and told to start confessing in earnest. For fifteen days he filled countless sheets of paper with confessions of his crimes as instructed by his jailers. This confession was perfected with the help of a Chinese fellow prisoner. By April the authorities decided that the priest was ready for yet another course of indoctrination. This went on throughout the spring and summer. At last, having signed a deposition that he had been fairly treated by his jailers, Father Tiberi was released on August 6. With twelve other priests, he was escorted to Tianjin where he was put on a ship and expelled from the country.

Five Beijing Missionaries[24]

Five missionaries from Beijing arrested in the summer of 1951, all bearing the scars of their confinement, arrived in Hong Kong on September 14, 1952. The five were Reverend Maurice Kavanaugh, Reverend Karel De Ryck, Reverend Albert Van Lierde, Reverend Ulrich Lebrun and Reverend Joseph Schyns [see below]. All told of hallucinations from lack of sleep as they were forced to stand or squat for days on end as their jailers attempted to force them to confess that they were secret agents of the imperialists. Father De Ryck, for example, believed that he had spent twenty days without sleep, although he admitted that he lost complete track of time. He was kept standing most of the time with his arms manacled tightly behind his back.

Father Kavanaugh had taken a strong public stand against the *San Zi Yun Dong*, and for that he was branded an imperialist secret agent. Like the others, he was forced to stand for several days without sleep, his hands handcuffed behind him. Still unwilling to confess, his guards forced him to "hunker" Chinese style, a position which was excruciatingly painful for him as he had broken his kneecaps earlier in life. When his guards discovered this fact, they kept him squatting for more than eighty hours inside a circled marked with chalk on the floor, jerking him upright whenever he fell over with a rope halter they had placed around his neck. Father Kavanaugh recalled falling unconscious four times during his interrogation. Long after his arrival in Hong Kong his legs still bore the ugly scars of the kicks and blows administered by his captors.

Father De Ryck was kept in chains during the entire ten months of his captivity. During his twenty sleepless days his guards pulled him around the cell by his beard whenever he dropped from exhaustion. Eventually every hair of his beard was pulled out by the roots. Father De Ryck, Father Van Leirde and Father Lebrun were each beaten more than ten times with sticks, clubs, ropes, leather straps and revolver butts. Father Lebrun was whipped in the face for more than two hours by two men with sticks until his face was swollen beyond recognition. The priest was also tied up by the feet and suspended from the ceiling.

Many of the priests were subjected to the "airplane ride," an especially cruel form of torture where the prisoner is tied securely with sticks behind his knees and elbows and suspended on a pole between two men. After suffering this treatment for more than two hours, Father Lebrun was unable to use his hands for several months. He was forced to eat his food like a dog because he could not lift the bowl to his mouth. More than one year later his arms and legs still bore the scars where they had been torn by the ropes.

The Chinese authorities were apparently confident that they would be able to "reform" the thoughts of their prisoners. All of the priests reported being approached by agents of the government promising freedom if the priests would promise to work for the communists in their native countries.

Father Joseph Schyns

Father Schyns spent one year in a Chinese prison and told an increasingly familiar story when he reached Hong Kong.[25] "In order to snatch confessions of crime invented by themselves," said the priest, "the communists make you pass through a series of tortures that gradually destroy your personality and reduce you to a state of hallucination during which you make a confession which is dictated to you."

Father Schyns, like his confreres, told of long days of sleep-lessness, and of being forced to "hunker" with his hands man-acled behind him during interrogations, sometimes lasting as long as twelve hours. He had only the thin clothing he had worn at the time of his arrest in August. When he shivered during an interrogation on a cold night in September the judge, in order to warm him up, ordered him to drag himself around the cell on his knees while a soldier beat him with a stick.

The most painful torture for Father Schyns was to be sus-pended from the ceiling. He was made to climb a pile of bricks with his arms handcuffed behind his back. A rope was attached to the chain of the manacles and his arms were hoisted up above the height of his head and the bricks removed. The weight of the priest's body disjointed his shoulders, elbows and wrists. His howls of agony were stifled with a dirty sock stuffed into his mouth by a soldier. Father Schyns was forced to endure this torture dozens of times, but, he reported thankfully, usually only for periods of 15 or 20 minutes. Some of his fellow pris-oners, whose cries of pain he could hear, had to endure the suspension for hours.

Father Schyns reported that his only source of strength each time he had to endure the unbearable pain of the suspension, was to begin the celebration of the Mass as his jailers mocked him. It is probably impossible to judge with any accuracy the effec-tiveness of these "brainwashing" or "thought reform" tech-niques. Though many intellectuals may have capitulated and published their self-criticisms in order to save their necks, and though the communist jailers proved themselves to be ex-tremely effective at extracting "confessions" from their prison-ers, there seem to have been only a very small percentage of cases involving the relatively more educated prisoners where the indoctrination program succeeded as intended.[26] At the same time, there were other cases involving Catholic priests where the prisoners turned the experience into a sort of med-itation, and seemed to grow spiritually from it.[27]

Over the years, however, the communists appear to have maintained their faith in these thought reform methods. Perhaps it was the faith of the true believer that Marxist dogma would eventually be accepted by the unbeliever. Even during the long prison confinements of Bishops Tang and Kung (*see below*) and others, where the prison authorities did not resort to physical brutality, the communists apparently believed that their prisoners would eventually abandon their "feudal superstitions" and embrace the truth of Marxism-Leninism-Mao Zedong Thought.

At the same time, the communists continued to exhibit a healthy respect, or even fear, of the power of the Christians' faith. In one case, security police disinterred the body of Archbishop Cyril Jarre of the Jinan Archdiocese in Shandong Province. The Archbishop had been imprisoned for several months before being removed to a hospital where he died on March 8, 1952. The body was handed over to local priests and prepared for burial in red Mass vestments signifying that the prelate had died a martyr's death in defense of the Catholic faith. It was to remove the red Mass vestments and replace them with a criminal prisoner's uniform that the police disinterred the body after burial.

Considerable confusion ensued, as the local Catholics rallied to prevent the authorities from carrying out their plan to clothe the body in prisoners' clothing. In the end it was agreed that the corpse should be clothed in white Mass vestments for reburial. A funeral Mass the following day was attended by all Catholics within walking distance of the city, and the body, still reported to be soft and flexible as though alive, was borne to the grave on the shoulders of the faithful. The *Mission Bulletin* reported that, "All the Catholics escorted the remains to the grave, to the acute astonishment of the police who failed to disperse them even with force."[28]

In Shanghai, the communist authorities continued to exhibit concern about the veneration of Father Beda Chang by the local Catholic community. They attempted to connect such veneration with the government propaganda claims that the United States was using germ warfare in Korea. It was said that the local Catholics were being contaminated with American imperialist "reactionary mental bacteria." Local Chinese priests were called in by the authorities to clarify their attitude toward Father Chang. And at least one priest reported being told that the police would hold Bishop Kung of Shanghai responsible for any miracles that occurred as a result of Catholics praying to Beda Chang![29]

Continuing Pressure on the Church

The years 1952 and 1953 were marked by the continuing expulsion of missionaries including many Catholic bishops, usually charged, among other crimes, with supporting the Legion of Mary. The government also persisted in its relatively ineffective efforts to establish the "independent" or "reform" church through the *San Zi Yun Dong*. And despite the fact that the Papal Internuncio had been expelled, bitter and vitriolic attacks on the Vatican continued uninterrupted. [See Chapter Six, Appendix 2.]

Of the more than 5,500 foreign Catholic missionaries in China before 1949, fewer than 2,000 remained at the beginning of 1952. In addition, at the beginning of the year, 23 Catholic bishops were in jail, five were under house arrest, and twelve more had been expelled.[30] As the end of 1952 approached, the *Missionary Bulletin* reported that 1,046 Catholic missionaries had left or been expelled from China during 1952. There remained at the end of November, 787 foreign missionaries of which 524 were priests, 210 were nuns and 53 were brothers. Of the Catholic hierarchy it was reported that two archbishops and two bishops had died in prison, fourteen more were still in prison, three were under house arrest, and 43 had been expelled.[31] In every issue of the *Missionary Bulletin* of these years, the "Mission Chronicle" section is full of accounts which begin, "Father Expelled," "Missionaries Expelled," "Prelate Jailed," "Prelate Under House Arrest," and, increasingly, from dioceses all over China, "Last Foreign Missionary Expelled."

All over China, Catholic schools, hospitals and orphanages had been taken over by the government. In those Catholic schools in which religious remained as teachers, they were stripped of authority over administration and curriculum. Mass arrests continued as well, associated with the continuing campaign to root out counterrevolutionaries and "spies" as well as the drive against the Legion of Mary. Indeed, as indicated earlier, association with the Legion of Mary in some form was the most common charge leveled at those Catholic missionaries who were arrested and expelled. Attacks on the Legion were usually highly visible and accompanied by charges in the press that quantities of hidden arms of various kinds had been discovered, or that the priests directing the Legion possessed radios and other paraphernalia used in anti-communist "espionage." A typical report, for example, claimed that the local Public Security authorities in the city of Taiyuan had seized "forty rifles and carbines, six pistols, one automatic pistol of German make, five tommy guns, one submachine gun, one light machine gun, three swords, over 570 rounds of ammunition and radio parts, etc. in the corridor and ceiling," of one Catholic Church and in the cow shed of another.[32]

The report did not detail how this arsenal, allegedly in the possession of the seven Italian Franciscans who were arrested at the time, was connected with the activities of the Legion of Mary.

At the same time, the government continued to press for the establishment of an independent Catholic Church through the San Zi Yun Dong. The movement had met with little success and, in fact, had encountered substantial resistance from faithful Catholics who for the most part continued to shun those priests who had been persuaded to go over to the "reform" faction. Moreover, the San Zi Yun Dong continued to suffer from the failure of the government to identify and recruit a prominent Catholic leader who would agree to head the movement. It was reported that Bishop Kung had been approached about leading the San Zi Yun Dong, but had refused.[33] There was even a story circulated by a Chinese businessman in Hong Kong who claimed that he had been allowed to leave China only on the condition that he make contact with Cardinal Tien, then living in the United States, to seek his agreement to lead the independent church.[34]

Judging from the relative ease with which the Three-Self Patriotic Movement had been accepted by Protestant churches, the government authorities probably did not anticipate the scale, strength or obstinacy of the Catholic resistance to this movement. As previously indicated, the movement was strongly opposed by the Catholic hierarchy from Rome down, and in this stand the Bishops were supported by the vast majority of their priests. Despite the vigorous efforts of the government, therefore, the movement in most places gained little or no acceptance by the local Catholic people. The account of the government's failure to force the establishment of an "independent" church in the Archdiocese of Lanzhou is typical of the reports brought to Hong Kong by expelled priests:

> In August 1951 the communists had tried to interest Catholics in the [San Zi Yun Dong] movement. All priests refused to have anything to do with it whereas the lay people stopped going to church as many of them feared both the authorities and any submission to the Independent Church.
>
> All mission work had already been greatly impeded by the communists when they placed Bishop Theo Buddenbroeck, six foreign priests and three brothers under house arrest in January 1951. In fact all foreign missionaries of the district were confined to the cathedral compound so as to stop all outside work. Then suddenly on November 7, 1952, the bishop, six priests and three brothers were removed to the police station; at the same time the Chinese rector of the seminary, Father Pius Chang, with twelve seminarians were forced to move to a spot outside the city on the pretext that they should observe the "land reform" process in action. Actually as soon as the decks were cleared, the communists brought in a "progressive" priest from the country district to head the "Independent Church" in Lanchow [Lanzhou].
>
> Force and strategy failed, for only a few stragglers attended church and all others resisted. After twenty days, the communists were forced to send away the "progressive" priest and bring back the bishop and his group from the police station. Likewise Father Chang and his seminarians were brought back and once more interned with the bishop in the cathedral compound. Father Chang is allowed to carry on religious services for the Catholics.[35]

So resolute were the Catholics in their resistance to the establishment of a reform church that the government slackened in its efforts to push the movement forward in the early months of 1953. The retreat by the government did not, however, signify its acceptance of defeat; it was merely the lull before an even more sustained onslaught against the Church which began in the summer months of 1953.

APPENDIX ONE
"An Analysis of My Thoughts Before Liberation"
By Chin Yuen-lin
Dean of the College of Arts and Chairman of the
Department of Philsophy, Tsinghua [Qinghua] University
(Beijing: *Renmin Ribao*, November 10, 1951)

I went to America to study when I was nineteen, and at the time of the May 4th Movement (1919) I had already spent two years in graduate work. It was at that moment that the attitude of arrogance and conceit of the intelligentsia began to take root in my mind. Due to this inclination to follow personal interests, I started to fall into the bottomless pit of the degenerate philosophy of the capitalist class. Upon my return to China, I engaged myself in the propagation of this sort of metaphysical philosophy dealing with the thought-patterns of various concepts, and even formulated a personal philosophy along similar lines. This system being altogether isolated from realities, we taught for the sake of teaching, and studied for the sake of studying, while to teach and study in conformity to prevailing social demands was deemed to be entirely out of the question. On the one hand I erred in misleading my pupils, while on the other hand I helped to build up Tsinghua's scholastic tradition of emphasizing personal interests.

Being strongly obsessed with the purely technical viewpoint, I put particular stress on abstract methods of analysis and on training in analytical technique. I have always been a follower of realism, and as such have resolutely sustained the materialistic aspects of realism, as well as waged some thirty years of constant war against the idealists. However, my emphasis was not upon the difference in viewpoint between materialism and idealism, not the wrong starting point of idealism, but on idealism's inability to put forward a thoroughly consistent system of thought. Though conceding that a man has the right to believe in idealism, I insisted upon pointing out that such thinking was not clear. In thus neglecting the trend of thought and only paying attention to the technique of thought, I further helped to develop Tsinghua's scholastic tradition of emphasis on the purely technical point of view.

As a result of my unwillingness to be concerned with politics, I exhibited, on the surface, an incomprehensible state of confused thinking. I was for communism but against the Communist Party. When we discussed in Kunming the possibility of communist liberation of Peking, I was perfectly prepared to accept communist leadership, but on the eve of the actual liberation of Peking I vacillated.

I started to "oppose" Chiang Kai-shek sometime during the year 1942–1943. However, I only offered lip-service, without taking any action, not even putting down anything in writing. I could not rid myself of my "compromising" nature. When the reactionary government was at its worst, I occasionally was able to whip myself up to the state of taking some action, but such moments never lasted for long. After five minutes, I usually returned to my customary state of laxity. On this point too I helped to build up Tsinghua teachers' practice of neglecting politics.

I wanted to resist Japan but I could not recognize imperialism. My idea of resisting Japan consisted of opposing Japanese occupation of Chinese territory, Japanese butchery of Chinese people, and especially Japanese rule over China. Together with numerous other intellectuals, we participated in the start of the War of Resistance, but we had no faith in the future of this struggle. Accordingly I longed for foreign assistance, especially British and American assistance. I then believed that the forces of autocratic monarchy would be defeated by the "forces of democracy."

My ignorance of imperialism further led me to indulge in muddled thinking on the question of international and national relations. I worshipped the political and military prowess of Britain and America, but I opposed their political and military aggression; I fundamentally despised American culture, yet actually I had long been an instrument of American cultural aggression. I thought of myself and numerous other teachers in Tsinghua as patriotic. But does it work to love our country in my way?

The above was, in brief, my concrete ideological state as a teacher before the liberation. It was, however, all confusion on the surface of it, completely without consistency and without any standpoint. But when I come to think of it now, it was consistent in its own way and possessed of its stand.

I am a middle-of-the-road intellectual of the petty bourgeois class. In economic status I belong to the petty bourgeois class while at the same time I also belong to the intellectual class. The intellectual class in China occupies a unique position in that, although it does not have the powers of the ruling class, it enjoys a part of the ruling class' privileges. Its progenitor may be either a scholar or an official. The salient ideology of an intellectual such as myself is a peculiar form of conservatism, a sort of "donkey-riding-ism." Though not exactly aspiring to become the man in front who rides the horse, yet I had no wish at all of becoming the man behind who has to push the cart. In fact, I was all for maintaining the status quo of the ruling class.

I honestly exhibited the standpoint of the people during the War of Resistance, though the contents of this standpoint were only founded upon the consciousness of the middle-of-the-road intelligentsia of the petty bourgeois class. I was honestly against the butchery of the Chinese people by the Japanese and Japanese occupation of Chinese territory, but what I was most worried about was, possibly, still the loss of my social position, my teacher post, and my personal interests. However that might be, not having thought of the matter in terms of the interests of the people, I could not be said to have exhibited the people's standpoint. Otherwise, I could not have lost faith in the future of the War of Resistance.

In teaching, I only helped Tsinghua in emphasizing personal interests, strengthening the pure technical point of view, and promoting the scholastic tradition of neglecting politics. When I started teaching in Tsinghua after the May 4th Movement, the progressive thoughts had already started to take root and a violent struggle had already started between the progressive forces and the reactionary forces. At such a moment, the scholastic tradition I was helping to establish could not but be an impediment to the progressive cause. The then prevailing students' movement had its progressive influences, but I was of no positive help to it.

In retrospect, from that time right up to the liberation, my way of thinking had been consistently confused, a sort of vacillating ideology of compromise aiming at the maintenance of the existing social order. A man thinking in such a manner must be an impediment to the forces of progress.

The third anniversary of the liberation of Tsinghua is only one month away. Though during all this time my thoughts have undergone some changes, there still are many undesirable aspects which have as yet to be exposed at the present state of the study movement. And though I have discovered a number of these through my own efforts, this is still inadequate, and I hope my colleagues in the discussion group will help me in unearthing my shortcomings and bringing about my reform. I am inclined to carry out changes slowly, yet now that the time is so pressing, I can no longer afford to proceed at such a slow pace.

APPENDIX TWO
"Anti-Vatican Cartoons"
Source: China Missionary Bulletin, 1952, pages 572–578

"The Vatican, Servant of American Imperialism"

梵 蒂 岡 教 廷 的 陰 謀

界天主教徒的朝拜聖地。
教廷建築崔峨，儼然莊嚴，從它的外表看很像一個世

The Vatican buildings are majestic and lofty, their appearance most imposing. Externally it looks like a holy place of worship for the Catholics of the world.

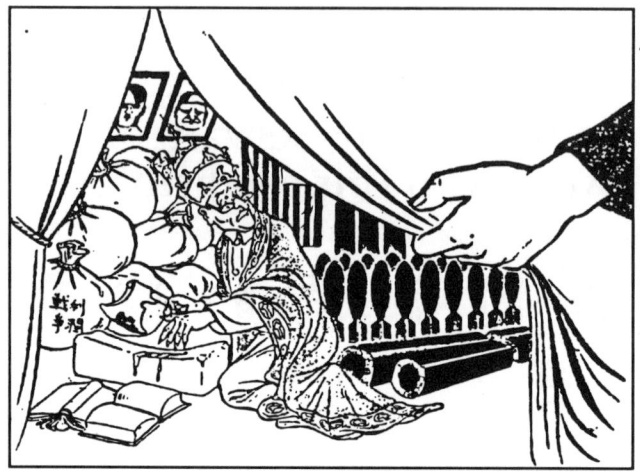

際資本主義反蘇反共反人民陰謀活動的中心之一。

可是骨子裡並非這樣，它的全部歷史說明了它却是國

However, it is not what it appears to be. Its whole history declares clearly that it is the principal center of the international capitalistic movement to oppose Russia, Communism and the people.

治外法權。

教廷在世界各種重要國家設立教區，派遣主教，享受

The Vatican sets up dioceses in every important country of the world and sends bishops who receive extraterritorial rights.

施，利用天主教報紙，宣傳美國政策。

出指示，要求：「無條件地擁護美國所採取的各項措

一九五〇年三月，教皇又進一步對駐各國紅衣主教發

In March 1950 the Pope went a step further in his instruction to the Cardinals of all countries, demanding: "Unconditional support for the American policies, and the use of Catholic newspapers to propagate American statesmanship.

工作。

國特務機關代表的聯席會議，討論怎樣加強反人民的

一九五〇年二月和十月，梵蒂岡曾兩次舉行教廷和美

In February and October of 1950 the Vatican twice convened meetings between church officials and representatives of American secret service organizations, to discuss ways of strengthening the opposition against the people.

間諜工作，美國特務將監督這項訓練工作。
梵蒂岡表示將特別訓練一批神父準備來到東歐去做

The Vatican announced that it would train a group of priests as spies for eastern Europe and American agents would undertake the work of their training.

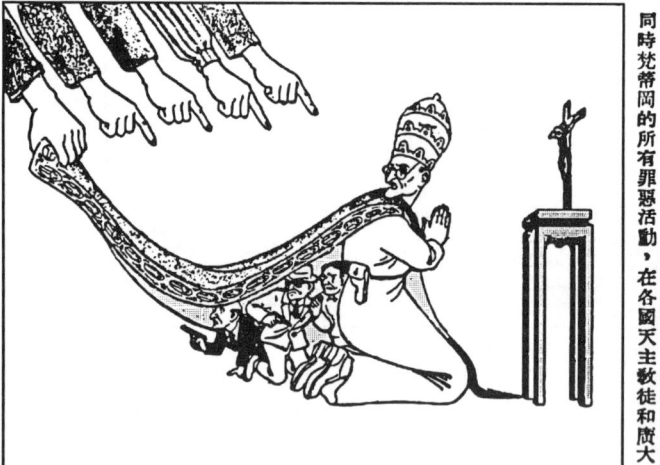

一落千丈。
的人民面前，由於暴露了他的赦免面目，更使它的影
同時梵蒂岡的所有罪惡活動，在各國天主教徒和廣大

The Vatican's evil machinations and aid towards criminals are becoming ever more clear to the Catholics and peoples of every nation. Its influence is falling by leaps and bounds.

Pope Pius XII recently issued another Encyclical on "Peace." Behind the mask of peace is a most hideous and repulsive face. On the one hand he uses hypocritical words of peace to hide from the eyes of men, and on the other hand he moves with fixed purpose along the road of war.

The Vatican has already set itself apart from those Catholics and people who sincerely desire peace.

和帝國主義戰爭販子的聯盟，只能有一個結局，它
正如馬廸懦在人民正義要求下所受到的裁判一樣，它

Just as (Msgr.) Martina was sentened upon the demands of the people, so the Vatican and its imperialist war-mongering allies can have only one end....

那就澈底的失敗！

That is utter destruction!

NOTES

1. Eric Hoffer. *The True Believer—Thoughts on the Nature of Mass Movements.* *New York: Harper & Row, 1951*, 78.
2. CMB no. 3, March 1952, 230.
3. CMB no. 2, February 1952, 138–139.
4. *Hong Kong Shui Pao.* December 23, 1951. *Cf.*, CMB no. 2, February 1951, 132.
5. Mao Zedong. "The Contradiction Between the Working Class and the Bourgeoisie is the Principal Contradiction in China," June 6, 1952, *Selected Works of Mao Tse-tung*, vol. V. Beijing: Foreign Languages Press, 1977, 77.
6. I have treated this subject in more detail in, James T. Myers, "Religious Aspects of the Cult of Mao Tse-tung", *Current Scene* (Hong Kong), vol. X, no. 3, March 10, 1972.
7. David E. Apter. *The Politics of Modernization.* Chicago: The University of Chicago Press, 1965, 223. I have discussed this aspect of the Mao cult in, James T. Myers, "Religious Aspects of the Cult of Mao Tse-tung", *Current Scene*, (Hong Kong), vol. X, no. 3, March 10, 1972. Also *cf.* James T. Myers, "Whatever Happened to Chairman Mao? Myth and Charisma in the Chinese Revolution," in Victor C. Falkenheim and Ilpyong J. Kim, eds., *Chinese Politics from Mao to Deng.* New York: Paragon House, 1989, esp. 22ff.
8. See, James T. Myers. "The Political Dynamics of the Cult of Mao Tse-tung," in Yung Wei ed. *Communist China: A System-Functional Reader.* Columbus, Ohio: Charles E. Merrill, 1972, 78–101. Also see, James T. Myers "The Cult of Mao Tse-tung: A Preliminary Attempt at Periodization and Description of Constructs," *Collected Documents of the First Sino-American Conference On Mainland China.* Taipei: Institute of International Relations, 1972, 177–209.
9. *Renmin Ribao*, Beijing, October 1, 1958.
10. *Renmin Ribao*, Beijing, October 13, 1960.
11. This is Ernest Becker's term. See his *Birth and Death of Meaning*, 2d ed. New York: The Free Press, 1971, esp. 119–120.
12. See James T. Myers. "Religious Aspects of the Cult of Mao Tse-tung," *loc. cit.*
13. Andre Malraux. *Anti-Memoirs.* New York: Holt Reinhart and Winston, 1968, 360.
14. Two especially interesting longer accounts of "brainwashing" experiences by Catholic priests are: Eleutherius Winance, O.S.B., *The Communist Persuasion—A Personal Experience of Brainwashing.* New York: P.J. Kennedy & Sons, 1959, and John W. Clifford, S.J. *In the Presence of My Enemies.* New York: W.W. Norton, 1963. Also *cf.*, Jean Monsterleet, S.J. *Martyrs In China.* London: Longman, Green and Co., 1956.

15. CMB, no. 4, April 1952, 310–311.
16. *Ibid.*, 311.
17. CMB, no. 5, May 1952, 415.
18. See Peter S.H. Tang. *Communist China Today, Volume I: Domestic and Foreign Policies*, 2d ed. Revised and Enlarged. Washington, DC: Research Institute on the Sino-Soviet Bloc, 1961. 390, ff. Also see, A. Doak Barnett. Communist China: The Early Years, 1949–1955, op. cit., 135, ff.; Richard L. Walker. *China Under Communism: The First Five Years op. cit.*, 95–97.
19. Peter S.H. Tang. *Communist China Today, op. cit.*, 392–393.
20. Peter S.H. Tang gives a figure of US $1,250,000,000, *op. cit.*, 393; elsewhere, he cites the "total sum derived from this campaign" as "US $2,200 million," *ibid.*, 353. A. Doak Barnett uses the figure US $800 million, *op. cit.*, 159. Richard L. Walker estimates the amount extracted by the campaign as "between one-half and one billion United States dollars," *op. cit.*, 97. The figure US $1,250 million is also cited in Theodore Hsi-en Chen and Wen-hui C. Chen, "The 'Three Anti' and 'Five-Anti' Movements in Communist China," *Pacific Affairs, vol. 26, no. 1, March 1953, 18, which also provides one of the most comprehensive accounts of the two movements.*
21. *Tang: Memoirs*, 39–40.
22. See Peter S.H. Tang. *Communist China Today, op. cit.*, 443, *ff.*; Richard L. Walker. *China Under Communism, op. cit.*, 212–213; A. Doak Barnett. *Communist China, op. cit.*, 125–134; also *cf.* Robert J. Lifton. "Brainwashing in Perspective," *New Republic*, May 13, 1957.
23. CMB, no. 8, October 1952, 681–683.
24. CMB, no. 9, November 1952, 764–765. All of the following stories plus several others are recounted in detail in Jean Monsterleet, S.J. *Martyrs In China*, trans. Antonia Pakenham, foreword by John C.H. Wu. London: Longmans, Green and Co., 1956, esp. 249, *ff.*
25. CMB, no. 10, December 1952, 854–855. Also see Jean Monsterleet, S.J. *Martyrs in China, op. cit.*, esp. 360–361.
26. One of the most celebrated "successful" cases involved Allyn and Adele Rickett. As the publisher's introduction to their book puts it, "They underwent a major ideological change and emerged from their experience convinced that there are correctness and value in the social experiment undertaken in China." Allyn and Adele Rickett. *Prisoners of Liberation.* New York: Cameron Associates, 1957, vii–viii. Also *cf.* A. Doak Barnett. *Communist China, op. cit.*, 104–115. Barnett describes his surprised reaction upon interviewing the Ricketts, whom he calls "Smith" and "Jones," when they crossed into Hong Kong in 1955. He writes, "Of course, my conversation with Mrs. Smith and Jones took place only during the first days after they had left China, so it is difficult to judge to what extent they will be able, slowly, to come out of their present trance-like state of mind

and adjust to a new environment during the months ahead. Their indoctrination may or may not wear off."

27. See, for example, John W. Clifford, S.J. *In the Presence of My Enemies.* New York: W.W. Norton, 1963.
28. CMB, no. 5, May 1952, 412–413.
29. CMB, no. 6, June–July 1952, 506.
30. CMB, no. 1, January 1952, 60–61.
31. CMB, no. 1, January 1953, 1.
32. "Quantity of Arms Hidden by 'Legion of Mary' Seized at Taiyuan," *Xinhua*, Taiyuan, January 13, 1952.
33. Richard C. Bush, Jr. *Religion in Communist China, op. cit.,* 118. Also, on the resistance of Bishop Kung and the Shanghai Catholics, see Bob Whyte. *Unfinished Encounter: China and Christianity,* London: Fount, 1988, 247–248.
34. CMB, no. 6, June 1953, 611.
35. CMB, no. 2, February 1953, 180.

SEVEN

THE CHURCH SUBDUED

> Venerable Brothers and beloved sons, the struggle imposed on you by divine law is undoubtedly not an easy one. But Christ Our Lord, Who said that they are blessed who suffer persecution for justice's sake, commands them to rejoice and be glad because their reward will be great in heaven.

Pope Pius XII
Ad Sinarum Gentem
An Encyclical Letter to the Chinese[1]

The year 1953 had begun in Shanghai with the organization by Bishop Ignatius Kung [Gong Pinmei] of a round-the-clock perpetual Rosary. All of the parishes in the diocese participated so that any hour of the day or night there would always be two Catholics reciting the Rosary. The aim of the perpetual Rosary was, "to obtain peace and God's blessing for China's church and its people."[2]

On March 29, 1953, a German engineer from Shanghai named Wolfgang Herman Gruen arrived in Hong Kong. He had been released after imprisonment for two years in the Ward Road Prison in Shanghai. It was in the Ward Road Prison in June of 1952 that Gruen met Father Aedan McGrath. The reader may recall that we met Father McGrath in Chapter Five and saw him arrested on September 6, 1951 for his work in forming the Legion of Mary in China.

Gruen had for many years had a keen interest in various religions but came to consider the Catholic Church too dogmatic and formal. Before coming into contact with Father

McGrath, however, his renewed interest in Catholicism had been aroused by a fellow prisoner. When it came to pass that his cell and that of Father McGrath were separated by only a small distance, he asked the priest to give him religious instruction. This Father McGrath did by writing religious instruction and answers to Gruen's questions daily on scraps of toilet paper which were given to the prisoners. Gruen was baptized into the Church when he reached Hong Kong. Asked how he felt about two years in a communist prison, he replied that he had no regrets because there he had "found Father McGrath and the true faith."[3]

For his part, the only message Father Aedan McGrath had Gruen take to the outside world was, "Tell them I have no complaints and am completely happy in jail."[4]

It was this sort of stubborn resistance, and the joyful acceptance of deprivation and suffering that the communist authorities had to contend with in their efforts to bring the Catholic Church in China to its knees.

The First Assault on Shanghai

Wang Xiaoling:

It was the day before our Senior III final examination in June, 1953. That morning as I entered the school compound I found two big character posters confronting me. The first read: "The Senior III graduation examination has been postponed until next Monday," and the second: "We support the government: arrest the counter-revolutionary Wang Rensheng" [Father Aloysius Wong, S.J., the school's headmaster][5].... [I] ran without stopping to the nearby Christ the King Church. I hoped to become calm again through prayer, and wondered what had happened to my parish. As I expected, the residence of the priests of Christ the King Church and the apartments all around were sealed off...only the church door was still open, and I walked in.... "Xiaoling! Our parish priest Father Francis Zhu [Francis Xavier Chu Shu-teh, S.J.] has been arrested," the first parishioner I met said to me, weeping. "And Father Palm is locked in his room. He may not come down!" said another parishioner with emotion....

I found myself bathed in tears as I knelt in the church. This was my most loved family, the community with whom I would remain, in life or death....

It seemed the sky was always overlaid with clouds, while pressure on our church grew stronger and stronger, and the enemies became more and more malicious in their methods. They tried their very best to vilify the Catholic Church using the mass media...and other channels of ideological propaganda. It was now no longer a question of whether the Church was under restrictions or whether there was freedom of religious belief. We had come to the point of having to do everything to keep our faith, to give up our future so as to guarantee its integrity, and to shed our own blood to preserve it. Yet, while the pressure was certainly great, the reaction was equally strong. Every Catholic was very well prepared for anything that might happen. By means of spiritual exercises and devout prayers we would be able to stand up against more serious tempests.[6]

The assault on the Church came on June 15, 1953. Armed police presented themselves at the residence of Father Francis Chu at Christ the King Church and began a search of his room. There they found a quantity of Legion of Mary handbooks. The books were considered evidence of the priest's guilt as the Legion had already been declared a counterrevolutionary organization. Father Francis was arrested and taken to jail, though it would be nearly seven years later, March 12, 1960, before he would be charged with a crime and sentenced to twenty years in a labor camp.[7] Arrested at the same time were at least nine foreign missioners, two French, and seven Americans, and a number of other Chinese priests. All of them were accused of espionage.[8]

Though the official accounts gave the total number of persons arrested as thirteen, only five were mentioned by name: Fathers Charles J. McCarthy, Thomas L. Phillips, Joseph P. McCormick, Fernand Lacretelle, and Joseph J. Deymier. These were no small fish. Father McCarthy was rector of the Jesuit Seminary, Father McCormick was the principal officer of the Office of Maryknoll Missions, Father Lacretelle was the superior of the Jesuit order, and Father Deymier was the provincial of the Lazarist Fathers.[9] The remaining arrested priests whose names were contained in letters from Shanghai were Fathers Thomas Phillips, John Houle, Joseph Getz, John Baptist, John Clifford and, of course, Father Francis Chu.[10]

On July 16, 1953, the communist authorities opened a propaganda barrage against the Shanghai Catholics. On that day the Beijing *People's Daily*, the official voice of the Communist Party Central Committee, published three major articles and an editorial against the Shanghai church. The four newspaper articles totaled nineteen single-spaced pages in the English translation.[11] The charges were by now familiar:

> The seized materials prove that this group of imperialist spies have for a long time engaged in criminal acts against the Chinese people. For long years the Mission D'Extreme Orient and the Jesuit Mission had done illegal remittance business in large volume, transferred properties, concealed arms, allured and compelled youths to receive reactionary training abroad, obstructed registration of members of the Legion of Mary, sabotaged agrarian reform and the campaign for the suppression of counterrevolutionaries.[12]

The propaganda campaign and the arrests appear to have had little effect on the spirit of the local Catholic community, however, or upon the resolve of Bishop Kung. The churches were filled to overflowing and the faithful seemed to show no fear at confronting the authorities. One foreign businessman arriving in Hong Kong reported that when the authorities tried to set up machine guns and take down crucifixes at the Jesuit complex at Zikawei, the site of the seminaries, of St. Ignatius Cathedral and several other church institutions, "young men crowded around and hustled the soldiers off by sheer force of numbers." And the businessman observed, "The communists made a mistake in persecuting [the Catholics], because they are stronger than ever and there will be a hundred new Catholics for every one they put to death!"[13] Attendance at the sacraments was reported to be greater then usual, numerous special devotions were offered and regular pilgrimages to the Marian Shrine at Zose outside Shanghai were organized.

In the face of this stiff Catholic resistance, the authorities were not prepared to abandon their efforts to force the Church into submission, but they did change their tactics. About the time of the Shanghai arrests in summer 1953, the communists apparently decided to abandon the *San Zi Yun Dong* in favor of a reform movement characterized as combining love of country ("patriotism") with love of church [*ai guo-ai jiao*]. This movement would eventually culminate in the creation of the Chinese Catholic Patriotic Association [*Tian Zhu Jiao Ai Guo Hui*] in 1957. At the same time the wave of arrests and accusations spread from Shanghai to other parts of the country.[14]

In the continuing battle for the minds of the youth of China, special attention was given to the activities of the Catholic Youth Patriotic Corps which was described as an "armed secret service organization," organized jointly by Belgian Father Raymond de Jaegher, "a Catholic imperialist spy, and the KMT secret agents."[15] The organization was accused of a wide range of activities including spying, plotting armed uprisings and murder. Youth groups were said to have been "unearthed" by the people's public security organs in Shijiazhuang, Beijing, Tianjin, Tangshan, Changping, Nankou and Kalgan [Zhangjiakou].[16] Nearly all of the specific allegations made against Father de Jaegher involved activities which took place before the communist victory in 1949. And while there can be little doubt about Father de Jaegher's anti-communist sympathies, the publication of these charges in the summer of 1953 was clearly a part of the large-scale national effort to arouse patriotic outrage by linking the Catholic Church once again to the imperialist enemy still fighting against China in Korea.

In the South, Canton, which had always lagged slightly behind the rest of the country in the implementation of national policy, the government moved to outlaw the Legion of Mary and a new push was begun to establish a "Patriotic" Catholic organization. As in other parts of the country in 1953, these moves were accompanied by an acceleration in the pace of arrests and expulsion of foreign missioners.

Archbishop Tang:
> On August 5, 1953, all the big newspapers of Canton carried on the front page and in large characters this alarming news: "Three Imperialists Hidden in the Canton Catholic Church, O'Meara, Egan, Limat, to be Expelled;" "The Great Counterrevolutionary Sheltered in the Canton Cathedral, Running Dog of the Imperialists, Major Counterrevolutionary Tam Tin-tak [Father Francis Tam]."
>
> When they read this news all the priests realized that the communists had raised the curtain on the second act of the destruction of the Church. At the begining of the liberation, it was already being said in Catholic circles that the communists would persecute the Church in three stages:
> 1) Attack the foreign missionaries and expel them from China;
> 2) Attack the Chinese clergy, arrest and imprison them;
> 3) Attack the Chinese Catholics, arrest them and close the churches....[17]

Late at night on August 4, 1953, the Public Security police entered and searched the residences of Father Edouard Limat of Shameen Church, Canton, Father O'Meara of Tung Shan Church and Father Egan of Yuet Sau Pak Church, and put them under house arrest. The next morning, Father Egan celebrated Mass in the chapel downstairs and was assisted by Paul Chan. Father Egan spoke to him in Latin during Mass, asking him to finish all the consecrated hosts and to inform me that he was safe. Some police were there at the time and asked Paul Chan what Father Egan had said. Paul Chan said that he was saying the Mass prayers....

On the morning of August 8, 1953, the Public Security police first ordered their luggage to be taken away and then brought the three fathers to the Canton South Railway Station. (Normally, this is the goods station.) They were put in separate carriages. Only when they arrived at Shamchun (Shenzhen) did they realize that they had all been expelled.[18]

At the same time, on August 5, the Canton Military Control Commission moved to suppress the Legion of Mary. All of the city's newspapers carried the message that the Military Control Commission had issued a decree ordering all members of the Legion of Mary to report to the Public Security Bureau to register their resignation and to acknowledge that the Legion was a counterrevolutionary organization.[19] Bishop Tang's response to this decree was to gather all his priests for a meeting. It was decided, and ordered by the bishop, that any priest who registered and admitted that the Legion was a counterrevolutionary organization would not be allowed to celebrate Mass. Any lay person who registered would not be allowed to receive communion. This would later constitute one of the most serious charges by the government against Bishop Tang.

Shortly thereafter, some 114 "patriotic" Catholics in Canton convened a "Preparatory Committee of the Canton Catholics Patriotic Association" on September 20.[20] Bishop Tang instructed his priests not to participate in the Patriotic activities, and few did. At the cathedral, most of the priests had been living and taking their meals with relatives. The Bishop decided that now they would all live and take their meals together. It was his hope that they could draw strength from their unity in order better to resist the intensified pressure from the government. In all of these matters they had the benefit of advice and examples from the resistance of the Shanghai Catholic community.[21]

For the Christmas celebration that year, the Bishop had a large stage constructed in the garden of the Carmelite Convent at Shek Shat, the site of the Bishop's Residence, where various religious programs were offered. The Bishop recorded that, "The whole garden was full of people, and the lights shone. We all felt very happy and excited."[22] The same night the Patriotic Catholics celebrated Christmas with very few people present.

Exodus

Throughout 1954 the pressure on Chinese Catholics to co-operate with the new "patriotic" associations continued, as did the consolidation and centralization of political control in Beijing. A new cabinet-level organization, the Bureau of Religious Affairs, designed to control and supervise the various religious groups in China, was established under the State Council of the Central People's Government. At the same time, the arrest and expulsion of foreign missionaries continued at an accelerated pace. Of the aproximately 5,500 foreign Catholic missionionaries in China at the time of the communist takeover, only 267 remained at the beginning of 1954, and 71 of those were in jail.[23] In May 1954, the number stood at 184,[24] and by August 1st it was down to 121, of whom 23 were in jail.[25] By December 1954, there were only 61 foreign Catholic priests remaining in China and of that number, 21 were in prison.[26]

Many of those arriving in Hong Kong noted the accelerated drive to get rid of foreign priests, and many predicted that the already strong pressure on the Chinese clergy to cooperate with the patriotic-independent movement would intensify once all of the foreign missionionaries were gone from the country.[27] A large number of those already jailed for long periods of time, including some we have met in earlier chapters, were released and expelled during the spring and summer of 1954. Father Francis X. Legrand, one of the organizers of the Catholic Central Bureau in Shanghai and founder of the *China Missionary Bulletin*, was released on April 28. Arrested in Shanghai along with Father Aedan McGrath on September 7, 1951, Father Legrand reached Hong Kong on May 2, 1954. He had been in prison for 933 days during which time he had lost more than sixty pounds. Father Legrand's account of prison tortures was sadly familiar. He reported that the worst torture session he endured was during March 1952 when he was kept standing, wrists chained behind his back, and questioned uninterruptedly for six days and nights, during which time he stubbornly refused to confess that he was a murderer.[28]

Father W. Aedan McGrath also arrived in Hong Kong on May 2. For seven months after his arrest he had been kept in a military prison. From April 1952, however, he had been kept in solitary confinement in the Shanghai Ward Road Prison. He reported that he had been able to deliver his toilet paper instructional tracts to fellow prisoners with the help of a White Russian prisoner who was given the task of bringing food to the foreign prisoners.[29] On July 6, Monsignor Fernand Lacretelle, S.J., one of those arrested on June 15, 1953 in Shanghai, reached Hong Kong though his confreres Father McCarthy and Father Houle remained in prison.[30]

Also reaching Hong Kong in July was Father Norbert Pieraccini, O.F.M., the last foreign missionary to be expelled from the Diocese of Tianjin. Father Pieraccini had spent much of the previous several years, at the request of the Chinese authorities, assisting the expelled missionaries who left China from the port of Tianjin. Father Pieraccini reported that the campaign against those who refused to join the reform movement was being stepped up. He also confirmed that a number of Chinese priests in Beijing who had been arrested the previous March were released and sent back to their native dioceses, usually in districts far away from Beijing. The effect of this move was that many small chapels and churches around the city, to which faithful Catholics had been going to attend Mass, were now closed, forcing the local Catholics to attend the churches under the control of the patriotic-reform group, or stay home.[31]

While many churches remained open in the cities, the "temporary" suspension of religious activities in the countryside during the period of land reform, combined with the expulsion of the foreign missionaries and the jailing and harassment of Chinese priests and religious, had effectively closed the rural churches and missions permanently.

The move by the government to accomplish the final expulsion of all foreign missionaries and the growing pressure on the Chinese clergy, were accompanied by a continuing consolidation and centralization of political control under the leadership of the Communist Party. A draft constitution was approved in June 1954, and in anticipation of the establishment of the formal organs of central power under a state constitution, the six great administrative regions which had existed since Liberation were abolished. The effect of this step was to place the provincial governments directly under the control of the central government. The First National People's Congress was convened on September 15, 1954, and the Constitution of the PRC was formally approved.

At the same time there was a move to accelerate the pace of collectivization of agriculture. Already in 1953 the director of the Rural Work Department of the CCP Central Committee had called for ending the Agrarian Reform program of the previous years and moving ahead with large-scale collectivization in agriculture.[32] The years 1954 and 1955 witnessed the push for the establishment of higher stages of producers' cooperatives which were, in effect, collective farms.

While the large majority of China's Catholics remained unmoved by the government's efforts to establish a Patriotic church, the government persisted in that effort, as it did in the search for a prominent church leader to step forward to lead the movement. At the opening session of the First NPC, Father Li Wei-kuang [Li Wei-guang] the Vicar-General of Nanjing and author of the Nanjing Manifesto (*see above*), himself a delegate to the Congress, denounced those uncooperative priests "who do not fulfill their patriotic duties."[33] In fact Father Li, the apparent *de facto* leader of the government's Patriotic-Reform movement, had already been excommunicated by name by the Holy See in 1952, though the decree was not published until 1955 in the hope that he might mend his ways.[34]

Collision Course

As 1954 came to an end, Pope Pius XII's encyclical *Ad Sinarum Gentem* ["To the Chinese People"], which he had written in October, was released on December 22.[35] This document is worth considering at some length as it sets forth with unmistakable clarity the position of the Holy See with reference to the government-sponsored movement for a "patriotic" and "autonomous" Chinese Catholic Church.

The Pope began by noting that in the three years since his Apostolic Letter to China, the situation "has in no way improved; on the contrary, accusations and calumnies have been increasingly directed against this Apostolic See and against those who remain faithful to it." The Pope congratulated and praised those who had been steadfast in their faith, but expressed his sorrow that:

> there are some among you who, deceived in good faith, or overcome by fear, or led astray by new false teachings, have recently adhered to insidious and dangerous "movements" which are promoted by those who are enemies of every religion, and above all of that religion divinely revealed by Jesus Christ.

The Pope praised the Chinese Catholics for obeying the public authorities "in those things which pertain to them," and lauded them for their patriotism and for fulfilling the duties of citizenship. At the same time, he declared the Holy See "greatly consoled" to know:

> that you have asserted, and do still openly assert, when necessary, that you can never forsake the precepts of the Catholic religion, never deny your faith in the Creator and Redeemer, nor ever abandon Him for Whose sake and for Whose love many of you have undergone torture and imprisonment.

The Pope defended the missionary effort and expressed his hope that there would soon be enough native Chinese priests and religious that there would be no need of foreign missionary assistance to carry on the work of the Church. He then turned his attention to each of the three "autonomies" demanded by the *San Zi Yun Dong*, administration, finances and propagation of the faith. Even when the Catholic Church in China no longer had need of the help of foreign missionaries, said the Pope, that church could not be ruled by the "so-called 'autonomy of government:'"

> For even then, in fact as you are well aware, it will be entirely essential that your Christian community, if it desires to form a part of our Society divinely founded by Our Redeemer, be subject in all things to the sovereign pontiff, the vicar of Jesus Christ on earth,

and that it must be most closely united to Him as far as concerns religious faith and morals.

These words, said the Pope, "embrace the entire life and work of the Church," and most especially the "two-fold sacred power" of orders and jurisdiction. The power of orders whereby the ecclesiastical hierarchy is constituted, he wrote, is obtained by receiving the Sacrament of Holy Orders. As to the power of jurisdiction, it is:

conferred on the Sovereign Pontiff directly by divine right, is derived to the bishops from the same right, but only through the Successor of Saint Peter, to Whom not merely the ordinary faithful but all bishops as well must be constantly subject and attached with the homage of their obedience and with the bonds of unity. Finally, by the same Divine Will, the people and the civil authorities are forbidden to interfere with the rights and with the constitution of the ecclesiastical hierarchy.

On the matter of finances, the Pope declared that money collected abroad for the Chinese was not done, "for any political reason or to further profane causes," but rather that these offerings had their origin in "that Christian charity whereby all those redeemed by the Sacred Blood of Christ are of necessity bound to one another by a brotherly alliance."

As to the autonomy of propagation of the faith, Pope Pius allowed that there could be variations in the "method" of teaching and preaching:

But—even the thought alone is absurd—by what right can men, of their own will, interpret differently from one country to another, the Gospel divinely given by Jesus Christ?...The sacred pastors of souls are not the inventors or authors of that Gospel, but merely its authorized custodians and its divinely appointed heralds. Wherefore we ourselves, and all bishops with us, can and must repeat the words of Jesus Christ: "My teaching is not my own, but His who sent me."

And if the message of the encyclical was not already clear enough, the Pope added this admonition:

You can easily see, therefore, Venerable Brothers and beloved sons, that no one can be considered a Catholic or glory in that name who professes or teaches something different from that which We have up to this point briefly explained, such as those who adhere to those dangerous principles on which the "three autonomies" are based, or to other principles of the same kind.

The promoters of the Independent and Patriotic church, said the Pope, were engaged in cunning "deception" when they declared that the only true Chinese patriots were those who adhered to the autonomous movement:

> In reality, however, their aim is, in a word, to establish in your country a so-called "national" church. Such a church, if it were set up, would no longer be Catholic, since it would deny the universality or "catholicity" in virtue of which the true society founded by Jesus Christ is above all nations and yet embraces each and all of them.

The Holy Father then again congratulated those who had remained faithful, especially those who had suffered and died for their loyalty, and he quoted the words of Jesus from St. Matthew's Gospel: "Everyone who acknowledges me before men, I will also acknowledge him before my Father in heaven. But whoever disowns me before men, I will in turn disown him before my Father in heaven." And perhaps mindful of the grim realities of the persecution awaiting those who followed his call, the Pope closed with an Apostolic Benediction and this prayer:

> May the holy martyrs of China assist you from heaven, they who serenely faced death for their true love of their fatherland and more especially for their fidelity to Our Divine Redeemer and His Church.

Had there remained before this time any question about the impossibility of accommodation between the Roman Church and the communist state, this encyclical should have put those questions to rest once and for all. The course of suffering and martyrdom for loyal Chinese Catholics was clearly set out by the Holy Father. Each of the three "autonomies" demanded by the Chinese authorities (and it is important to remember that this was a government sponsored and controlled movement), and most particularly the important autonomies of administration and propagation of the faith, were specifically and emphatically denied by the Pope.

The Chinese authorities were, however, equally resolute in their determination to bring the Church under state control. The stage was thus set for a major showdown.

Wang Xiaoling:
> Though our parish had lost a great number of priests and our activities were restricted, one branch of the vine was sufficient to bear fruit. Not only were there many vocations among the young

people, on big feasts, baptisms, and first communions were very numerous. When we could not have a retreat in our parish I brought the young people to another parish to make one. When there were no buses running directly to Our Lady's Shrine at Sheshan [Zose] we went by train and boat and made our devotions before Our Lady's altar. I felt that God was richly blessing the work and life of the parish and that they were prospering. When people thought that all was without meaning, then we truly lived. But the atmosphere was one of foreboding—the lull before the storm. So it was that I, at the age of eighteen, went to meet the summer of 1955.[36]

The Arrest of Bishop Kung

The exodus of foreign missionaries continued during the early months of 1955. Most of the freed missionaries brought to Hong Kong with them harrowing stories of their prison experiences. A typical account published by the *China Missionary Bulletin* is included in the Appendix of this chapter. At the same time there were growing reports in every number of the *Bulletin* of arrests, imprisonment in labor camps and, increasingly, of executions of Chinese priests. It was clear, as Bishop Tang had expressed the fear, that with most of the foreign missionaries expelled from the country, the Chinese authorities were now turning their attention to native priests and religious.

In addition to the struggle taking place in Shanghai, loyal Catholics in Beijing were also under great pressure. In March of 1954 there had been a mass arrest of Chinese priests who refused to cooperate with the reform movement.[37] Defections to the reform movement were still few, but the government made the most of those priests who were willing to cooperate. Much publicity was given, for example, to a visit to China in August 1954 by a British Labor Party delegation headed by former prime minister Clement Atlee. Mr. Atlee met on August 17, amid much fanfare, with a group of Christian leaders in Beijing. Among this group were two Catholic priests, Father Li Yin-t'ao and Father Ma Wen-chun. Father Ma, the pastor of the Dong Tong Church, was a "progressive" priest in bad standing with the Vatican. Father Li, pastor of the Nan Tong Church (Immaculate Conception Church), was one of two priests—together with Father Li Wei-guang—who had been excommunicated by name by the Holy See, and his church placed under interdict. It is not known whether Atlee knew who these two priests were, nor was any mention made of the dozens of Catholic priests in jail in Beijing at the time.[38] Mr. Atlee did observe the following day that, "the object of government is not the power of the state, but the happiness of individuals."[39]

The Beijing authorities likewise gave publicity to an ordination which took place in the capital on July 10, 1955, and which they claimed to be the first ordination of a Catholic priest since Liberation. This claim was clearly incorrect, even as it pertained to the Archdiocese of Beijing. Perhaps the government news agency meant to convey that this was the first ordination to take place under the authority of a Catholic bishop who was cooperating with the Patriotic-Reform movement. The name of the presiding bishop, variously given as Tung[40] and Chang,[41] may have been Alphonse Chung Huai-mo, O.F.M. [Chong Huai-mo] of the Luan Diocese in Shanxi Province who had taken up residence in Beijing. Bishop Chung had been cooperating with the "progressives" as had the Beijing vicar general Father Lee Kuen Wu [Li Qun-wu], and the excommunicated Father Li Yin-t'ao. Father Li was reported to have been offered the post of rector of the seminary from which the new priest had graduated, though it was not clear at the time whether he had accepted the post or not.

What was clear was that the pressure on the Church was beginning to yield for the authorities some of the desired results. As evidence of the success enjoyed by the reform movement by the middle of 1955, authorities in Beijing could point to the fact that the seminary, all four of the parish churches open in Beijing, including the vicar general's cathedral parish, and all but one of the city's chapels were in the hands of the reform faction.[42] Nevertheless, the *Missionary Bulletin* reported that more than fifty priests in the diocese remained loyal to Rome,[43] and there is considerable evidence, especially from later testimony, that the vast majority of the laity remained suspicious, if not openly hostile, to the "progressive" priests.

With almost all of the foreign missionaries now out of the country and with the Church encircled and besieged, the government apparently felt that the time was at hand to strike a mortal blow at the most recalcitrant and defiantly loyal Catholic stronghold in China, the Catholic community of Shanghai.

In mid-summer 1955 the government launched yet another drive against counterrevolutionaries. A *Renmin Ribao* editorial of July 3 called for the liquidation of "hidden counterrevlutionaries."[44] This call was picked up and repeated throughout the country over the next several weeks. On July 27, in his speech to the Second Session of the National People's Congress, Minister of Public Security Luo Rui-qing detailed cases of counterrevolutionary activity which had already been uncovered. Referring specifically to the Catholic Church, Minister Luo told the Congress that:

> counterrevolutionary elements were still working under the cloak of religion; between May 1953 and April 1954, close to 200 dugouts, some large enough to contain 100 people, had been discovered. These had been used by secret organizations under the name of the Catholic Church in [two] regions of Hopei [Hebei] Province.[45]

A nationwide mass campaign was organized to mobilize people to discover and report counterrevolutionaries. Those who were most successful in detecting these criminals were singled out for special recognition and praise. One especially diligent citizen was cited as a "grade-A model of treason-preventer and security-protector" for turning in 281 counterrevolutionaries and other criminals.[46] This campaign also coincided with a major purge of two of Mao's rivals within the Communist Party, and with a renewed attack on intellectuals highlighted by an attack on and the arrest of the well-known veteran communist literary figure, the writer Hu Feng. All of these activities signaled a continued turn to the "left" in Chinese politics which could not fail to mean additional trouble for the Church.

Close on the heels of Public Security Minister Luo's July 27, 1955 speech, the Shanghai *Liberation Daily* [Jiefang Ribao] began to carry a steady stream of letters attacking the Catholic Church in general and the "criminal activities of the counterrevolutionary Kung Pin-mei group" in particular. The charges were the now-familiar ones: gathering information for the enemy, organizing acts of violence, encouraging the resistance movement, spreading rumors, poisoning the minds of the youth, killing babies in Catholic orphanages, listening to the Voice of America, etc. Several nasty incidents resulted from this agitation and a few priests were arrested.[47] It was clear that the big confrontation was at hand, and on September 8, 1955, the government struck.[48]

On the night of September 8, Bishop Kung, an unspecified number of priests and other religious, and several hundred Catholic lay people were arrested in a massive police sweep.[49]

Wang Xiaoling:
> It was the hottest time of autumn. That evening I had had a bath and changed into my pajamas. I was going over the name list of the catechism class in the dining room. My grandmother, my mother and others were sitting around in the doorway and in the courtyard of our house taking things easy. I put the name list beside the music books on the piano. Suddenly, three men in ordinary clothes burst in through the back door. They immediately asked bluntly, "Which of you is Xiaoling?" I replied directly, "I am." They immediately took out a pair of handcuffs and put them on my wrists. At the same time, they summoned to the living room my father and sisters who had already gone upstairs to bed. In the name of the Bureau of Public Security, they announced that I was being arrested as a "reactionary."[50]

Over the next several weeks the attacks on the Church spread. Radio Beijing announced on September 11 that a large group of Catholics in that city, including at least one priest, had been arrested for counterrevolutionary activities. On September 14, Radio Beijing warned that Catholics who did not withdraw from the Legion of Mary would be "very severely punished." The following day the authorities announced the arrests in the East [Zhejiang Province] and South [Fujian Province] of a number of individuals who had "infiltrated Catholic organizations to carry out anti-revolutionary activities." All of those arrested were denounced as "faithful running dogs of the imperialists."[51]

On November 10, the communist authorities gave wide publicity to a letter said to have been signed by 74 priests in Shanghai addressed to fellow priests and Catholic laymen discussing the case of Bishop Kung.[52] The letter made extensive use of the lengthy confession which had been signed and tape-recorded by Father Lacretelle before his release from prison and expulsion from China.[53] The letter cited Father Lacretelle's "confession" that he had "assisted Bishop Kung Pin-mei in opposing the various activities led by the People's Government."[54] The Bishop was accused in the letter of having celebrated Mass in honor of certain "counterrevolutionaries," of having given shelter to "traitors, special agents and counterrevolutionaries," of opposing the Chinese participation in the Korean War, and other now-familiar crimes against the People's Government.

On December 10, the *Renmin Ribao* devoted considerable space to the case of Bishop Kung and published an editorial on the subject. The lead *Renmin Ribao* article, which runs to four long single-spaced pages in translation, reviewed the history of Bishop Kung's non-cooperation and of his various "counterrevolutionary crimes" in considerable detail.[55] The editorial, titled "Counterrevolutionaries Will Never Be Allowed to Exploit Religion for Subversive Activities," was almost as long as the article and covered pretty much the same familiar ground. It is certainly a measure of how seriously the government regarded the challenge represented by Bishop Kung and the Shanghai Catholics that so much space and publicity should be given the problem in the official news organ of the CCP Central Committee, the nation's most important newspaper.

It was rumored that Bishop Kung would shortly be brought to trial,[56] though this was not to occur until March 1960.

In Shanghai, following the September arrests of virtually all of the Chinese priests loyal to Rome, the administration of church affairs, for all practical purposes, came to be effectively under the control of the "progressives." Shortly after Bishop Kung's arrest the priests of the diocese with no ecclesiastical authorization elected the 76-year-old Father Chang Shih-lang [Zhang Shi-lang] as their bishop. Father Chang was never consecrated as bishop, though he took over direction of the affairs of the Shanghai Diocese. Father Chang asserted that for a long time he had been "cheated and oppressed by the imperialist Kung Pin-mei and his counterrevolutionary group."[57] There was, however, still considerable evidence that the Catholics of Shanghai ignored Father Chang, regarded those priests they considered unreliable with great suspicion, and resisted participating in activities organized or conducted by the Patriotic Reform group.[58]

A similar story was repeated in many other parts of the country. In the Hankow [Hankou] Archdiocese [Hubei Province], for example, the administrators of the archdiocese and of the Hanyang Diocese were arrested on September 15, along with a number of priests. The remainder of the priests not arrested were said to have been placed under house arrest in the Hankow Cathedral. A newspaper campaign similar to that conducted against Bishop Kung was begun for the purpose of attacking Father Odoric Liu, the administrator of the archdiocese.[59] September also brought the arrest, in the Taichow [Taizhou] Diocese of Zhejiang Province, of Bishop Joseph Hu, one of that small group of Chinese priests who were the first of their nation to be consecrated as bishops by Pope Pius XI in 1926.[60]

All over China the pressure on the Church was intensified. On the night of December 5, the bishop's residence in Swatow [Shantou, Guangdong Province] was surrounded by security police. The deputy bishop and all the priests were arrested. At the same time, almost all the other priests in the city were also rounded up by the Public Security Bureau. Within less than two weeks, the police sweep in eastern Guangdong Province had netted most of the priests in the surrounding villages as well, including a certain Father "Joseph Zhang" from whom we shall hear more later.[61] To the west of Swatow, in the city of Canton, several priests and other religious and some Catholic lay people were arrested,[62] but at least for the moment, Bishop Dominic Tang remained at liberty in Canton.

The Chinese Catholic Patriotic Association

The Catholic Church had suffered a terrible blow in 1955. It was a church surrounded and besieged on all sides. In many places the organization and administration of church affairs was entirely in the hands of those priests who, enthusiastically or unenthusiastically proved willing to cooperate with the Patriotic-Reform Movement. The pressure on the Church was, however, as it had been from the beginning, applied somewhat unevenly from one place to another. Thus there were still individual prelates such as Bishop Dominic Tang Yi-ming, S.J., of Canton, and Bishop Peter Joseph Fan Xue-yan of the Baoding Diocese in Hebei Province, who remained free of confinement and steadfast in their refusal to cooperate with the "progressives."

The years 1956 and 1957 were an interesting and complex period in Chinese Communist history. These years encompassed the "Hundred Flowers" campaign, the "Anti-Rightist" movement, the completion of the First Five-Year Plan, and the plans for launching the "Great Leap Forward" in 1958, the latter a great watershed in the history of the Chinese communist movement and government which set the nation on course for the cataclysmic "Great Proletarian Cultural Revolution" in 1966. It might be said that these were the years in China in which the transition to a dictatorship of the Communist Party was completed, and in which the move toward the dictatorship of one man, Chairman Mao Zedong, was begun. While this may be an oversimplification of the complexities of Chinese politics during this important period, such a statement does reflect the general trend of political events in China in the years leading up to the Cultural Revolution.

The precise nature of the original motives of the Chinese leadership in launching the "Hundred Flowers" movement are still somewhat in dispute by China scholars, but the course of the movement and its results are fairly clear. The name of the movement derived from a call issued by Mao Zedong at a meeting of the Supreme State Conference in May 1956 to, "let one hundred flowers bloom, let one hundred schools of thought contend." Intellectuals were invited to express their thoughts openly and to use their creative and innovative powers. In the first phase of this campaign, from the late spring of 1956 to February 1957, intellectuals responded with great caution, perhaps recalling the harshness of the drives they had witnessed over the preceding several years. From about March to June 1957 there was a period of big "blooming and contending," following another address by Chairman Mao to the Supreme State Conference in which he delivered his famous speech, "On the Correct Handling of Contradictions Among the People" (*see above*, Chapter Two).[63] A huge campaign was launched nationwide, especially among intellectuals and the united front groups, to encourage dissidents to speak out so that they might be gently "corrected" rather than suppressed.

The storm of criticism which resulted was apparently a great shock to the leadership, in terms of both breadth and intensity. In one violent incident, for example, more than 1,000 students rioted in the city of Hanyang, Hubei Province, attacking the

Party headquarters and demanding Chairman Mao's resignation. The Party's response to this particular "innovation" was to execute several score of those involved, including the dean of studies and vice principal of the Hanyang Middle School.[64] By June 1957, the "blooming and contending" had been shut down with a vengeance, to be replaced with a campaign against "rightists" [fan you pai yundong]. The Anti-Rightist Campaign would eventually claim many tens of thousands of new victims, and usher in a period of even stricter control and indoctrination of students, intellectuals, and disaffected members of the various united front groups.

The beginnings of the Anti-Rightist Campaign also coincided with the decision of the Party Central Committee at the end of 1957 to abandon the Stalinist developmental model of the First Five Year Plan, and to launch a Great Leap Forward with the Second Five Year Plan beginning in 1958. It was Mao's great revolutionary plan to substitute manpower, which China had in abundance, for those inputs of development which were extremely scarce in his poor and backward nation, namely technology and capital. The year 1958 saw vast agricultural communes formed all over China, each encompassing at least 2,000 peasant households. The Great Leap also brought with it other campaigns of mass mobilization on an enormous scale. There were one hundred million workers daily involved in water conservation projects, and some two million or so backyard steel furnaces, tended by more than sixty million Chinese, which were intended to help China become self-sufficient in steel production almost immediately, and to surpass Great Britain in industrial output within fifteen years. None of these programs achieved the desired results. Steel from the backyard furnaces proved to be useless for the most part, and in every other respect the Great Leap can only fairly be described as a failure of colossal proportions. Indeed, some of the political and social reverberations of the policy decisions taken by the Chinese leadership in the late 1950s were still being felt at the end of the 1980s.

It was against the background of these events that the Chinese Catholic Patriotic Association [Tian Zhu Jiao Ai Guo Hui] was created in 1957.

As indicated above, a shift in the emphasis of the *San Zi Yun Dong* to a movement of "love of country and love of church" [*ai guo-ai jiao*] had already taken place, and government-sponsored Catholic organizations emphasizing "patriotism" had been established all over the country. In the wake of the police sweeps of 1955 which removed from the roster of active participants large numbers of those priests and religious loyal to Rome, the government moved ahead with plans to organize a national organization of "Patriotic" Catholics.

In July 1956 Premier Zhou En-lai called a meeting in Beijing of some 38 individuals to attend a "Preparatory Conference for the Preparatory Committee of the Catholics' Patriotic Association."[65] According to Chinese press reports, the meeting lasted six days and was attended by four bishops, nine vicars-general, twelve priests and eleven lay Catholics. A second meeting was called in Beijing from February 12–16, 1957, chaired by Ho Ch'eng-hsiang [He Cheng-xiang], Director of the Bureau of Religious Affairs of the State Council. It might be noted parenthetically that at the time of the February meeting, there were only twelve foreign priests still in China (including Bishop Walsh), of which eight were in prison. In addition there were eleven sisters, Franciscan Missionaries of Mary, who had been allowed to remain in Beijing where they ran a school for the children of foreign diplomats.[66]

The Hong Kong *China News Analysis* observed that if four of the five invited bishops attended the February conference, there were still some 25 Chinese bishops in residence in China who did attend the conference, and that the ecclesisastical status of some of the vicars-general was in doubt.[67] Nevertheless, the government pressed ahead and, after a delay of several months, a conference was called for June 17,[68] again under the direction of Religious Affairs Bureau Director He, for the purpose of organizing a national Chinese Catholic Patriotic Association (CCPA). The conference was finally officially convened on July 15, 1957. The initial Xinhua report called for the conference to last six days, though in fact, it did not conclude its work until August 2.[69]

Official press reports indicated that a total of 241 priests, religious and laity, representing more than one hundred dioceses, attended the meeting. Considerable publicity was given to the meeting and to the formation of the CCPA, including a long statement attacking "rightists" in the Church made to the Fourth Session of the first National People's Congress, also meeting in Beijing during the month of July, one of the authors of which was the excommunicated Father Li Wei-guang.[70]

During the course of the conference, the participants adopted a statement of protest to the Vatican for its refusal to recognize the election by the progressives of a vicar capitular of the Shanghai Diocese following the arrest of Bishop Kung. Rome insisted on recognizing the order of succession established by Bishop Kung before his arrest.[71] Finally, on August 2, the establishment of the CCPA was announced. A committee of 150 was elected to lead the organization, and Archbishop Ignatius P'i Shu-shih [Pi Shu-shi] of the Shenyang Archdiocese [Liaoning Province] was elected chairman.[72] The Archbishop, it might be noted, had spent years in prison and under house arrest, and his will was apparently broken.[73] The Chinese Catholics, *Xinhua* announced, "took a solemn decision to cut political and economic ties with the Vatican because of its persistent hostility to the people's regime and its blatant intervention in internal matters of China which had nothing to do with religion."[74] The conference resolution declared that Chinese Catholics would obey the Vatican in "matters of dogma and morals," but would, "resolutely oppose any scheme concocted by the Vatican in the form of religion which interferes with our country's internal affairs or violates its sovereignty, and damages our Patriotic movement against imperialism."[75] The day following the close of the conference, the *Renmin Ribao* published an editorial in which they declared the decision of the conference to keep church administration in the hands of Chinese Catholics "a matter of fundamental principle."[76]

For those still refusing to cooperate with the CCPA, the pressure intensified.

Archbishop Tang:
   [In 1957] the communist government and the Bureau of Religious Affairs set up around the bishop's residence...a public address system and broadcast loudly every day over the loudspeaker material accusing me. They shouted loudly and endlessly: "Tang Yee-ming,

you should repent quickly" and so on, to frighten me. Posters were stuck everywhere on walls and inside the house with the slogan: "Tang Yee-ming, the most loyal running dog of the reactionary Vatican." The Catholics were angry and tore them down secretly....

More than ten "struggle" meetings were held in the premises of the CCPA. Before and after every meeting, I went to the chapel to pray, asking for God's protection. During the "struggle" meetings, I kept quiet in the hope that I, too, could have my share of suffering for the Church. Before my arrest, I went very often to Confession to prepare my soul in a peaceful manner.[77]

In the months following the close of the conference, "preparatory" meetings and conferences were held all across China for the purpose of organizing official provincial-level units of the CCPA.[78] In the course of these meetings the participants usually affirmed their acceptance of the leadership of the Communist Party, and "uncovered" and "criticized" the "rightist" elements in the ranks of the local Catholics. It soon became clear that the days of freedom were numbered for the few prominent holdouts loyal to Rome who had not yet been taken into custody. The "preparatory" meeting in Baoding [Hebei Province], for example, criticized, in unmistakable language, Bishop Peter Joseph Fan Xue-yan, Bishop of the Baoding Diocese and one of the strongest voices resisting the CCPA who was still at liberty. The Bishop was "unmasked" as a "rightist element" who had, "all along adhered to the anti-party and anti-socialist stand, openly defended the Vatican's reactionary political nature, undermined the anti-imperialist and patriotic movement, and claimed that participation in the Patriotic Association constituted 'betrayal of and schism in the Church,' and that to be anti-imperialist and patriotic was 'sinful.' "[79] Like the renewed attacks on Bishop Tang in Canton, the tone of this attack on Bishop Fan left little doubt as to what his fate would be.

On February 8, 1958, the Chinese press announced that the Canton Municipal Public Security Bureau, "acting on information given by the masses and following a prolonged investigation, broke the counterrevolutionary case of Teng Yi-ming [Dominic Tang], Bishop of the Canton Diocese, hiding in the Catholic Church." The report revealed that, acting according to law, the Bishop had been arrested on February 5.[80] A short time later Bishop Fan was also arrested in Baoding.[81]

Archbishop Tang:

[On February 5, 1958], I saw four big fellows standing in front of the garden of the cathedral as if waiting for someone. I felt that something was going to happen. I returned to the chapel of the bishop's residence (Carmelite Convent) to say five decades of the Rosary and went to Confession to Father Anthony Ngan....

It was quite cold; I put on my coat. Suddenly at around 8:00 P.M., a cadre from the local police station came to the bishop's house leading some policemen. He asked Father Joachim Lau to take him to my room; then Father Lau left. A policeman pointed a revolver at me and ordered me to raise my arms and at once I was handcuffed.... While I was being arrested, I was happy; for priests and many Cathoics had also been arrested because they had obeyed my orders; they had not joined the CCPA nor had they admitted that the Legion of Mary was counterrevolutionary. How could I not be like them?[82]

The arrests of Bishops Tang and Fan left the Catholic Church in China effectively without a visible pro-Vatican leadership. The open break with Rome was at hand with the first unauthorized consecrations of "Patriotic" bishops in 1958. Still ahead, too, was the storm which would break over the heads of the Patriotics who had tried to bend themselves to the will of the government.

APPENDIX
"They Made an Ass of Me"
By Father Alber Sohier
(CMB, March 1955, 189–195)

On November 8, 1954 at 12 o'clock noon the SS Hupeh took off from the Tientsin waterfront carrying me away from China. I had not wept when leaving my parents and my own country seven and a half years ago, but today, leaving this land of China where my heart remains, the tears ran down over my hands and on the guard rail. My mind went back to the last moments of imprisonment. Today I was starting to write a few of the events of that unhappy period.

We Broke Your Back
Last Friday the judge in Peking said to this prisoner about to be freed, "That your back was broken here is a fact. We do not ask you to deny it but we do ask you not to exaggerate the facts." Another official standing by added, "If you are objective you will admit that we no longer beat prisoners. We have made mistakes in the past but our methods have been improved; time was required to get the situation in hand."

It is true that I had neither seen nor experienced the brutal beatings in 1953 and 1954. But severe punishment did not cease and it was a common thing to see prisoners chained hand and foot when they refused to confess as ordered.

On July 25, 1951, I was arrested and put in jail in Peking. The prison interrogators started their work on me at 10 o'clock that evening. One of them stated first, "Of course you know why you were arrested." My answer was, "Either because there is some misunderstanding about my conduct or I am in prison for religious reasons." The judge corrected me saying, "The communist program allows freedom of worship and therefore it is not a question of religion. But you have opposed the interests of the People's Government."

Burying People Alive
They questioned me that night on the date of my arrival and on my various activities in China. After the interrogation

I was put in a cell with six Chinese prisoners. The cell chief said he was in prison for burying people alive. The prospects under such a man were not very bright. He rebuked me severely the next morning when I made the Sign of the Cross at mealtime. A little later he advised me to be very frank and confess everything during the interrogations. If I did so, he said that I would be rewarded with generous treatment and soon be released. Meanwhile, I was being given a view of things to come. We were called out to participate in a "criticism" or accusation meeting which was to "help" a certain Wong confess his crimes. He stood at attention for several hours surrounded by a group of prisoners who screamed at him and threatened him if he did not confess his crimes.

Shackle Irons Applied

The second night in prison I was brought up again for interrogation. The subject of the questions was, for the most part, my relations with Father De Jaegher, a Belgian priest whose anti-communist activity was notorious. I admitted having known him personally after my arrival in Peking but not before. I was asked if I knew his assistant Ts'ao Ly-shan. I knew a Father Alexander but did not know if Ts'ao was his surname. The same questions were asked in a thousand different ways, but I always gave the same truthful answers. The magistrate lost patience and angrily threatened me because I was not frank and honest in my answers, he said. After a long threatening lecture he suggested that I go back and carefully think over my crimes. But I was left alone for only two hours and then called back again for more questions by the same two individuals. I, too, became impatient and protested vehemently when they questioned my honesty. As punishment for the protest my hands were handcuffed behind my back and iron fetters weighing about twenty pounds were fixed to my ankles. With that they sent me back to my cell for more reflection.

The No-sleep Torture

The cell chief, following instructions no doubt, decided that I should not be permitted to sleep. He appointed fellow prisoners to watch in turn and keep me awake. During the four weeks following I slept only sixteen hours altogether. Four hours sleep was allowed on the order of the judge after I pleaded with him to let me get some rest. Four hours were allowed at another time after I fainted during one of the beatings. One night I got eight hours sleep between two days of continuous rain when there was no interrogation.

During the third night of interrogation the magistrate asked me again if I had known Father De Jaegher before coming to China. When I persisted truthfully that I had never seen him before coming to China, I was ordered to sit on the ground, stretch out my legs and lie back on my shackled wrists in a way that made the handcuffs dig into the wrists until they bled. The pain finally made me falsely confess that I had met him in Rome in 1939. As a matter of fact, Father De Jaegher had been in China continuously since 1931. I was asked to sign and thumb-print questions and answers after each period. When I protested that the answers were not correct, the interrogators promised to make rectifications at the next period, which of course was never done.

Confess and Be Forgiven

The interrogations went on night and day for three months. Two to six sessions were held every 24 hours, most of them at night. I was bold enough to express great indignation at the methods of the communists in forcing confession of crime. But this seemed to make no impression. Lies had been circulated which said that I had a radio transmitter. They said that a young lad at a public trial had confessed that I had directed him to write reactionary slogans and to paste them on the city walls. I was accused also of sabotage, espionage, of having concealed guns, and of preparing an army for insurrection.

When I related all these accusations to the prisoners in the same cell, they said it was simply a matter of confessing all these crimes to clear the record, and so, they urged me to confess. I half-believed them. Then when the suffering, sleeplessness and fatigue of repeated interrogation became unbearable, I accepted the proposal of cell-mates and gave out a fantastic confession of the following crimes: (1) At the time of the Red Army liberation of Peking I had concealed a radio-sending set. Later I had set it up and collaborated with Tiao Hwa-jen in organizing an information net to cover the city of Peking. I said that in the summer of 1950 Tiao Hwa-jen had left for Hong Kong and that I had communicated with him through secret or code messages, assisted by a certain Sung Wei-ly. (2) I had organized a group of twenty or thirty children to paste anti-government slogans on the city walls, to throw stones at the windows of schools, public buildings, street lamps, etc.

A Web of Lies

The magistrate warned that I should reflect on the gravity of these confessed crimes and so I began to retract the lies with great relief. He then said, "Weigh your words well, for if your first confession was false you have deceived the government and that in itself deserves punishment." Caught in a web of lies I felt discouraged and said, "I have not been permitted to sleep for many days and I have been beaten repeatedly. My exhausted mind now wanders like a man dreaming and I can no longer distinguish between imagination and fact."

The cell chief had kept me from sleeping now for 110 successive days because he asserted that I needed the time to reflect on my crimes and make a good confession. I was forced to stand continuously day and night. When the prison doctor saw my swollen legs he gave orders to let me rest. The cell chief then permitted me to sit down but not to lie down except for brief periods, and they still kept me from any sleep. If I nodded they slapped me or jabbed chopsticks into my ribs or pinched me. This treatment could have been the idea of the cell chief, but it was not stopped by the police who frequently looked into the cell.

Approved Torture

After each interrogation I had to repeat to the cell-mates what had been asked and what I had answered. The cell-mates, under the direction of the chief, criticized my answers and then proceeded to "help" me confess sincerely. All this pressure was according to the prison regulations, but it is supposed to have been stopped since 1953 except under official instructions for some cases. The help was frequently punctuated by punches on the nape of the neck and in the ribs or jabs in the stomach with stiffened fingers. Sometimes I was ordered to stand up with my arms overhead or was ordered to sit on my wrists which were held tightly in shackles. The cell chief repeatedly forbade me to moan or to cry out from pain under the threat of more severe beating. In spite of it all I was unable to keep from crying out many times. I am sure that the guard outside could hear me but he did nothing to stop it. Once I complained to the interrogating judge but this also did no good. It drew a severe reprimand for my attitude and refusal to confess. This convinced me that the authorities after all did approve of the torture and coercion directed by the cell chief, so there was nothing to do but put up with it.

To "help" in what I should say, the chief made repeated suggestions and threats. Hence I concluded that he was acting under expressed instructions from the prison authorities.

A False Witness Exposed

My strong protest against their imputation and absurd lies they wanted me to tell was considered rebellious. As a result they applied feet shackles which I wore for four weeks and my ankles bled and my legs were dangerously swollen. I had denied that I knew a certain 14-year-old boy or told him to paste up anti-communist slogans. He was brought in to confront and accuse me. I tried to remember if I had ever seen him but could not. The judge again declared that I was not frank and honest. He then ordered me to sit on my handcuffed wrists until the torture made me admit that I had told this lad named Tchang to write the slogans and that I had paid him to do so. They also brought another accuser, Sung Wei-ly, who said he had sent secret messages to Hong Kong for me. His accusation did not hold water since I was in the hospital recovering from an operation on the day he mentioned. A few hours later the judge told me that although the date might not be correct the other details of his accusations were true. I denied the whole trumped-up case with firmness and self-assurance. As a result I was again submitted to the shackle torture.

Fears, Worries, Threats

On August 21, 1951, after one month in prison, the warden ordered the fetters removed from my feet. The ankles were now bloated and infected and it caused me much pain. My wrists were also cut and sore where the shackles were on and off at the anger and whim of the interrogating judge. I felt a great relief those few hours. But that same evening I was again accused and questioned on matters which I denied. The judge declared that I was lying and ordered my wrists shackled once more behind my back. The chains were taken off again after interrogation and I was told to sleep that day and the next day, for they would soon call me back and they expected the proper answers. The fears and worries, and threats of the judge kept me from sleeping. Alternate treatment of severity and leniency are regularly used by the communists to extract confessions.

Demonic Torturers Unleashed

In the afternoon of August 23, a light chain, without the twenty-pound weight this time, was again fastened on my ankles. When the interrogation started that evening, only a few words were exchanged. The judge declared, "I see that you cannot be frank and honest in your answers." I replied, "I want only to give honest and satisfactory answers; I hope I can find some way to answer properly." The judge then added, "I'll find a way for you." He then gave an order to the guard who went out immediately. A few minutes later he returned with five other gendarmes who ordered me to squat on my haunches. Since I was weak and unable to stay in that position, they had me sit on a brick. Two men seized my knees and pulled them outward while the chains pressed into the ankle flesh; another held my feet down; the fourth tied a string to the wrists chained behind my back, then pulled my arms upwards; the fifth gendarme applied a towel gag over my mouth to stifle the screams; the last one, the biggest, jumped on my back for 10 to 15 minutes at a time to force me to confess. This same torture was repeated seven times during that night. The last period of torment was at dawn August 24. Suddenly my head dropped and struck the floor between my feet. The back was broken and I was doubled over in agony. They left me lying on the floor.

My legs were numb and powerless. I could not sit up even braced against the wall. The torturers came back and tried to make me sit up but it was impossible.

Hounds at the Kill

An hour later a man came to me who spoke French. He questioned me as I lay helpless on the floor, about Father De Jaegher's activities. When the pain allowed me to talk I slowly told him what I knew. The awful agony would let me speak no more, so I begged him to wait until some later time for further questioning. I felt that my mental and physical condition made me incapable of answering anything rationally, and besides I knew nothing more than I had already told.

Under torture in the past I had made up several stories on the subject and I dreaded repeating them now since death seemed only a short way off.

Carried Out on Stretcher

They decided to take me back to my cell. I was supposed to walk resting on the arms of two gendarmes but it proved impossible; my useless legs refused to respond so they dropped me to the floor. An hour later the prison doctor came to examine me. He found that the back was broken so I was finally loaded on a stretcher, carried back and left on the cement floor of the cell unable to get up. The unbearable suffering kept me twitching on the cement floor for relief. Ulcer sores soon formed in many places on my back. No medical help was given except to smear iodine on the sores. The cell chief forced me to sit up as exercise, resting on my arms propped against the wall. Since I could not bear this position for more than a few minutes I was showered with insults from the cell chief. After some weeks the guard ordered the cell mates to place me on a board bed. Another fifteen days went by. Three large festering wounds had now formed; one was at the base of my spine, the other two on the hips. When the stench got so bad that the prisoners complained, the doctor made up his mind to do something about it. Bandages were now applied to the ankles, wrists, knees, and elbows, and renewed regularly. The back sores were dressed daily and shots of penicillin were also given.

Pitiless Torture

For many months I had to lie on my stomach with my toes pressing into the boards. My toes and ankles were gradually being twisted out of shape. The doctor took note of it and ordered the cell chief to keep a bundle of clothes under my shins so as to let the feet hang free. But the cell chief refused to carry out the instructions after his departure. I dared not complain, for complaint would only bring me more torture. As a result of lying in this position for the greater part of the year, one of my ankles is still badly twisted and the big toe of each foot is bent under the other toes. A partial paralysis as well as pain still continues to be felt in the toes and feet, but this is probably an effect of the broken spine.

The cell chief decided he was going to cure me, and he and the fellow prisoners started shaking my legs to give them exercise. Their intentions may have been good, but their handling was so rough that I could not refrain from screaming. The warden heard the noise, came to our cell, and personally forbade them to continue their "help." Communism does not leave its followers much room for charity. Many times I had to go full days without a drink of water since the cell mates would not take the trouble to bring me a drink.

Two months after my back had been broken, the judge came to my cell on November 21 and said, "The confessions you have written up to now are useless. You have exaggerated many facts and you have omitted others. Hence nobody can make anything out of them. You are to start from the beginning and write another confession and you must make it sincere and honest this time."

Another Cell, Another Confession

They moved me to another cell. Since I could not write I was told to dictate my confession. The cell chief who was to take it down said, "You must revoke everything which was incorrect in your former confession." I began by saying that I was hereby contradicting three main points that I confessed before..."I have no radio-sending set, I have had no connection with Tiao Hwa-jen or any other spy-net; I did not direct any children to sabotage and did not organize them or anyone else for that purpose." The surprised cell chief put down his pen and said, "I see that you are not yet prepared to be honest. We shall write a confession when you are better disposed."

"Help" for Confession

Although the punishment was less brutal than in the first cell, I was still subjected to "help" stunts by cell-mates to make my confession properly. They struck my biceps, slid chopsticks between my fingers and squeezed them, twisted my ears until they tore and bled, jabbed chopsticks into my neck just under the jawbone, etc. I was completely helpless against it all since the broken back would not allow me to move. The torture went on for a month until December 20 when the warden ordered them to stop it. In January there was evidently a change in government policy on the severity of prisoners' treatment. Officials and cell chiefs had to hold criticism meetings and report all their excesses and guilt in this regard.

From then on the treatment was considerably less brutal. However, prison life did not suddenly become pleasant. I was slapped violently when my answers did not please. I was also severely beaten several times because I was noticed praying. Although the government professes freedom of religion, the facts do not bear this out. The only way I could pray was in secret and unnoticed. But I did manage to say the Rosary on my fingers everyday and when the cathedral bells not far away rang out for the Angelus, I always said the Angelus in secret. But a man under the conditions that I was under could not pray very much.

Communist Courtesy

On the 25th of July, the first anniversary of my arrest, the judge came in to my cell and asked, "What do the cell-mates think of you?" I answered, "They are evidently not pleased because they say I have made little progress toward making a good confession of crimes. They are also displeased because I have dysentery most of the time, cannot take care of myself and dirty the cell." He replied, "Who else makes such a mess? It is not a man who dirties his clothes and his bedding. It is an ass. Your whole conduct is that of an ass." And after ten more minutes of continued insults he concluded, "After a full year it is now high time that you clear your conscience and confess your crimes properly."

For several days after that the acting cell chief beat and tortured me thoroughly. He was sent to another cell after severe criticism for his excesses. All my cell-mates were changed about the first of August and after that I suffered no more physical torture. But I was still the object of jibes, painful criticism, and mean insults.

Two days after the last mistreatment by fellow prisoners and the change, I was brought to the Tung-jen Hospital. My feet and spine were examined by a doctor who took two x-ray plates of my loins. I never heard anything of what the x-rays showed and no treatment was applied as a result of them.

Learning to Walk Again

It was a year now since my back had been broken and I thought I might be able to use my legs again. I started to stand on them for a few moments resting against the wall or a small table. Some weeks later I could even take a few steps from the wall to the bed. By November, after three months' exercise and trial, I could walk as far as the toilet but with difficulty. The officials thought I was well enough to start writing again so they pressed me to write confessions about all the people I had known in China and they told me I should also write all my own personal activities. I made up my mind to write fully all the details of my deeds and actions since coming to China whether they seemed criminal or not. First I submitted an outline and then I wrote little by little, day by day, and handed in the finished document a month later in December.

Interpolated Confessions

Now that I was able to walk a bit, they started a series of weekly or bi-weekly interrogations in January 1953. I retracted the former declarations about having a radio-sending set and about directing children's sabotage. The cell chief still urged me with threats to admit these false accusations again but this time I refused. When April came around I was required to write whatever I knew about the Legion of Mary members. When that was finished I was told to do the same about all the priests, brothers, and nuns of the Peking Archdiocese. The dictated material was written by a scribe but many suggestions and interpolations were written into it, suggested by fellow prisoners. They no longer used violent methods but my terror experience of the past prevented me from objecting. In July, I was again taken daily for questioning by another judge. Everything that I said was written down. And then I was asked to sign.

The next move was to send me to another office where the document was translated into French with the aid of a Chinese interpreter. From the French text we made a parallel Chinese translation and I was required to sign both. There were four parts to this latest deposition or confession: (1) my relations with spies and the Kuomintang special agent, De Jaegher; (2) the letters written to my parents and other relatives; (3) the counterrevolutionaries and sabotage activities including the "reactionary organization," the Legion of Mary; and (4) my activities in opposing the Independent Church movement. In between times they had me write letters to Legion of Mary members, telling them that it was a reactionary organization and they should confess all their criminal activities. But it is not necessary to go into all these details.

Re-write as Instructed

In May 1954 I was called into the office of a government official whom I had never met. First, he asked about my physical condition. Producing the general confession which I had written under four points in 1953, he said "You are going to re-write this but leave out the lengthy passages. It is not necessary to write about your letters home. You may also omit what concerns the three autonomies (Independent Church) movement." I went back to my cell to start writing the new French text immediately, which was finished the next morning at 8 A.M. During the day I was permitted to take a few hours rest. In the evening I was brought to another office to make a Chinese translation assisted by an interpreter. We worked through the night and the next day when the work was finished rather late. I was then brought before the interrogator who studied the text. He ordered me to make many changes in the French text to correspond with the translation into Chinese which he had made. The changes distorted many of the facts and added guilt in more damning terms. It was supposed to be my own confession but the finished product was far from it.

Tape Recording and Photos

They gave me a short recess when this task was finished and then I was led into a large hall. On the desk was a microphone wired to a recording machine on a side table. The agent who had forced me to write the changes into the text now ordered me to sit down at the desk and read clearly. He was standing with a secretary (who knew French) close by, in order to watch me read every word. When the recording was over they took a picture of me reading the text into the microphone. I don't know whether the confession was broadcast over the radio but I presume it was.

I'll skip the intervening episodes down to November 4, 1954, when I was once again brought before an interrogator. The interrogating judge asked me, "What do you think of your crimes?" In substance I gave him just about the same views that were expressed in my recorded confession. It was useless to say anything else although I knew many of the statements were untrue. One gives up protesting when it does no good. Thirty months of communist prison ordeal had taught me that much.

During the conversation the judge said to me, "You must realize that the gravity of your crimes deserves at least a 10-year sentence in prison. Concerning your relations with De Jaegher it is quite possible that as a newcomer to China you did not realize exactly what you were doing. But you have certainly helped De Jaegher who is an enemy of the Chinese people." On November 5, 1954 at 9:30 A.M. the judge did notify me that a decision had been made to expel me instead of serving a long prison term. Expulsion was supposed to be an act of leniency. At least it was an act of mercy to deliver a man from their prisons.

Sentenced at Last

After nightfall I was taken together with my luggage in a jeep to the meeting hall for government agents. The interrogating judge was there flanked by two gendarmes and another individual I had never seen before. This last man stood up and slowly read a document stamped with a large government seal: "The Peking Military Administration Commission, Military Justice Section, concerning the accused, Su Chih-yuan (my Chinese name), hereby declares he is guilty: (1) of having provided military information to the special agent De Jaegher before liberation; (2) of having organized and led the reactionary activities of the Legion of Mary after liberation; and (3) of having provided economic and political information to imperialists after the liberation. Therefore we sentence him to four years in prison but have decided instead on his immediate expulsion from the land of the People's Republic of China." And so after almost three and a half years in prison they have given me a sentence. I was asked if I had anything to say about the verdict. Any words were useless now so I answered, "Nothing to say." Then I was led to the automobile and immediately taken to the railroad station at Tien Men (Heaven's Gate). It had a special meaning for one just released from Hell, so to speak. Escorted by two gendarmes I reached Tientsin about midnight and was taken to the prison of the fifth police division. The following afternoon I was led through customs to the steamer Hupeh to leave China "forever" with much grief in my heart.

The End of It All

This brief account of the long years in prison was written during my first week of freedom, as the ship sailed from Tientsin to Hong Kong. No "help" or torture was applied to make this "frank and honest." I am not a writer and can only be simple, frank and honest and, I hope, objective—as my friends, the communists, ordered. They are my friends, fellow creatures created by God and I bear them no malice, though they call me an enemy.

The editor of *Mission Bulletin* read my notes, asked me to condense them and let him publish the account. I consented because it shows how weak and useless I was when I should have been a hero or perhaps a martyr.

During my seven weeks in St. Paul's Hospital, Hong Kong, I have typed out my notes. Just before taking off in a plane for Belgium, I add this little note to end it all:

I am really guilty of many sins but not the ones the communists accused me of and I hope to make amends for my sins. The perjuries, lies, and cowardly acts as a communist prisoner weigh heavily on me. I hope that the world will understand and that God will forgive his poor servant. "The spirit is willing, but the flesh is weak" under torture. I myself feel like the ass in La Fontaine's fable, *"Les Animaux Malades de la Peste."* After all, the judge had called me an ass and in this accusation he was right: I am that and nothing more.

NOTES

1. *Ad Sinarum Gentem*, "Paternal Exhortations in the Present Difficult Situation." An Encyclical Letter of His Holiness Pius XII. Done October 7, 1954, released December 22, 1954. Unofficial Translation in CMB, no. 2, February 1955, 87–90. An English translation of this document may also be found in *Papal Documents Related to the New China 1937–1984*. Ed. Elmer Wurth, M.M. New York: Orbis Books and Hong Kong: Holy Spirit Study Centre. Two volumes, 1985, vol. I, 38. All citations are to the CMB translation.
2. "Round-the-Clock Year Rosary," CMB, no. 4, April 1953, 402.
3. "Co-Prisoner Instructed by Father McGrath," CMB, no. 6, June 1953, 600–601.
4. CMB, no. 5, May 1953, 499.
5. Father Wong was arrested on July 7, 1953 and died in the White Lake labor camp in December 1960 with Father Francis Chu at his side. See: *If The Grain of Wheat Dies, op. cit.*, 42, 94. This account gives both December 2 and December 22, 1960 as the date of Father Wong's death. Father Francis Chu would spend most of his life at this camp, though he was transferred to the prison in Hefei, Anhui shortly before his death from a heart attack on December 28, 1983.
6. *Xiaoling: Memoirs*, 34–38.
7. *If the Grain of Wheat Dies...Father Francis Xavier Chu Shu-teh, S.J., (Hong Kong. n.p., n.d.)*, 5, 35, *passim*. Hanson's account of this incident is incorrect. [Eric O. Hanson, *Catholic Politics in China and Korea, op. cit.*, 51.] He gives the name of the arrested priest as Father Vincent Zhu. In fact Father Vincent Zhu [Chu Hung-sheng, S.J.] was the assistant parish priest at Christ the King in 1953, [*cf. Xiaoling: Memoirs*, 37.] It was reported in the *China Missionary Bulletin* that all of the priests at Christ the King were arrested at the time except for Father Vincent Zhu who was placed under house arrest. [See "Translation of a Letter from a Shanghai 'Catholic' June 17, 1953, 6 p.m.," CMB, no. 7, July 1953, 697.] Father Vincent was pastor of Christ the King at the time of his arrest in Shanghai on September 8, 1955 along with Bishop Kung, more than twenty other priests, and several hundred leading Chinese Catholics. [*Cf.*, CMB, November 1955, 805.] The two priests were from different branches of the same famous family which had provided numerous priests, brothers and sisters over the decades.
8. The official number of those arrested was given as thirteen. *Xinwen Ribao*, Shanghai, June 16, 1953. *Cf.* CMB, no. 7, July 1953, 696–697. Father Ladany cites seven arrests including two Belgians, though the Belgians were apparently arrested several months earlier. See CNA, Hong Kong, no. 186, June 28, 1957, 4.

9. *Ibid.* Also, "Smash Wrecking Activities of Imperialism Through Catholic Church: Two Espionage Cases Broken in Shanghai, "*Renmin Ribao*, Beijing, July 16, 1953.

10. CMB, no. 7, July 1953, 696.

11. "Smash Wrecking Activities of Imperialism Through Catholic Church: Two Espionage Cases Broken in Shanghai, *Renmin Ribao*, Beijing, July 16, 1953; "Stamp Out Imperialist Elements Hidden in the Catholic Church," *Renmin Ribao* editorial, Beijing, July 16, 1953; Tu Pei-lin, "Sanguinary Evidences of Crimes: The Shanghai Exhibition on Criminal Imperialist Wrecking Activities Through Catholic Church," *Renmin Ribao*, Beijing, July 16, 1953; "The 'Catholic Patriotic Yough Corps': An Armed Reactionary Secret Service Organization," *Renmin Ribao*, Beijing, July 16, 1953. All four articles are translated in SCMP, no. 617, July 24, 1953.

12. "Smash Wrecking Activities of Imperialism Through Catholic Church," *Renmin Ribao*, Beijing, July 16, 1953.

13. CMB, no. 2, February 1954, 192.

14. See, for example, "Case of Counterrevolutionary Activities Under Cover of Catholic Church Broken in Xianxian, Hebei," *Renmin Ribao*, Beijing, September 7, 1953.

15. "The 'Catholic Youth Patriotic Corps': An Armed Reactionary Secret Service Organization," *Renmin Ribao*, Beijing, July 16, 1953.

16. *Ibid.*

17. *Tang; Memoirs*, 58–59. Father Tam would spend the next thirty years as a prisoner, first in prison and then in labor camps. Most of this time was spent in a labor camp in the northeastern province of Heilungjiang. It was common practice for prisoners from the south to be sent to Heilungjiang where they found the sub-zero cold especially hard to endure. Father Tam was finally released in October 1983.

18. *Ibid.*, 62–63.

19. *Ibid.*, 48–49.

20. *Wen Hui Pao*, Hong Kong, September 24, 1953.

21. *Ibid.*, 66–68.

22. *Ibid.*, 73.

23. CMB, February 1954, 180.

24. CMB, September 1954, 601.

25. CMB, September 1954, 665.

26. CNA, Hong Kong, no. 186, June 28, 1957, 4.

27. See, for example, CMB, April 1954, 389–390.

28. CMB, September 1954, 602–605.

29. *Ibid.*, 690–691.

30. CMB, October 1954, 790–791.

31. CMB, November 1954, 889–890; also from several interviews with Father Pieraccini at his residence in Hong Kong.

32. For a discussion of these developments see, Peter S.H. Tang, *Communist China Today, op. cit.,* 300–3327.
33. CNA, Hong Kong, no. 186, June 28, 1957, 4.
34. *Ibid.*
35. See Chapter Seven, Note no. 1.
36. *Xiaoling: Memoirs,* 41.
37. CMB, December 1954, 984.
38. *Xinhua,* Beijing, August 17, 1954. Accounts of this meeting are also contained in CMB, November 1954, 889; also *cf.* CNA, Hong Kong, no. 49, August 27, 1954, 4.
39. CNA, Hong Kong, no. 49, August 27, 1954, 4.
40. CMB, September 1955, 624, quoting the Chinese government dispatch.
41. Richard C. Bush, Jr, *Religion in Communist China, op. cit.,* 122. Bush does not name the Bishop in his account of the ordination, but on the previous page he refers to "Bishop Alphonse Chang of Peking." CMB reported that the bishop who ordained Fr. Laurence Cha, "was no doubt Bishop Alfonse Chung (sic!), O.F.M., from Luan [Shanxi Province]." [CMB, September 1955, 624.] However, Fr. Angelo S. Lazzarotto writes, "According to my records, Alphonse Chong Huai-mo, O.F.M., was the Bishop of Yantai (or Chefoo) in Shandong [not Shanxi].... Born in 1904, he was made Bishop of Yantai in 1952. As for the 'Bishop Alphonse Chang of Peking' mentioned by Bush (p. 122), I think he was really not an ordained bishop; in China a Vicar General is sometimes referred to with that title by the people. In fact only in summer 1959 (some sources say 1960) a new bishop was ordained for Beijing... [which may be] the reason for having an outsider (whoever he might have been) to ordain the priests mentioned in the event." [Personal correspondence with the author, January, 1991.]
42. *Ibid.,* 122–123.
43. CMB, September 1955, 624.
44. *Renmin Ribao,* Beijing, July 3, 1955.
45. *Renmin Ribao,* July 29, 1955; reported in CNA, Hong Kong, no. 186, June 28, 1957, 4.
46. Peter S.H. Tang, *Communist China Today, op. cit.,* 275. Tang gives an excellent account of this drive, 274–276.
47. See CMB, February 1955, 143–146 for an account of the events leading up to the arrest of Bishop Kung.
48. This is the correct date, not September 7 as it is given in Bush, Hanson and Whyte. See the *Xinhua* dispatch, Beijing, November 10, 1955, which begin with the words, "On September 8, 1955, Kung Pinmei...and others were arrested according to law by the public Security Bureau for counterrevolutionary crimes." Also, "Shanghai Public Security Authorities Proceed with Examination of Kung Pin-mei

Counter-Revolutionary Clique," *Renmin Ribao*, Beijing, December 10, 1955, which states that, "the Shanghai Public Security Bureau on September 8, 1955 broke a counterrevolutionary group hidden in the Roman Catholic Church and led by King Pin-mei... [They] were arrested according to law." Wang Xiaoling also gives the date of her own and the Bishop's arrest as September 8: *Xiaoling: Memoirs*, 42, 46. Also *cf.*, *If the Grain of Wheat Dies*, *op. cit.*, 29, which gives a chronology of events in the Shanghai Diocese.

49. The precise number of those arrested is not clear. The earliest report published in the CMB [November 1955, 805] cited information provided by Father Luis Bolumburu, a Spanish Jesuit from Shanghai who reached Hong Kong on September 18. He gave the number of those arrested in addition to the Bishop as 23 priests and "some two or three hundred of the leading Chinese Catholics." Sixteen of the priests were identified by name. CMB [February 1956, 144], quoting the *Hong Kong Times* [Nov. 2, 1955], which relied on Chinese government sources, claimed a total of 74 people were arrested, of which 16 were priests, 33 were mission employees, and 25 were Catholic lay people. The Hong Kong paper, however, claimed that in fact more than 530 people were arrested, though more than 400 were later released. Bush [124], Hanson [73], and Whyte [248], all apparently relying on each other and/or the same source [which Hanson cites as a Union Research translation] gives the numbers as 21 to 23 priests, 2 Carmelite nuns, and 200–300 Catholic Laity. In addition all three cite an additional 15 to 20 priests and 600 to 700 laymen arrested on the night of September 26. The two Carmelite nuns arrested on the night of September 8–9 are also mentioned in CMB, as are two more Caremelite nuns arrested during the night of September 26–27 [CMB, February 1955, 146–147]. Wang Xiaoling simply states: "During that night [September 8, 1955], several hundred Catholics were arrested, among them Bishop Ignatius Gong Pinmei, priests, religious brothers, nuns, Catholic teachers, doctors and young people." [46]

50. *Xiaoling: Memoirs*, 42.

51. For a summary of all of these reports see CMB, November 1955, 806.

52. *Xinhua*, Beijing, November 10, 1955. CMB, March 1956, 220–223.

53. Hanson has an interesting account of this episode, drawing on the analysis of Father Jean Lefevre [*Shanghai: les Enfants dans la Ville*, Paris: Casterman, 1956]. He acknowledges that he places more emphasis than did Father Lefevre on the importance of Father Lacretelle's prison confession extracted from the Jesuit superior by withholding medical aid several times and then reviving him when he was near death. Hanson credits Father Lacretelle's confession and its attack on Bishop Kung with creating a split in the Shanghai

clergy. [*Chinese Politics in China and Korea, op. cit.,* 78.] His interpretation may well be correct, yet the letter of the 74 Shanghai priests attacked Bishop Kung for writing to Father Lacretelle on the day he arrived in Hong Kong, "I hope you are healthy as ever, and that in a short while you will continue to lead us openly. I know in fact you have not abandoned your leadership" [CMB, March 1956, 220], indicating that perhaps more complex motives were at work here than the grievances of Chinese priests against foreign missionaries.

54. CMB, March 1956, 221.
55. *Renmin Ribao,* Beijing, December 10, 1955. CMB, March 1956, 223–227.
56. CMB, February 1956, 143, quoting the *Hong Kong Standard* of December 28, 1955.
57. *Renmin Ribao,* February 8, 1956. Quoted in CNA, Hong Kong, no. 186, June 28, 1957, 5.
58. *Ibid.;* also *cf.* CMB, December 1956, 761, which translated a part of a letter from a young Catholic woman in Shanghai reporting on conditions there.
59. CMB, January 1956, 66–67.
60. "Lettre De Famille," CMB, December 1955, 907.
61. This is from the typewritten account of Father "Joseph Zhang's" (pseud.) experiences written after his arrival in Hong Kong. Father "Zhang" was arrested in December 1955 and imprisoned until 1980. He has asked that his true identity not be revealed. Unpublished document in the author's possession.
62. *Tang: Memoirs,* 81.
63. Mao Zedong, "On the Correct Handling of Contradictions Among the People," *Selected Reading From the Works of Mao Tse-tung,* (Beijing: Foreign Languages Press, 1967), 350–387.
64. For a detailed discussion of this period see: Peter S.H.Tang, *Communist China Today, op. cit.,* 449–455.
65. *Xinhua,* Beijing, July 26, 1956; also, *Renmin Ribao,* Beijing, July 27, 1956. CNA, Hong Kong, no. 186, June 28, 1957, 5 discusses this meeting in some detail. Bush gives the number of those invited as 38 and of those attending as 36 [*Religion in Communist China, op. cit.,* 132]. Both *Xinhua* and Father Ladany [CNA] give the number as 38. There was a later meeting in February 1957 to which two of the expected participants begged not to attend. See CNA, no. 186, 5.
66. CMB, February 1957, 130.
67. *Ibid.,* 6.
68. *Ibid.,* 186.
69. "Catholic Leaders Meet," *Xinhua*—English, Beijing, July 15, 1957. Bush incorrectly gives the dates of this meeting as June 17–July 13 [134]. Whyte also gives the opening date as June 17 [277], though he has the August 2 closing date correct. Hanson also gives the dates of

the "first conference" of the Patriotic Association as June 17–July 13, though in a footnote he indicates correctly that another "preparatory" meeting took place over these days, while the official inaugural meeting opened July 15 [69; fn. 53, 71]. Also *cf.*, L. Ladany, *The Catholic Church in China*, New York: Freedom House, 1987, 23–24.

70. Li Wei-guang and Hu Wen-yao. "Rightists Warned Against Looking for Markets Among Catholics," (A Statement to the 4th Session of the 1st National People's Congress, July 12, 1957), *Renmin Ribao*, Beijing, July 20, 1957.

71. "Chinese Catholics Protest to Vatican," *Xinhua*—English, Beijing, July 30, 1957.

72. "Chinese Catholics Define Link with Vatican," *Xinhua* English, Beijing, August 2, 1957.

73. *Cf.*, L. Ladany, *The Catholic Church in China, op. cit.*, 24.

74. "Background to Catholic Decision," *Xinhua*—English, Beijing, August 2, 1957.

75. "Chinese Catholics Define Link with Vatican," *loc. cit.*

76. *Renmin Ribao*, editorial, Beijing, August 3, 1957.

77. *Tang: Memoirs*, 85–86.

78. See, for example, "Conference of Catholic Representatives Convened in Sichuan Province," *Xinhua*, Chengtu [Sichuan Province], December 23, 1957; "Catholics in Anhui Hold Forum," *Anhui Ribao*, Hofei [Anhui Province], December 29, 1957.

79. *Hobei Ribao*, Baoding [Hopei Province], December 12, 1957.

80. *Wen Hui Pao*, Hong Kong, February 8, 1958.

81. I have not been able to discover the precise date of Bishop Fan's arrest. Most sources, including Amnesty International which worked for years for his release, simply state that he was arrested "in 1958." See, Amnesty International, *China: Prisoners of Conscience in the People's Republic of China*. New York, June 1987, 15–16. We do know that by July 1958, the Patriotics in Baoding had elected a new bishop to replace him, Father John Wang, who was consecrated without Vatican approval on July 20, 1958. See, CMB, January 1959, 74.

82. *Tang: Memoirs*, 90–91.

EIGHT

"AWAY WITH ALL PESTS"

On this tiny globe
A few flies dash themselves against the wall
Humming without cease,
Sometimes shrilling,
Sometimes moaning,
Ants on the locust tree assume a great nation swagger,
And mayflies lightly plot to topple the giant tree.
The Westwind scatters leaves over Changan,
And the arrows are flying, twanging.
So many deeds cry out to be done,
And always urgently;
The world rolls on,
Time presses.
Ten thousand years are too long,
Seize the day, seize the hour!
The four seas are rising, clouds and waters raging
The five continents are rocking, wind and thunder roaring.
Away with all pests!
Our force is irresistible.

Mao Zedong[1]

The first illegal consecrations of bishops in China—that is, consecrations in the face of specific Vatican disapproval—took place on April 13, 1958 in the city of Wuhan [Hubei Province]. The two men, both Franciscan priests, Father Bernardine Dong Guang-qing consecrated as Bishop[2] of Hankou, and Father Marcus Yuan Wen-hua consecrated as Bishop of Wuchang [Hankou and Wuchang together with Hanyang are the three cities which make up the Wuhan metropolis], were elected by assemblies of local priests on March 18 and 19.[3] *Xinhua* reported that the consecration was performed by Bishop Joseph Li Tao-nan [Li Dao-nan] of the nearby Puqi Diocese and attended by three other bishops and a number of priests and laymen from provinces in China.[4]

Following the elections, but before the ordinations, cables were exchanged with Rome, the contents of which were not revealed, but which apparently informed Rome of what had taken place, and asked for Vatican approval of the elections and coming ordinations. This approval was denied. As the Chinese press put it, "[the] Vatican, which ever regarded the Chinese people with hostility, sent a wire to the two new bishops respectively on March 26 and 29, irrationally refusing to recognize the elections. The Vatican described the elections as 'invalid,' 'worthless,' and 'void'...."[5] The Vatican also described the penalty of excommunication which would fall on Bishop Li and of the two newly-elected bishops should they proceed with the consecrations. The Chinese press described this "threat" as "shameless" and asserted that the Vatican was "under the control of U.S. imperialism."[6] As Father Ladany points out, however, the Pope did not impose excommunication, he merely quoted canon law which stipulated that in such cases excommunication was automatic.[7]

Over the next several months similar elections and consecrations took place in a number of parts of the country. The *Mission Bulletin* calculated that by October 1958, 23 such Patriotic consecrations had taken place.[8] By mid-1959, the number of confirmed Patriotic consecrations had reached 26, though it was possible the number was even higher.[9] Among the consecrators were Archbishop Pi Shu-shi of Shenyang, who had originally refused to participate in such activities. Other consecrators included Bishop Li Tao-nan assisted by the first two bishops he had consecrated in Wuhan in April 1958.[10] All of those involved in these consecrations were considered by the Vatican to have suffered the censure of excommunication.

The local election of Patriotic bishops in China, and the Vatican reaction to those events, raised a host of questions about "what might have been" in terms of the relationship between the Holy See and the communist rulers of China.

Decades later there is still disagreement as to who should bear the blame for the hostile relations between the two parties.

Church and State

The problem of relations between the Catholic Church and the Chinese state is an unusually complex one because of the fact that the Church is not simply a religious institution. The Holy See also functions as a state which maintains state-to-state diplomatic relations. Technically, that is, it is the Holy See and not Vatican City which maintains these diplomatic relations, though the headquarters of the Church for both religious and diplomatic purposes is commonly referred to simply as "the Vatican." This is true even though diplomatic relations were conducted by the Church for many years prior to the creation of Vatican City in 1929. It should be important to separate these two aspects of the problem, the religious and the politico-diplomatic, but it appears to be virtually impossible to do so as the head of the Vatican state, the Pope, is also the head of the Church. Moreover, the Pope is the head of a Church which is Catholic—that is, universal—and within which obedience to the Supreme Pontiff on certain matters is required, based on his position as successor to St. Peter. Pope Pius XII's encyclical to the Chinese, cited in Chapter Seven, makes this point rather forcefully. Within such an institutional structure—"One Holy Catholic and Apostolic Church"—the concept of a "national" Catholic Church, Chinese or otherwise, is clearly a contradiction in terms.

Even with these considerations in mind, however, we may still ask what the Chinese state wanted from the Catholic Church after 1949, and we may ask if there was anything the Chinese Catholics and/or the Vatican could have done to prevent the terrible abuses which, as we have already seen, were suffered by the Catholic faithful, natives and foreigners alike.

In the diplomatic domain, the PRC would certainly have insisted that the Vatican withdraw its diplomatic recognition of the Republic of China on Taiwan. Indeed, in more recent times, this has usually been put forward as the first condition which must be met on the way to improving relations. But, as we have seen, this was not a major issue in the years we have reviewed thus far. Indeed, the principal demand made of the Vatican up to the year of the "illegal" consecrations was that the Vatican cease its "interference" in internal Chinese affairs. And from about 1957 onward, the emphasis was on the Chinese Church severing "financial and political" ties with Rome.[11] The main thrust of government policy during this period thus appears to have been the splitting of the Catholic Church in China away from the Roman Catholic Church, not the establishment of better relations with Rome under any conditions. It is important to remember in this connection that the Papal Nuncio did not leave China of his own volition. As Father Ladany points out, "The Nuncio [Monsignor Riberi] intended to move, with other ambassadors, from [the nationalist capital at] Nanjing to Peking [Beijing]; he was turned down and expelled."[12]

At the time of the establishment of the CCPA it was asserted that the Catholic Church in China would continue to maintain the "traditions" of the Roman Church and would obey "all doctrines and precepts of the Church which should be believed and enforced."[13] As evidence of this obedience it was pointed out that, "the Pope has decreed that we should believe in the Assumption of Our Lady," and that this had been observed "by all clergy and laity without a single exception."[14] Yet, as Pope Pius XII's encyclical points out, the principle of autonomy of propagation of the faith raises fundamental questions even in the area of the purely religious authority of the Holy Father. In any case, the claim of such "obedience" would soon disappear as well. In the period following the Second Vatican Council, when the rest of the Catholic world changed the form of the liturgy and adopted the local vernacular for its language, the Mass in China continued to be celebrated in Latin in the older Tridentine form. Indeed, in the 1980s when many Catholic churches were permitted to reopen, and when priests learned of Vatican II and new liturgical materials found their way into China, visitors could distinguish the clergy loyal to Rome from those of the Patriotics by the form of the Mass which they celebrated.

In the matter of the local election of bishops, it has been argued that the Vatican had, in some cases, permitted a degree of local participation in this process, especially in Franco Spain, and that it was because of the strong anti-communist feelings of Pope Pius XII that the Vatican took such a hard line stand in the Chinese case.[15] It is further claimed that the assertion of such local rights in the selection of bishops was not "unreasonable" against the "monarchical claims of the papacy."[16] It is difficult to argue with the notion that if the government of China had been friendlier, the Holy See might have adopted a different position as to some degree of local participation—as distinguished from local election—in the selection of Chinese bishops. The consecrations of 1957, however, clearly presented Rome with a *fait accompli*. It was not consultation which was the desired outcome of the exchange of cables between Beijing and Rome, but a test of strength. Under the circumstances, it is difficult to see how the Pius XII could have acted differently than he did. It also seems unnecessary, under the circumstances, to make excuses for the Pope's anti-communist feelings.

There is the further issue of context to be considered. These consecrations were not the subject of an abstract debate on theology or canon law. They occurred in the context of ten years of bloody and bitter persecution of the Catholics in China, both foreign missionaries and native clergy and, by 1957, of vast numbers of Chinese lay Catholics as well. Thousands of Catholics had been brutalized, tortured, and executed. Uncounted thousands languished in prisons and labor camps. All but a small handful of foreign missionaries had been expelled, including the Papal Nuncio; the Church had been relentlessly vilified in the Chinese press. The Vatican and the loyal adherents to the Roman Church had been endlessly charged with, and punished for "crimes" of every manner and description. Whatever one might have thought of the missionary enterprise in China, such a series of actions by the Chinese government can scarcely have been said to be conducive to a friendly relationship with the Vatican. Nor, as suggested above, does it appear at any point during this period, that such was the desire and intention of the Chinese authorities.

This brings us back to the point from which we began. What, after all, did the Chinese authorities want from the Church, and was this something that the Church could possibly have delivered in the interests of peace and harmony? Both Eric

Hanson, and Bob Whyte following him, assert that the aim of the Chinese government was not the suppression or eradication of the Church, but rather its penetration and control. With the understanding that there is a very fine line between control and suppression, we may still pursue this argument briefly.

Hanson sees the government of the PRC as a successor to the traditional Chinese state. He writes, "Chinese state religious policy seeks to penetrate, regulate, and control institutional religions."[17] And he further asserts, "The difficulties of the Catholic Church in the People's Republic are not primarily due to Peking's Marxist ideology, but to a re-emergence of a strong Chinese state with a continental political ideology."[18] Whyte contends that PRC religious policy "must be understood as aimed at control rather than suppression."[19] He further asserts:

> It is wrong to narrow this question down to the issue of Christianity *versus* Communism. What Christians confronted in 1949 was a newly revived Chinese State which could at last free itself of foreign interference and which could therefore pursue certain traditional concerns of Chinese government through to the end....[the objective of which] was not so different from that of successive dynasties throughout Chinese history.[20]

There can be no doubt that the government of the PRC made every effort to penetrate, regulate and control the Catholic Church in China. The rest of the traditional Chinese State model, however, is a bit more troubling. One might well argue, for example, that the power to regulate and control is in fact the power to destroy. We have earlier quoted Justice Oliver Wendell Holmes, Jr.'s concerns in this regard. But that still does not get to the question of the ultimate *motives* of the Chinese authorities as they confronted the Catholic Church.

Both Hanson and Whyte assure us that Marxism or communism had little or nothing to do with the confrontation, with the exception, possibly, of the use of certain Leninist organizational techniques.[21] The view expressed here in the preceding pages from Chapter Two onward, however, is a very different one. This view sees the confrontation between Catholic Church and communist state in terms of a clash of two alternate versions of the truth, a "religious" war, if you will. Furthermore, I have asserted, and attempted to demonstrate, that the ultimate aim of the communist state was not merely to regulate and control the Catholic Church and the Catholic religion, but to destroy it and all similar "feudal superstitions" along with it. There are, of course, many different types and degrees of control and regulation. The United States, for example, which places a very high value on religious freedom, and which adheres to a Constitution, the First Amendment of which declares that Congress shall make no law prohibiting the free exercise of religion, in fact controls and regulates religion in a variety of ways. Plural marriage is forbidden, for example, as are religious rites which involve the sacrifice of animals, or dangerous religious practices such as the handling of poisonous serpents. Nevertheless, one need not be a judge or a political philosopher to distinguish between this sort of regulation under law and the types of policies adopted by the government of the PRC to penetrate, regulate and control the Catholic Church in China. Nor have the communist authorities in China been the slightest bit reticent when it comes to announcing the long-range goals of these policies. They have, in fact, been quite open in publishing their views about the ultimate disappearance of religion as they progress toward socialism and communism, and about the role of state policy in hastening this development. We have already discussed the theoretical foundations of these views in Chapter Two.

On a more practical level, however, the Chinese authorities have been so bold—and so helpful to our understanding of these events—as to publish a blueprint for the development of government policy toward the Catholic Church. This is not a plan of action which has as its ultimate objective mere control and regulation. It aims rather, as it clearly states, "to destroy it" [the Church]. This it asserts, "is the objective to be obtained and that is what we are fighting for."

The interesting document from which these revelations come is the so-called "Li Wei-han Document," named for its author who was at the time of its publication the director of the United Front Work Department of the CCP Central Committee. Several versions of this document, the authenticity of which has never been seriously questioned, have circulated over the years. Li Wei-han originally wrote his "Program of Action" in

1959 in order to instruct the Communist Party of Cuba on the experience of the Chinese Communist Party in dealing with the Catholic Church.[22] This document is, therefore, worth considering here briefly.

Li began his treatise with the assertion that, if the people's democracies are to continue their advance to socialism and communism they must, "do away with the influence of the Catholic Church and with the activities which it carries on." To this end, Li offered to his Cuban comrades a "program of tactics" which had been "applied with success" in China, the purpose of which was "to liberate the Chinese people from the influence of the Imperialist Catholic Church of Rome."

The program called first for the creation of a religious affairs bureau within the government, followed by the creation of national, regional and local organizations of Catholics under its direction. This move, said the action program, would call forth the opposition of those "counterrevolutionaries" who oppose it. These opponents in turn must be made to appear as "unpatriotic criminals who follow the imperialist instructions issued by the headquarters of the Catholic Church, the Vatican." At this stage, vigilance is extremely important: "The party militants must direct the work of the reform committees," and they must "eliminate" the reactionaries whom they encounter among the masses. During this initial phase of the program, said Li, it is important to have the ecclesiastical authorities assure the masses that their religion has become "purer" now that it has been "freed from criminal and unpatriotic elements." Also: "With the exception of spiritual affairs, every indication or expression of liaison with the Vatican will have to be spurned as being motivated by imperialist interests and supporting counterrevolutionary activities."

This brings us to the next stage of the "attack," the destruction of the link existing between the Catholic Church in China and the Vatican. At this stage, wrote Li Wei-han, "It is the task of our militants to convince the masses that the individual may have his religion, without the Vatican directing the affairs of all churches of the world." Li advised that a preparatory campaign should be carried out before the establishment of an independent church was publicly proclaimed, and that any clergy who had resisted the movement should be denounced at public meetings for the purpose of eliminating their influence with the laity. The simplest way to accomplish this was said to be through anonymous accusations brought by Party militants. At the same time, the task of the Party militants was to lead the Catholic associations in a movement requesting the government to authorize the establishment of an independent church, "in order to remove from the Catholic associations any unpatriotic stain caused by elements still attached to the Vatican. The People's Government will give the authorization, and the Independent Church will be organized."

"And now," wrote Li Wei-han, "we have come to the last stage." The separation of the Church and the Vatican having been accomplished, "we can proceed to consecrating the leaders of the Church chosen by us." This, in turn, said Li, would lead to the ultimate objective:

> Once the key posts of the clergy are in our hands and submitted to [the will of] the People's Government, we will proceed progressively to eliminating from the liturgy those elements which are incompatible with the People's Government. The first changes will affect the sacraments and prayers. Then, the masses will be protected against all pressure and all obligation to put in an appearance in the church, to practice religion, or to organize [religious] associations.... We know full well that when the practice of religion becomes no more than an individual responsibility, it is slowly forgotten. New generations will follow the old, and religion will be no more than an episode of the past, worthy of being dealt with in the history of the world communist movement.

It might be argued that Li Wei-han was excessively optimistic in his estimate of the ease with which this plan could be executed, as well as his prediction of its ultimate success in eliminating religion from Chinese (or Cuban) society. It is much more difficult to argue, however, based on this rather clear documentary evidence (combined with ample historical evidence as well), that the aim of the People's Government was merely control and regulation, and that had the Catholic Church been more flexible or conciliatory it might have achieved some sort of accommodation or *modus vivendi* with the new communist governors of China after 1949.

Prison Life

Following his arrest on February 5, 1958, Bishop Dominic Tang was kept for a brief time in a detention center. Then, on February 15, he was transferred a short distance away to the Number 1 Prison of Guangdong Province and there given the number "2202." For the first two months or so of his imprisonment he was interrogated daily about the affairs of the Canton Diocese, the Legion of Mary, the CCPA, and about fellow priests whom he was encouraged, but refused, to denounce. Life was generally not easy under the best of circumstances for the ordinary people of a poor and backward China; in prison, daily life was especially grim. It was, if anything, even more so for Bishop Tang who was never formally convicted of any crime and therefore never sentenced to a specific prison term. He would eventually serve 22 years in prison, seven of those years in solitary confinement.[23]

Archbishop Tang:

It was prescribed in the rules of the prison that all prisoners could write home once a month to ask their relatives to send them clothing or other things; but in the first few months, I was not allowed to do so.... [Finally], I was allowed to write a letter. When the priests at the cathedral received my first letter, they immediately told [someone] to bring me a parcel of clothing and other daily things, such as soap, toilet paper and a packet of sweets [sent by my mother] from Hong Kong. I was so excited and happy when I received them that I cried. Then I shared them with the other prisoners....

During the few years after 1959, and especially after the three years of natural disasters [the famine following the Great Leap Forward], we were given two meals of *congee* [rice gruel] daily. In the beginning we had one and a half bowls each daily. This was reduced to one bowl only, with neither vegetable nor oil. Owing to malnutrition, my knees and lower limbs were swollen [from beri beri].

For a certain period, a year and a half, we had to paste together cardboard boxes in the cell.... My companion and I had to paste over ten dozen daily; thus, apart from the time for interrogation and meals, we had to spend all our time pasting boxes. If the work was not done well, we had to re-paste them. Though we produced so much, there was not, on that account, the slightest improvement in our living conditions. We usually ate *congee*. At times we had rice mixed with sweet potatoes; it seemed a big bowl full, but very soon we felt hungry again. There was a time when we had lunch at 8:00 A.M. and supper at 4:00 or 5:00 P.M., so we felt hungry at midday.

Later, we had lunch at 11:30 A.M. and supper at 5:00 P.M. After we had eaten supper we had to wait for many hours till 11:30 A.M. the next day before we could eat again, and each time we had only half enough. So, around 10:00 A.M. every day, we felt great pangs of hunger and sometimes we would shiver all over with hunger and would break out into cold perspiration.

For a period I was physically very weak; I had headaches and blurred vision, and my pulse was irregular. I could neither eat nor sleep; besides I had beri-beri and a hernia. Truly, I was only half alive. The prison doctor did not dare to treat me....

I was weak and often felt dizzy and had headaches. At night, the prisoners slept along the walls on each side of the cell, thus leaving only a small passage for me to go to the toilet bucket. When my legs were unsteady and weak, I would fall over the other prisoners, who would then scold me. Afterwards, I did not dare to walk upright, but crawled on all fours to the toilet bucket....

In the first 13 years of my imprisonment, the government gave me only two pairs of underpants. So in summer my shoulders were bare. In winter, I had only a single garment and I put on a cotton padded coat over it. My padded coat and padded quilt were mended in such a way that one could not see what the original cloth was like. As I had no trousers, I had to use the cloth bags in which people sent things to prison. I used the lid of a Tiger Balm tin to cut them and turn them into triangular-shaped underpants....[24]

Eventually Bishop Tang was placed in solitary confinement. He was locked in a small cell for seven years, 24 hours a day. His life was one of routine and monotony, morning to night, day after day, year after year. He, and others who survived, have testified to the large numbers of those who went mad under such conditions. Many committed suicide. It was only through the conscious strengthening of his will and of his faith, and through an extraordinary exercise of discipline, said the Bishop, that he was able to avoid succumbing to this cruel form of mental torture.[25]

Archbishop Tang:

The daily time-table was set in such a way that there were no changes. In the morning after rising, I was allowed to stretch my legs for a while, tidy my cell, do some physical exercises, etc. Then I had to sit in a fixed place until dusk. At 4:00 P.M. they allowed me to do fifteen minutes physical exercises, after which I had to sit down again until bedtime at night. The daily activities were fixed by rules; there were more than ten rules; everything was controlled...the warders would peep through a small hole to spy on what I was doing; they had to see whether I was keeping the rules. They were careful when opening and closing the door of the spy hole so that I could not find out when they were watching me....

While in the cell, I had to face the dark and dull walls; no air came into it. My eyes became very tired and I was afraid that I should become blind....

In prison, I always asked God to grant me the grace to progress in virtues, e.g., humility and obedience. I considered the prison authorities my superiors. I obeyed them. Obviously, I obeyed only the regulations which did not conflict with the principles of my faith.... There were many opportunities for practicing virtue in the prison.

Besides following the prison regulations and time-table, I also set my own time-table. Every morning, after rising, I recited the prayer of the Apostleship of Prayer, offering the day to God. I would say the "Veni Creator" (Come, Creator Spirit) because every day there were many events which needed the light of the Holy Spirit. Then I would do half an hour of meditation, meditating on the deeds of Jesus, his miracles; I meditated especially on the mysteries of the Holy Rosary. I liked best to meditate on the Passion of Jesus, and to recite some Latin prayers of the Mass which I remembered. (But in the last years I remembered very little.) I would recite the prayers of the Conse-cration of the Body and Blood of Christ and then make a spiritual Communion. This became a habit. I recited daily fifteen decades of the Holy Rosary in place of the Divine Office. I would also recite five decades more asking Our Lady to protect the Diocese of Canton. As I had no rosary beads, I had to rely on my fingers for the counting of the beads.

Every day I prayed, meditated and sang hymns so that I had no free time. These spiritual exercises were the same every day and supported me for the long years of prison life and gave me strength to overcome both material and spiritual hardships and to have a serene heart. God gave me the grace of an optimistic spirit, encour-aging me to look constantly at the good side of things and seldom at the bad side. I was imprisoned for God, for the Church; my con-science was at peace, as I had done my duty toward God and the Church. If I were to die some day, I would die in peace. If I were released, I would continue to serve God and the Church. These happy thoughts and feelings, this peace in the depth of my soul, supported my spirit during the 22 long winters and summers of my prison life.[26]

Wang Xiaoling served slightly more than one year during her first imprisonment, from September 8, 1955 to October 10, 1956. Like Bishop Tang and the others, she underwent long interrogations during the early part of the prison stay. As a young teenager she admitted to terrible bouts of homesickness, fear, and despair. She, too, was subjected to intense psychological pressures to "confess" and to denounce her fellow Catholics of the Shanghai Diocese.

Wang Xiaoling:

> I could describe in detail the many kinds of torment I had suffered since I was detained: filthy living conditions, food which was not even good enough for animals, the thought of my relatives whom I had left behind, the alternating threats and promises of the interrogation sessions, the loss of human dignity and freedom including the fact that one could not pray openly. All this inhuman torture, more terrible than death itself, was too much for me. I was in the bloom of youth with the possibility of a successful future; I had a wonderful family, high ideals, and confidence in my own abilities; but now, I thought, "Shall I be deprived of all these or shall I be able to keep even a part of them?" My mind went back over these thoughts in perplexity and, in my state of depression, I felt uncertain. At one point, I felt too weak to endure, but God protected me and preserved my faith, so that I did not lose my way even under pressures of every kind. I bit my finger and with my own blood wrote down my desires on toilet paper, "Protect me, Our Lady of Sheshan [Zose]. Guide me and give me back my freedom."[27]

Following her release from prison in October 1956, Wang Xiaoling remained at liberty for two years, until October 10, 1958, when she was arrested again. Her second arrest coincided with the violent turn to the "left" in Chinese politics which characterized the implementation of the Great Leap Forward in 1958. It will be recalled that the Great Leap was Mao's bold plan for rapid economic development and to make China economically self-sufficient, ("walking on two legs" was the slogan), by mobilizing China's vast reservoir of human labor power through mass communal organizations. The Church did not fare well under these strident leftist policies and, as we have already seen, 1958 was the year of the arrest of Bishops Tang and Fan, among many others.

October 1958 also brought the arrest of the last foreign bishop left in China, Bishop James E. Walsh, M.M., who had been under house arrest in Shanghai since 1953.[28] Though taken into custody in October, Bishop Walsh's arrest was not announced by the authorities until December 15.[29] It would be

March of 1960 before Bishop Walsh, Bishop Kung, and a number of others were finally brought to public trial.

Wang Xiaoling was arrested at her place of work on October 10, 1958, handcuffed and taken to the Ward Road Prison. She would spend the next twenty years in prisons and labor camps before finally being released in the summer of 1979. In prison, she once again recalled the boredom, the loneliness and, most of all, hunger.

Wang Xiaoling:
> The utterly monotonous life, among complete strangers, without freedom or material necessities of life, caused intense suffering and drove many prisoners to desperation and despair. The greatest material pressure came from hunger. Time seemed interminable, so naturally the two meals became the focus of the prisoners' interest. The kidney-shaped bowl...contained enough rice, but the rice was coarse, and the vegetables were cooked without oil so our hunger was never really satisfied.... The size of the rations changed according to the overall national economic situation so that during that period [the Great Leap Forward] and the following three years of natural disasters, in every [prison and] reform by labor camp, prisoners suffered much from hunger, and many died of salt addiction, edema or malnutrition.[30]

It is perhaps worth noting that the Great Leap Forward worked mighty hardships on the entire Chinese people, not alone on those confined to prisons and labor camps. The radical leftist policies of Mao Zedong and his followers that were carried out through the Great Leap proved to be a disaster of immense proportions for China. The attempts at revolutionary social and economic engineering, combined with some unfortunate weather conditions, produced what may have been the greatest famine in the long history of China, and one of the worse the world has ever seen. Calculations based upon relatively complete demographic statistics, which are now available from China, reveal that the Great Leap Forward and the ensuing famine created a population deficit in China of upwards of 30 million people.[31] It is probably not surprising, therefore, that prisoners reported their prison rations during the years of the "natural disasters" were barely adequate to sustain life.

Reform Through Labor

We have already noted that a number of Catholics were confined not in prison but in "labor camps." The purpose of these camps, in theory, was to change the thoughts or attitudes of the criminal and political prisoners and to return them to society as reformed and productive members of the community. There is no doubt that "reform" was an important part of the "Lao Gai" reform through labor system, and indoctrination classes were an important part of the daily camp schedule. But the camps also played a significant role in the economic construction of the country. This economic role of the reformation through productive labor program was in fact very likely even more important than its political role, for the many hundreds of thousands or millions of inmates of these camps provided a vast, readily available source of unpaid (formerly, but now unfashionably, known as "slave") labor upon which the state could draw for its ambitious economic development programs.

The state made no effort to hide the character of this labor which the Minister of Public Security described as "forced, unpaid, and subject to strict control."[32] Indeed, Chinese government authorities pointed with some pride to the economic contributions of this forced and unpaid labor. The *Renmin Ribao*, for example, claimed that, "Production from corrective labor is producing considerable effects in its coordination with the economic construction of the state."[33] Such corrective labor production, which was not confined to agriculture but also included industrial and mining enterprises as well as the operation of kilns for the making of tiles and bricks, was said to be, "coordinated with the capital construction of the state, and supply in part the livelihood of the people."[34] As examples of this contribution, the *Renmin Ribao* cited the hosiery works of the Beijing Prison which in 1953, "produced 32 percent of all the socks produced in the whole North China region." The bricks and tile works of Hebei Province, operated with forced labor, was said during 1953 to have raised their daily output from 80,000 to 155,000 bricks, "leading to an increase of wealth for the state of 4.7 billion yuan per year."[35] Special emphasis was also given to the labor camps in the sparsely populated border regions where forced labor was used to create farms out of virgin soil, to build roads and to open mines.[36] It was to these types of forced labor that Wang Xiaoling, Father Joseph Zhang, and many other Catholics were condemned during the 1950s.

On March 4, 1960, Wang Xiaoling was taken from the Ward Road Prison in Shanghai and transported by truck to Jilin Province to undergo reform through labor at the Qingshan Knitting Factory.[37] She was housed in a large warehouse where the bedding consisted of two tiers of wooden planks, each "bed" intended to sleep twenty prisoners. She was assigned to the hosiery department where her job consisted of finishing stockings or socks. The prisoners worked ten hours per day with an additional two hours set aside for political "purification" through study. Four months after her arrival at the knitting factory, there was large-scale transfer of prisoners. Wang Xiaoling makes the interesting observation that it was only later that she realized that people in the camps were constantly being moved; this was apparently in response to the demands of the output quotas of the various manufacturing units in the forced labor system.

Wang Xiaoling herself was transferred to the Muyuan Silk Manufacturing Unit in Heilungjiang Province in July of 1960. Her description of the journey to the new camp is reminiscent of images of nazi prisoners being shipped to concentration camps.

Wang Xiaoling:
   Toward dusk, after another roll-call, we were ordered to get into a truck, bringing our baggage with us, to go to the railway station. All around stood PLA [People's Liberation Army] men on the alert. We were moved as secret cargo. We reached the station, and after another roll-call we carried or dragged our baggage into the wagon. So this journey of suffering began. The wagon in which we found ourselves was usually used for transporting coal, pigs, and so on. It was small, dirty, and with no opening apart from a hole in the roof which served as a ventilator. A five candle-power bulb cast a gloomy light inside the wagon and made us look like shadows. We were so crowded that one could only sit on one's baggage. We were given two long loaves each, and we knew that the journey would not be too long. As soon as the large open wooden barrel which was to serve as a toilet had been carried in and put in a corner, the door was shut and heavily locked on the outside.

The train travelled slowly on. We could not tell if it was day or night. The bread was finished and our lips began to crack with thirst. With the vibration of the train, the barrel, now full of the excreta of over a hundred people, began to shake and the contents spilled over on to the floor, adding to the already nauseating stench. I was weary, utterly weary....

The train seemed to have run for a day and a night. It stopped at noon. We alighted from the wagon and looked at each other and we felt like bursting into tears. As it was a coal train, we were all covered with coal dust, our faces, our clothes and hands, and we found we had become strange mottled figures. In the end we did not know whether to laugh or cry. I followed the others, but because my baggage was so heavy I could scarcely keep up with them. The cadres shouted at me telling me to hurry up. Fortunately, some other prisoners came to my assistance. So, goaded on by the cadres and aided by my companions, I reached the end of this painful journey and arrived at the Muyuan Silk Manufacturing Unit.[38]

At the Muyuan Silk Manufacturing Unit, Wang Xiaoling learned that she was in the lowest of the three categories of inmates of the camp: prisoners undergoing labor reform, those not convicted of crimes (such as errant cadres) undergoing re-education through labor, and detainees who had completed their sentences but who had not been permitted to return to their homes. The prisoners worked the longest hours, received no pay for their work, and had the worst food and housing and the most restrictive regulations. Wang Xiaoling spent four years at the Muyuan labor camp.

Wang Xiaoling:

During this period of reform by labor, China was suffering from "the three years of natural disasters 1959–1962." Our factory adopted the system of two-shift work, with twelve hours a shift. Often when I stood beside the weaving machine, I felt completely numb.... There was enough food to stave off the pangs of hunger, but the food consisted mostly of dried potatoes, bitter wild plants and tree bark, all very difficult to swallow.[39]

Father Joseph Zhang, last seen by the reader under arrest in Fujian Province, was shipped to the Northeast in the fall of 1958 where he was condemned to life in prison, and where he would in fact remain in labor camps until February 1980. The priest and 1,200 prisoners were packed into boxcars with little ventilation and only enough room to sit back-to-back for the four-day journey to a labor camp near the city of Darien [Dalien] in Liaoning Province. Father Zhang was one of a group of 600 prisoners unloaded at the Wu Shun Machine Tool Factory. He reports that there were approximately 2,000 prisoners in his section of the labor camp, the job of which was to produce screws, abrasive sheets, and drills.

Conditions at the Wu Shun Machine Tool Factory were extremely harsh. The food was plain and rough and the work was backbreaking. Frequently during the winter months, the prisoners worked at temperatures which reached 25 below zero F. During the Great Leap Forward, conditions became even worse:

> [W]e worked twelve hours a day and oftentimes they added more time so that we were completely exhausted. My eyes became bloodshot, and when coming back from work, tired out with aching legs, we all dropped down to sleep in our clothes. They pushed an intolerable situation beyond human endurance. We were allowed to rest only five or six hours a day.

Nevertheless, Father Zhang considered himself fortunate to have been sentenced to an industrial labor camp rather than an agricultural labor camp:

> In the farm prison, conditions are primitive. One lived in a thatched hut without any basic convenience at all. The work was backbreaking. The hours of work simply unbelievable. Anyone sentenced to over twelve years of prison labor was never sent to a farm prison because he would die before the sentence was up.

It must have been a source of frustration, or perhaps of amazement, to his captors that they were never able to succeed in Father Zhang's re-education through more than two decades of forced labor. Like the other Catholic survivors, Father Zhang credited his strong Catholic faith with sustaining him during the long years in prison:

> [E]ven in these unbearable circumstances, I always recited five decades of the Rosary every day, and the litany of the Blessed Mother for the souls in purgatory. Ever since entering the prison, while lying on my bed, I could recite the entire Mass from memory.... [T]here was a good deal of scripture of which I had little profound understanding in the past, but now thinking about them again, I discovered the inexhaustable treasures of love and justice they contained. They gripped my heart and brought spiritual consolation to my tired soul. While

under the throes of these pagan practitioners of power, I welcomed these insights into sacred scripture like a gift from God which helped me not to bear any grudge against heaven or earth, never to become pessimistic or lose hope.[40]

For all these unfortunate prisoners, things would get even worse with the coming of the Cultural Revolution in 1966. Indeed, they would need all the faith and inner strength they could muster to see them through that terrible time. For Wang Xiaoling personally, her life took a dreaded turn for the worse almost two years earlier.

Wang Xiaoling:
On the 20th of November [1964], the daily routine was abandoned. Early in the morning, we were awakened by the whistle and then told to pack our belongings. Amid roll-calling and group-forming another transfer was beginning.

At the urging of the cadres, we piled into ten trucks with our luggage. And as we moved out slowly along the winding road, we realized that we were heading for a newly opened farm on barren land which was not too far away.[41]

Prelude to the "Ten Years of Disorder"

The year 1958 was not only an economic watershed for the PRC, but a watershed in terms of elite politics as well.

It became clear only later that the plans for the Great Leap Forward had been put into action by Mao Zedong and his supporters over considerable opposition from within the top ranks of the Chinese Communist Party. The immense failure of the Great Leap, which was becoming clear in the spring and summer of 1958, only deepened the already existing divisions in the top party leadership. Indeed, the outbreak of the Cultural Revolution in the fall of 1966, was the culmination of a decade-long struggle in the top ranks of the CCP over policies relating principally, though not exclusively, to domestic Chinese economic and political programs.[42]

The immediate issue of the Great Leap policies was joined at three important Party Central Committee meetings in 1958 and 1959. The first of these meetings was the Sixth Plenum [full meeting] of the CCP 8th Central Committee held in Wuhan in November–December 1958, the second was the Seventh Plenum in April 1959, and the third was at the Eighth Plenum convened in Lushan [Jiangxi Province] in September–October 1959. It was at the Sixth Plenum that Mao, under pressure from his opponents, announced his decision not to stand again for election as the chairman of the PRC. At the Lushan Plenum, Mao's opponents pressed their attack and he was openly opposed by his minister of defense, Marshal Peng Dehuai.

The political result of these meetings was a kind of compromise or standoff. Mao gave up his title as State Chairman, though he remained until his death Chairman of the Party. Marshal Peng and his supporters lost their army and government posts, but they were not (yet) physically eliminated, nor were they expelled from the Party. It was almost immediately following the Lushan Plenum that the enormous buildup of the Mao personality cult, which we described in Chapter Seven, was begun.

Chairman Mao, the symbol as well as the man, was too intimately involved in the whole fabric of communist rule in China for the Party to permit his image to be tarnished by the failure of the Great Leap. Yet Chairman Mao was also intimately connected with the entire range of Great Leap policies and with the philosophy which lay behind the movement. It is in this paradox, perhaps, that we can find the origins of the tremendous cult of personality which grew up around Mao over the next decade. Likewise, Mao was the apparent, if not actual, victor over all his rivals and dissenters, especially as he formed a close alliance with the new defense minister—the man eventually hailed as Mao's chosen heir and successor—Marshal Lin Biao. Under Marshal Lin's direction, the rhetoric emanating from the Party Center, and from the Maoist-controlled propaganda machine, over the next years assumed a decidedly radical tone. It was only with the onset of the Cultural Revolution that it would become clear that during these years there had also been quietly unfolding a general offensive against the Maoist line and policies in a number of areas of domestic politics, carried out by those in the top level of the CCP who controlled the administration of party and state affairs.

It should be worth noting that during this time, not only did the Chinese leadership suffer the disasters of the Great Leap—together with the ensuing great famine—and the political struggles cited above, but 1959 was also the year of the Tibetan uprising and of the flight of the Dalai Lama to India, and it was the year of worsening relations between China and the Soviet Union which culminated in the sudden withdrawal of all of the Soviet advisors to China in the summer of 1960. It is probably not entirely coincidental, therefore, that a few months after the close of the divisive Lushan Plenum, in a situation of political crisis, when the central government was eager to demonstrate wide popular support for its policies, that highly-publicized trials featuring Bishops Kung and Walsh were conducted in Shanghai.

The government press reported that the trials were held in the Shanghai Intermediate People's Court between March 16 and 17, 1960, before more than 500 spectators of "various circles" in Shanghai. Shanghai Bishop Kung Pin-mei, identified as the "chief culprit" of the "traitorous counterrevolutionary clique" was sentenced to life imprisonment on March 17, 1960. Thirteen other "major culprits" were given sentences of from five to twenty years imprisonment.[43] The charges against Bishop Kung were the now familiar ones:

> Due to active support by U.S. imperialism, the traitorous counterrevolutionary clique under the cloak of religion, persisted in their efforts to undermine the various political movements in the country and the implementation of state policies, laws, and decrees. They persisted in their efforts to sabotage the anti-Imperialist and Patriotic movement of Catholics all over the country, persecuted Patriotic Catholics, invented and circulated rumors, advocated aggressive war by U.S. imperialism, undermined the peace movement, colluded with and offered shelter to imperialist spies and collected restricted state information, harbored special agents and counterrevolutionaries and worked to undermine the land reform movement and the movement to suppress counterrevolutionaries, set up secret counterrevolutionary organizations and trained special agents, incited young people to flee the country, secretly stored arms and ammunition, and maintained clandestine radio communications, coordinating their actions with US imperialist aggression and the efforts by the Chiang Kai-shek gang to make a comeback.[44]

The following day, Bishop James Edward Walsh, M.M., described as,"the veteran U.S. imperialist spy who personally directed the Kung Pin-mei traitorous counterrevolutionary clique," was sentenced to a term of twenty years in prison.[45]

The trials were given considerable publicity throughout China. *Xinhua* reported nationwide support for the verdicts in a dozen or so articles over the month following the end of Bishop Walsh's trial.[46] When the U.S. Secretary of State, Mr. Christian Herter, condemned the sentencing of Bishop Walsh, China responded with an attack on Secretary Herter by Archbishop Pi Shu-shih, the chairman of the Chinese Catholic Patriotic Association[47] which was also given wide publicity, and which was followed by similar "denunciations" by various religious "circles" around the country.[48] At the same time, the Patriotics in Shanghai convened the first session of the First Representative Conference of Shanghai Catholics from April 23 to 26. The conference, which denounced the Holy See as a "tool" of United States imperialism, formally established the Shanghai Catholic Patriotic Association and also elected Father Chang Chia-shu [Zhang Jiashu] as Bishop of the Shanghai Diocese. *Xinhua* reported that the conference was attended by 683 fathers, sisters, and representatives of various districts within the Shanghai municipality. Also attending were Archbishop Pi, as chairman of the CCPA, Patriotic Bishops Li Wei-kuang and Chao Chen-sheng as vice chairmen of the CCPA, and 37 other, "bishops, fathers and Catholics" from Beijing, Hebei, Shandong, Anhui, Jiangsu, Hubei, Zhejiang, and Fujian.[49]

With the trial and life sentence of Bishop Kung and the election by the Shanghai Patriotics of Father Chang as Bishop of the diocese, the long, bitter battle of Shanghai was over. The government was at last victorious as the leaderless faithful Church was scattered and defeated.

In the years of the early 1960s leading up to the Cultural Revolution, less and less news of the Catholic Church in China reached the outside world. No longer was there a stream of missionaries reaching Hong Kong with news of those left behind. Nor was the government any longer busy prosecuting the Catholics faithful to Rome and reporting those prosecutions in the Chinese press. The faithful Catholics, including many thousands of lay people as we have seen, were safely locked away in prisons or labor camps. Likewise, the Church was greatly reduced in size compared with ten years earlier. Everywhere in the countryside the churches were closed. Hospitals, schools, orphanages and the like had all been confiscated. Many urban and suburban churches had been lost to the government as well, as these properties were confiscated and converted to various non-religious uses. So, too, were the income-producing commercial and rental properties owned by the Church taken over by the government, most of them never to be returned. And the ranks of the clergy were decimated by the expulsion of thousands of foreign missionaries and the jailing or killing of large numbers of their Chinese brethren. Even in the churches which remained open, attendance at the Sacraments was reported to be extremely low.[50] Many were no doubt fearful of practicing their faith in public; others, we know from later testimony, continued to practice their faith in private while refusing to receive the Sacraments from Patriotic priests whom they regarded as unsound or unfaithful.

For those Patriotics who remained, life in the 1960s went on with what came to pass for normalcy in the daily life of the battered and shrunken Catholic Church in China. The government-controlled press continued to discourse occasionally on the "freedom of religious belief" in the PRC,[51] and to report regularly on the celebration by Chinese Christians of the major Christian holy days such as Christmas and Easter.[52] Occasionally the Patriotics also expressed their outrage or condemnation of U.S. imperialism, such as the condemnation of "U.S. war provocations" in Viet Nam.[53] But the big battles were over, and there was very little real interest in or attention paid to the broken and truncated Catholic Church by the Chinese authorities in the years 1960–1966.

The real interest, in fact, was concentrated on what would become a life and death struggle over the line and direction of the Chinese Communist Revolution.

In retrospect, much of the political maneuvering in the years preceding the Cultural Revolution appears curious indeed. As already noted, this period coincided with the tremendous build-up of the personality cult of Chairman Mao. In terms of his public image, Mao was in the process of being elevated almost to the status of a demigod. Even those who opposed Mao politically joined in singing the Chairman's praises. Behind the scenes, however, the effort went on to dismantle the policy and machinery of the Great Leap Forward, and to de-radicalize Chinese political life. Indeed, Mao would later accuse his opponents of "waving the Red Flag to oppose the Red Flag," that is, of publically extolling the virtues of radical Maoist policies while secretly attempting to undermine and oppose those same policies.

Several attempts were made by the Maoists at high-level Party meetings to reverse the course of domestic politics decisively in favor of the radical Maoist vision of the revolutionary future, but each of these attempts was deflected in turn by Mao's more moderate opponents in the Party leadership. In the end, Mao felt himself increasingly isolated within the Party which he had headed since 1936. His revolution, he felt, had changed course and aborted; many of his old revolutionary comrades had deserted him. In an extrordinary interview in 1966 on the eve of the Cultural Revolution Mao told Andre Malraux:

> The thought, culture, and customs which brought China to where we found her must disappear, and the thought, customs, and culture of proletarian China, which does not yet exist, must appear.[54]

Mao bemoaned the "arrogance of intellectuals" who did not want to get their hands dirty,[55] and he complained that, "Neither the agricultural nor the industrial problem has been solved." Still less, said Mao, had the youth problem been solved: "Revolution and youth must be trained if they are to be properly brought up.... Youth must be put to the test."[56] And then, at the end of the interview, as the two men walked alone to Malraux's waiting automobile, Mao expressed his sense of isolation. "I am alone with the masses," he said. "Waiting."

It was the "masses" that Mao called upon to launch his attack on the Party which had let him down, to sweep away those insignificant "pests" who were holding back the march of the revolution toward the millenium. Mao especially relied upon the younger masses, the Red Guards, in his attempt to cleanse and purify the Party; to steel the young generation in the crucible of revolutionary struggle, and to put the revolution back on the correct path. It was a storm of almost unparalleled violence which Mao unleashed in the late summer of 1966, a storm which would not completely subside until his death in 1976. Mao's attempt to revitalize his revolution brought China almost to the brink of anarchy, and its devastating social and economic consequences were still being felt by the China of the 1990s.

So far as China's Catholics were concerned, with the Catholic Church faithful to Rome already destroyed as a functioning institution, it was the Patriotic Catholic Church which was swept up in the holocaust of the Great Proletarian Cultural Revolution.

NOTES

1. Mao Zedong. "Reply to Kuo Mo-jo [Guo Mo-rou]," (February 5, 1963), *Xinhua*—English, Beijing, December 31, 1966. This poem was carried on that day in all three major national daily newspapers in China. See: James T. Myers, Jurgen Domes, Erik von Groeling, *Chinese Politics: Documents and Analysis, Volume One—Cultural Revolution to 1969*. Columbia: University of South Carolina Press, 1986, 266.
2. Some accounts give Father Dong's title as "Archbishop," perhaps because Hankou was the Archbishop's See. CNA and *Xinhua*, however, refer to him as "Bishop." See CNA, June 1958, 607–608.
3. "Archbishop of Hankou and Bishop of Wuchang Elected," *Changjiang Ribao* [Yangtze Daily], Wuhan, March 21, 1958. Also, "Catholic Representatives Meet in Hankou Protest Against Vatican's Sabotage Plot," Changjiang Ribao, Hankou, April 18, 1958.
4. CNA, June 1958, 607. Also *cf.*, *Changjiang Ribao*, Hankou, April 18, 1958, which reported that 82 representatives from 20 provinces were in attendance.
5. "Catholics in Wuhan Solemnly Announce Freedom from Control of Vatican and Independent Administration of Church," *Changjiang Ribao*, Wuhan, April 11, 1958.
6. "Catholic Representatives Meet in Hankou Protest Against Vatican's Sabotage Plot," *Changjiang Ribao*, Hankou, April 18, 1958.
7. L. Ladany, *The Catholic Church in China, op. cit.*, 26.
8. CMB, June 1959, 601.
9. CMB, December 1959, 1066–1067.
10. CMB, December 1959, 1066–1067.
11. See, for example, Li Wei-guang and Hu Wen-yao, "Rightists Warned Against Looking for Markets Among Catholics," Joint Statement to the 4th Session of the National People's Congress, (July 12, 1957), *Renmin Ribao*, Beijing, July 20, 1957.

12. L. Ladany, *The Catholic Church in China, op. cit.*, 26.
13. See, for example, Zhou Jian-zhong, "The Catholic Church in China," *Xinhua*, Beijing, July 22, 1957.
14. *Ibid.*
15. Bob Whyte. *Unfinished Encounter. op. cit.*, 279. In Spain, Franco apparently asserted the traditional right of Spanish monarchs to approve Vatican appointments of bishops. There is no record that Gen. Franco ever failed to approve any Vatican appointments.
16. *Ibid.*
17. Eric O. Hanson, *Catholic Politics in China and Korea, op. cit.*, 85.
18. *Ibid.*, 86. This is not the place to argue with the central thesis of Hanson's book which he gives as "the People's Republic continues the traditional Chinese State religious policy of seeking to penetrate, regulate and control institutional religions and to obliterate heretical sects"[112]. I would simply suggest that in the rapidly changing world of the post-WW II era, the idea of attempting to analyze the politics of the PRC as a continuation of the Chinese imperial tradition strikes me as being of extremely limited utility. As evidence, I would point to the intellectual gymnastics required by the author to explain why the successor state of the Republic of China on Taiwan has not behaved in the same "Chinese" fashion toward the Catholic Church. The notion of a "continental political ideology," I find plain silly. Does the United States have such an ideology, for example?
19. Bob Whyte. *Unfinished Encounter. op. cit.*, 250.
20. *Ibid.*, 251. Whyte chooses to ignore the question of the Republic of China on Taiwan's very un-"Chinese" behavior in this regard. Perhaps he believes the ROC not to be free of "foreign interference." He follows most of Hanson's argument but does not tackle the issue of Taiwan at all. For his part, Hanson—quoting Professor John K. Fairbank—describes Taiwan as the "last treaty port" [Hanson, 84], an analytical concept as nonsensical in the 1990s as it was in 1974 when it was first advanced.
21. *Ibid.*, 251. Whyte calls these "Marxist organizational techniques."
22. I have two versions of this document, "The Catholic Church and Cuba: A Program of Action" by Li Wei-han, which was originally published in Spanish "for the exclusive use of the Latin-American Section of the Liaison Department of the Chinese Communist Party" by the Beijing Foreign Languages Press, 1959. One version published by the US Government Printing Office as an appendix to hearings by a subcommittee of the Senate Judiciary Committee is an English re-translation of a French translation of the Spanish language original. See: "Li Wei-han Document," Appendix, *Communist Exploitation of Religion*, Hearing before the Subcommittee to Investigate the Administration of the Internal Security Act and Other

Internal Security Laws, of the Committee on the Judiciary, United States Senate, Eighty-Ninth Congress, Second Session, "Testimony of Rev. Richard Wurmbrand," May 6, 1966. Washington, D.C.: US Government Printing Office, 1966, 27–30. A second version in English, translated from the Spanish original, was published in *The Mindszenty Report*, first in September 1965 and re-published in June 1983, vol. XXV, no. 6 (The Cardinal Mindszenty Foundation, P.O. Box 11321, St. Louis, MO 63105). The document is hereafter cited as "Li Wei-han." All citations are to the US Government Printing Office version.

23. I have recounted some of Bishop Tang's prison experiences in, James T. Myers. "Catholics and the Cultural Revolution," *America*, (New York), vol. 152, no. 21, June 1, 1985, which reproduces a portion of a long interview which I conducted with the Bishop at his residence in Wah Yan College, Hong Kong, on July 10, 1984.

24. *Tang: Memoirs*, 100–113.

25. James T. Myers, "Catholics and the Cultural Revolution." *America, loc. cit.*, 449.

26. *Tang: Memoirs*, 115–128.

27. *Xiaoling: Memoirs*, 49.

28. CMB, May 1959, 490–491.

29. CMB, April 1959, 393–394.

30. *Xiaoling: Memoirs*, 83.

31. See Basil Ashton, *et. al.*, "Famine in China, 1958–61," *Population and Development Review* (New York), vol. 10, no. 4, December 1984, 613 ff.

32. See "Corrective Labour Camps (1)," CNA, (Hong Kong), no. 53, September 24, 1954, 2. Also *cf.*, CMB, December 1954, 977.

33. *Renmin Ribao*, Beijing, October 6, 1954.

34. *Ibid.*

35. *Ibid.* Aslo *cf.* "Reforming Criminals," CMB, February 1955, 142–144.

36. *Ibid.*

37. *Xiaoling: Memoirs*, 92–98.

38. *Ibid.*, 96–98.

39. *Xiaoling: Memoirs*, 99–102.

40. Father Joseph Zhang, unpublished manuscript in the author's possession.

41. *Xiaoling Memoirs*, 109.

42. For a detailed discussion of these developments see, Jurgen Domes and James T. Myers. "General Introduction." James T. Myers, Jurgen Domes and Erik von Groeling. *Chinese Politics: Documents and Analysis— Volume One: Cultural Revolution to 1969*, Columbia, SC: University of South Carolina Press, 1985, 1–3, *passim*; also *cf.*, chapter one.

43. *Xinhua*—English, Shanghai, March 17, 1960; SCMP, no. 2223, March 24, 1960.

44. *Ibid.*

45. *Xinhua*—English, Shanghai, March 18, 1960; SCMP, no. 2223, March 24, 1960.

46. See, for example, "Religious Circles in Peking Support Sentences of the Kung P'in-mei Clique and American Spy Walsh," *Xinhua*, Beijing, March 20, 190; "Religious Circles in Tientsin Support Sentences Passed on the Kung P'in-mei Counter-Revolutionary Clique and US Spy Walsh'" *Xinhua*, Tianjin, March 20, 1960. "Chinese Religious Circles in Shanghai, Kiangsu, Chekiang, and Other Places Support Sentences on Counter-Revolutionary Traitors and US Spy," *Xinhua*, Shanghai, March 19, 1960; SCMP, no. 2224, March 25, 1960.

47. "Leading Catholic in Peking denounces Herter's Statement," *Xinhua*–English, Beijing, March 22, 1960.

48. See, for example, "Peking Religious Circles Condemn Herter's Statement," *Xinhua*—English, Beijing, March 23, 1960. "Shanghai Religious Circles Denounce Herter's Lies," *Xinhua*—English, Shanghai, March 22, 1960.

49. *Xinhua*, Shanghai, May 6, 1960.

50. See Richard C. Bush, Jr., *Religion in Communist China, op. cit.*, 158–163.

51. See, for example, Chang Chih-yi, "Correctly Understand and Implement the Party's Policy on Freedom of Religious Belief," *Minzu Tuanjie* [Nationalities Unity], no. 4, April 1962; in *Survey of China Mainland Magazines*, (Hong Kong), no. 318, 1962.

52. See "Christians in Peking Mark Christmas Eve," *Xinhua*—English, Beijing, December 24, 1962; "Easter Marked by Christians in China," *Xinhua*—English, Beijing, April 22, 1962; "Easter Marked by Christians in Shanghai," *Xinhua*—English, Shanghai, April 14, 1963; "Chinese Catholics Celebrate Easter," *Xinhua*—English, Beijing, March 29, 1964.

53. "Patriotic Catholics Condemn US War Provocations," *Xinhua*—English, Beijing, February 11, 1965.

54. Andre Malraux. *Anti-Memoirs*, New York: Holt, Rinehart and Winston, 1968, 360.

55. *Ibid.*, 370.

56. *Ibid.*, 366.

NINE

UP FROM THE ASHES

It doesn't matter if the cat is black or white as long as it catches mice.

Remark attributed to Deng Xiaoping

The Cultural Revolution plunged China into 10 long years of political, social, and economic chaos. All over China essential activities ground to a halt. Schools and universities were closed; factories and other workplaces were riven by political factional disputes. Uncounted tens of thousands of citizens, especially intellectuals and others suspected of revolutionary impurity, were rounded up, tormented, "struggled" against, tortured and killed by roving bands of Red Guards.

The Communist Party itself was all but destroyed as a functioning institution and many of its functions were taken over by the newly-formed "Revolutionary Committees" in the provinces and localities of China. With few exceptions, the top leadership of China was purged of all of Mao's old revolutionary comrades, including the General Secretary of the CCP, Deng Xiaoping, who would later engineer not one but two successful comeback attempts. Other top leaders, such as the party's long-time number two man, Liu Shaoqi, and former defense minister Peng Dehuai, met their deaths in the early stages of the movement, and would only be "rehabilitated," *post mortem*, years later.

The movement, which exploded in mid-August 1966, would not end officially until Mao's death in September 1976. Catholics in prison or labor camps found these years to be bitter indeed, and for many the sufferings became unbearable. Those priests who had tried to cooperate, the Patriotics and their followers, soon also found themselves arrested or scattered, as all remaining churches were closed and religious practice of any sort was placed under complete governmental interdict. For most of China's Catholics, even Chairman Mao's death would bring no relief; it would be several years after Mao's death before the lives of most Catholics would improve in any significant way.

"Don't Be Afraid of Disorder"[1]

At 7:15 P.M. on August 10, 1966, Chairman Mao met with the "revolutionary masses" in Beijing. The official account of this meeting declared, "There was no telling how many hearts throbbed with excitement, how many eyes shone with tears of joy and how many hands reached out toward him." Those who had been lucky enough to shake hands with him told others, "Come and shake hands with me! My hands have just touched those of Chairman Mao!" And, the report continued, "Like a spring wind, the happy news that the most respected and beloved great leader... Chairman Mao, had met the revolutionary masses in the capital swept through the rest of the country."[2] This meeting was a prelude to the enormous mass rallies in Tiananmen Square at which Mao greeted millions of young Red Guards and others caught up in the mass hysteria of the early stages of the Cultural Revolution.

The upsurge of revolutionary hysteria unleashed a wave of vigilante violence which eventually reached every corner of China. Considerable literature has grown up in the years since Mao's death, the literature of the "wounded" as it became known, offering personal testimony to the horrors of the Cultural Revolution.[3] Indeed it was a horrible, dark period in the history of the PRC, and in the "reform" period of the 1980s it became fashionable, and politically acceptable, to blame virtually all of China's problems on the "ten years of disorder." As we have already seen, however, the horrors suffered by the Catholic Church in China predated the Cultural Revolution by some years.

In fact, there was very little of the Catholic Church left to destroy when the Red Guards began their rampages. The attempt to destroy the Church as an independent functioning institution was, as the previous chapters have attempted to demonstrate, a deliberate policy conceived at the top levels of the Party and executed with ruthless singlemindedness over a period of years. It was not the work of roving groups of adolescent Red Guard vigilantes responding to what would later be described as Chairman Mao's "gross mistakes"[4] during the Great Proletarian Cultural Revolution. This is not to suggest, however, that the Red Guards did not destroy whatever they could find that offended their youthful revolutionary sensibilities, especially those things which could be classified under one of the "four olds": old thinking, habits, culture, and customs, any or all of which could easily be applied to religion.

The Red Guards were quick to move against those remnants of the Church which were still operating in August of 1966. Churches were attacked and stripped of their religious symbols. Stone crosses, statuary and other architectural features were chiseled or blasted from the exteriors of the churches in an attempt to remove any religious identification. Virtually all churches were ransacked and looted, and most were converted to use as warehouses, workshops, or the like. Protestant, Moslem and Buddhist places of worship received the same treatment. Many Buddhist temples and monasteries, because of their large size, were converted to factories. Indeed, it was not uncommon even as late as the 1980s to still find famous Buddhist shrines which operated as factories, and in which the Great Hall of the Sutras was locked and piled high with boxes and cartons of items manufactured on the premises.[5]

The only known foreign Catholic missionaries left in China by 1966 were the small group of eight nuns, Franciscan Missionaries of Mary, who had remained in Beijing to operate a school for the children of foreign diplomats. On the morning of August 25, 1966, Red Guards broke into the grounds of the Sacred Heart Academy. The nuns were locked in their rooms and the building was ransacked and wrecked. The Chinese press reported two mass rallies on August 26 and 28 at which the authorities announced first, the confiscation of the school and second, the immediate expulsion of the sisters.[6] The eight women were placed on the train under armed guard, and crossed into Hong Kong on August 31. The following day,

Sister Eamon died, apparently as a result of the exhaustion of the week-long ordeal.[7]

For Wang Xiaoling at the remote Caotai Prison Farm, and for the other Catholics in prison or labor camps, the Cultural Revolution brought even greater horrors than those they had already experienced. Wang Xiaoling described the inhuman conditions of life on the forced labor farm in the mid-1960s, where prisoners were forced to work in sub-zero temperatures during the bitter Manchurian winter.

Wang Xiaoling:
Old and shabby clothes were insufficient to protect the body from cold, so we had to work harder and harder in order to generate more heat, otherwise we would freeze to death. As you worked the soil with the hoe or other farming tools, up and down the field, your hands and feet would crack until they bled....

And what about summer? Things then were even worse—eight to nine hours laboring under the hot sun, wet through with sweat and dried by the sun alternately until there appeared a white powder of salt all over your clothes. No shade for you to take a rest, no time to wipe away your sweat, constant thirst and exhaustion....

The hygiene of the labor camps in the countryside, namely on a farm, was very rudimentary. The biggest difficulty came from the poor water supply—you had to carry water from a mile away. Mosquitoes and flies were everywhere....

As for the lavatory, you would not want to go there on account of the maggots crawling everywhere, day and night.[8]

In October 1966 Wang Xiaoling completed her prison sentence. Because she was not yet "reformed," however, she was kept at the Caotai Labor Farm as an "employed detainee." As she herself observed, she was still in a "concentration camp," still undergoing six two-hour sessions of political study per week, and still performing back-breaking labor. Yet, there were some improvements in life which came with this curious status—employed detainee—devised by the Chinese penal authorities. The detainees received a small amount of pay for their labor. They could write letters freely and they could spend leave at home once each year. In addition, family members could occasionally visit the camp and spend several nights. The detainees could use their small salary to buy extra food; they were permitted to leave the camp for shopping on Sundays and holidays, and they were permitted to date and marry. Wang Xiaoling had been in detainee status for about one year when the Cultural Revolution erupted.

Wang Xiaoling:

> During the 1960s in Chinese society, the Cultural Revolution raised the senseless banners "Rebellion is Justified," "Revolution First," and so set off a chain of shootings, killings, looting that led to utter chaos and disaster. The effects of all this were felt even more intensely in the labor camps. In their fanaticism the cadres came to relish the "criticism-struggles," the cruel killings and the wailing of the "reptiles" under their feet. To demonstrate their loyalty to the "Line of Mao Zedong Thought," every day they picked out a target for "criticism-struggle...."
>
> Things that had never been heard before or seen or even thought of, these were now heard and seen. This labor camp was just like a hell on earth, a camp for killing. People were chasing one another, beating one another, mocking one another, abandoning reason and killing in a cruel frenzy. Every night we could hear the piteous cries of those in solitary confinement, the moaning, as if they were at death's door, of those who had been tortured, the slogan-shouting of those butchers of the great and small "criticism-struggle" meetings, the jangling of chains and fetters and the sounds of the other instruments of torture. All this stretched our nerves to the breaking point and threw our minds into turmoil. Those who were most affected were the kindhearted and compassionate people who could not get away yet could not bear to watch what was taking place.
>
> I myself feared that my turn would probably come for "criticism-struggle"... I could not understand this strange sudden frenzy. I wanted to avoid these murderous and demented surroundings but I was worn out. In this inhuman and turbulent atmosphere there arose from the depths of my heart but one faint cry: "Lord, how will you protect your little lamb?"[9]

Father Joseph Zhang gave a similarly grim assessment of life in the labor camps during the Cultural Revolution. He wrote, "In those miserable dreadful days of tragedy and terror, how many jumped from heights, drank poison, split open their bellies for release from this hell of torture. The prison became truly among men a hell on earth."[10]

Wang Xiaoling also recounts the tortures endured by her friend Xiaolong at the Caotai Prison Labor Farm. "Xiaolong" was, in fact, Margaret Chu, the niece of Shanghai Bishop Kung Pin-mei. "Xiaolong's" brief, moving personal account of her own prison experiences is reproduced as Appendix One of this chapter.

The End of the Cultural Revolution

The violent phase of the Cultural Revolution came to an end in April 1969 with the convening of the Ninth National Congress of the Chinese Communist Party. Many serious problems and divisions remained to be resolved, but the Party leaders had at least achieved a level of accommodation which permitted them to convene a Party Congress and issue a new constitution for the CCP. It was a fragile peace, however, and it was tested more than once over the next years. The peace was shattered briefly in 1971 by the attempted *coup d'etat* by Lin Biao, (and the reported plot to assassinate Chairman Mao), which cost the defense minister his life. It was not until September 1976, however, with the death of Mao Zedong and the quick arrests of his widow, Jiang Qing, and her chief supporters at the Party center, the so-called "Gang of Four," that the Cultural Revolution came finally to an end.

In the complex and sometimes Byzantine world of Chinese Communist politics, Deng Xiaoping had, in the period following the Ninth Party Congress, made one comeback under the protection of Premier Zhou Enlai. But Premier Zhou died in January 1976, eight months before the death of Mao Zedong, and by April of that year Deng was out of power once again. The successor to Mao Zedong as Chairman of the Party and head of the government was Hua Guofeng, a man plucked by Mao from relative obscurity and designated by Mao to succeed him. It was widely reported that Mao had told Hua, "With you in charge, I am at ease."

Chairman Hua Guofeng did not, however, have a sufficiently strong base of support in the Party, and within a few years, Deng Xiaoping was attempting his second comeback and challenging Hua as the ultimate leader in the PRC. The power struggle was waged at the Eleventh National Congress of the CCP in August 1977 and decided at the Third Plenum of the Eleventh CCP Central Committee in December 1978. There, Deng Xiaoping presided over the defeat of Hua and his "Two Whatever" Faction ["Firmly uphold whatever policy decisions Chairman Mao made and unswervingly adhere to whatever instructions Chairman Mao gave"]. Indeed, in the era of Deng Xiaoping which would follow, the Third Plenum of the Eleventh Central Committee was usually cited by Chinese officials as the watershed event after which everything was substantially improved in China.

What were the important decisions of this Central Committee meeting, what was the nature of the "reform" of the Deng era, and what implications did this have for the Catholic Church in China?

It might be useful here to recall the general trend of political events in China in the years before the Third Plenum of the Eleventh Central Committee. As far back as 1971 under the leadership of Premier Zhou Enlai, and after the death of the former Defense Minister Lin Biao, China had gradually been moving in the direction of a more open stance toward the outside world. The PRC had mounted a successful effort in 1971 to obtain the permanent seat of "China" on the United Nations Security Council, a seat up to that time held by the rival government of the Republic of China on Taiwan. There was even an opening crack of religious freedom in that year as a few priests were released from prison and the Nan Tang Church in Beijing was re-opened, though only for foreign visitors to China and not for native Catholics. United States President Richard Nixon made his historic visit to China in 1972 and signed the Shanghai Communique, opening an era of improving relations between the two nations. The improving relationship with the United States culminated in the formal recognition of the PRC by President Jimmy Carter in 1979 after almost three decades of hostile relations.

During this time the Chinese also revived the notion of united front in domestic politics. The Fifth Chinese People's Political Consultative Conference [CPPCC] was convened in February 1978 after fourteen years of inactivity. The reader may recall that the CPPCC originally served as the legislature of the PRC up to 1954 when the First National People's Congress [NPC] was convened. Following the establishment of the NPC, the CPPCC had for approximately ten years served as the principal body through which China's "united front" groups were organized. After a meeting in January 1964, in the political atmosphere of the gathering storm of the Cultural Revolution, the CPPCC had ceased to function.

Now, with the return of the concept of a united front of all patriotic Chinese, working together for the modernization of their country, the CPPCC was resuscitated. Elderly members of nearly extinct political parties such as the Revolutionary Kuomintang and the China Democratic League, many in their late 1980s, joined "Patriotic" Christians [Protestants], Catholics, Buddhists, women, trade unionists, and representatives of various mass organizations, in a congress designed to show that the bad old days of the Cultural Revolution really were a thing of the past.

It was in this context, at the Third Plenum of the Eleventh Central Committee in December 1978, that Deng Xiaoping was able to assemble the coalition of forces which wrested control of the Party leadership from Hua Guofeng. Hua kept some of his titles and positions for a time, but his star was clearly in decline. In addition to marking Deng's second return from political obscurity, the Plenum also set China on the road to the "Four Modernizations": the modernization of agriculture, industry, science and technology, and the military. These modernizations were to be accomplished by undertaking both economic and political reforms.

A look at China in 1979, at the time of the undertaking of Deng's modernization policies, might cause the observer to ask what had happened. Thirty years after the end of the Chinese Civil War and the proud and hopeful declaration by Mao Zedong that "China has stood up," the China of Deng Xiaoping remained one of the world's poorest and most backward nations. All of China's universities had been closed during the Cultural Revolution, and when they reopened once again to educate the youth of China their facilities and quality of instruction left much to be desired. The debate over whether it was better to be "Red" (politically reliable) or "expert" (technically competent) had raged for years. It was finally decided decisively in favor of "Red" during the Cultural Revolution when intellectuals were classified as one of the nine "stinking things."

As a result, the China set on its new "modernizing" course

by Deng Xiaoping was almost everywhere staffed by individuals who owed their positions not to technical or managerial competence, but to revolutionary reliability, or perhaps even more commonly, to *"guanxi,"* an important feature of Chinese life best translated as "connections." One small example might serve to illustrate the point: of those employed in the administration of justice in China at the end of 1982, including the personnel of the courts, the Procuracy, and the various levels of the Ministry of Justice, only 3 percent had any higher education, while 70 percent had no education at all, that is, not one day of formal schooling![11]

One possible explanation for this state of affairs has already been hinted at in Chapter Six: the notion of the triumph of the true believers. An enormous amount of energy was released in China during the years between the communist victory in 1949 and the accession to power of Deng Xiaoping in 1979. Looking back, it is easy to identify the major convulsions, most of which we have previously discussed at least superficially: land reform, suppression of counterrevolutionaries, Aid Korea—Resist America, Three-Anti, Five-Anti, Anti-Rightist, Hundred Flowers, Great Leap Forward, Socialist Education Campaign and, of course, the Great Proletarian Cultural Revolution, to list only the major mass mobilization efforts. But all these campaigns, this immense release of systemic energy, was wasted in a futile effort to transform the character of the Chinese people according to a Maoist revolutionary image, not at making China more prosperous or more modern. And I would argue that the revolutionary true believers who came to power with Mao Zedong in 1949 really believed that such a revolutionary transformation could be more or less rapidly achieved. It was hubris, therefore, the pride and conceit of the revolutionary true believer, coupled with some stunningly bad political management, which can account for the failures of the Chinese Communist Revolution.

Deng's formula for overcoming this thirty-year revolutionary bad start was to implement policies which bore a strong resemblance to those which he and his comrades, such as the late Liu Shaoqi, had proposed in opposition to the radical Maoist policies of the late 1950s. The key to the modernization of agriculture was to be reform of the incentive structure. If the peasants would not work for Marx and Mao, maybe they would work to put a few more *yuan* in the family coffers. The great agricultural communes were abolished and replaced by a contract-responsibility system based upon individual peasant households. The more the peasants produced, the more they were allowed to keep for the benefit of themselves and their famililes. Peasants were encouraged to get rich; the most successful, the "ten thousand *yuan* households," were cited as models of individual hard work and enterprise under the new order. China, said Deng, should first get rich and then build socialism.

At the same time, there was a move to reduce the amount of central control and central planning in the government and economy and to reduce or eliminate the harsh ideological element which had been such a persistent feature of Chinese life under Mao Zedong. Deng was widely quoted as saying that he did not care about the color of the cat as long as it caught mice, indicating that ideological purity would have to take a back seat to practical results. Huge numbers of "foreign experts" were invited into China to teach English and other skills. Foreign trade was encouraged as was the formation of Chinese and foreign joint ventures. By the early 1980s, due to the extreme shortage of living space, foreign businessmen were almost literally standing in line to get into China, and famous hotels such as the Beijing Hotel had little room for travellers as their space was filled on a permanent basis by foreign companies of every description.

All of this gave rise to the hope that China was truly on a new path to modernization and development characterized by "rational" rather than "revolutionary" behavior. Deng Xiaoping made a successful tour of the United States where he was photographed wearing a cowboy hat. He was widely characterized as "moderate" and "pragmatic." He became Time Magazine's "Man of the Year." Even more encouraging from the Catholic perspective was the fact that the government indicated its willingness to permit the resumption of normal religious activities beginning in 1979.[12] In the major cities of China, church buildings began to be returned to their previous owners. Priests and pastors returned to the churches from the obscurity to which they had been banished, and all over China the gates of prisons and labor camps were opened to Catholics who had been imprisoned there.

Free At Last

Wang Xiaoling was finally set free in the summer of 1979. Also, among many others released from detention in 1979, Bishop Fan returned to Baoding and Father Francis Xavier Chu returned to Shanghai. For Wang Xiaoling it had been a long journey indeed. In the spring of 1969 she had been transferred from the Caotai Prison Farm to another farm labor camp about one hundred miles away. Shortly after her transfer, she had the opportunity to renew her acquaintance with Qiao, a young man she had known in Shanghai who was a detainee on another prison farm. In December 1969 they received permission from the authorities to marry. Qiao came by train to Xiaoling's camp and there they were married and spent a week-long honeymoon. Wang Xiaoling added this postscript to her memoir:

Wang Xiaoling:
> At the end of our honeymoon my husband had to return to his reform by labor camp which was thousands of miles away in the Southwest. Two years later I joined him there. When our first child was four years old we applied for permission to leave this camp and also China. One day during the summer of 1979, we crossed the bridge at Lowu into Hong Kong. I thanked God from the bottom of my heart.[13]

Several years later, Wang Xiaoling and her family were able to move to the United States where they settled in the Northeast. Wang Xiaoling's parish priest, Father Vincent Chu, arrested in 1955 and tried with Bishop Kung in 1960, was allowed to return to Shanghai because of illness in 1978; he was released from detention in 1980. Bishop Ignatius Kung would remain in prison until July 1985.

In February 1980 Father Joseph Zhang was released from his labor camp in Manchuria and permitted to return to his home in the South. Several months later, on June 9, 1980, Bishop Dominic Tang was suddenly released from prison in Canton. Up until shortly before his release, Bishop Tang had still been working barefoot in a vegetable field pulling up weeds.[14]

Archbishop Tang:

On the morning of June 9, 1980, when I was going to work outside as usual, the warder suddenly came and asked me to go back to pack up my things. I dressed myself, took my meager luggage and followed him to the prison office. To my suprise, reporters and photographers were there waiting for me. When the officer-in-charge of the prison returned my rosary, the reporter took our photos at once; it was the rosary which had been confiscated from me 22 years before when I was arrested. The officer said they would give me four *yuan* (RMB) in compensation for my episcopal ring which had a ruby. When I was arrested, they took 200 *yuan* (RMB) from me; they deducted a sum for certain expenses, and returned fifty *yuan* (RMB) to me.[15]

Upon leaving the prison, Bishop Tang reported that the warden said to him, "We have not been able to change your ideas from the day you arrived here."[16]

Although he was no longer under detention, Bishop Tang found that he was not entirely free, nor had he been "rehabilitated." At the time of his release from prison, the head of the local Bureau of Religious Affairs declared, "Tang Yi-ming is a counterrevolutionary; he refused many times to reform, and so he was arrested. Now the government, with great clemency, has released him; but from now on, he is no longer the Bishop of Canton."[17] The CCPA sent a Miss Tsang Mei-mei [Ceng Mei-mei] to watch over him. Bishop Tang observed that although Miss Tsang was reputed to be a Catholic, "never saw her go to receive Holy Communion, and I never saw her kneel during the Consecration of the Mass."[18]

Many Catholic visitors who wanted to see the Bishop were turned away by the CCPA functionaries and the Bishop was refused permission to celebrate Mass in public because his Latin "was not good enough." It was September 1981 before the Bishop was permitted by the CCPA to celebrate Mass in the cathedral, at a side altar and behind closed doors.[19]

All over China churches began to reopen. In many places promises were made by the government to return to the churches property which had been confiscated from them at an earlier time. In many ways the first year or so of the new religious tolerance after 1980 was quite remarkable. For one thing outsiders were able to gain a glimpse of the condition of the Church in China. I was personally able to visit churches in a number of parts of China in 1982, though all but one of the visits were spontaneous, involved no official permission, and were accomplished alone.[20] Many had thought that the Church was mortally wounded by 1960, and few dared hope that the Church could survive the holocaust of the Cultural Revolution. Even the most optimistic believed it might be decades—or perhaps centuries—before the Church could recover from the damage it had received. What we discovered was quite different indeed.

One of the most remarkable accounts came from William Hinton, the author of *Fanshen*. In Chapter Three we encountered Hinton's account of the destruction of the Catholic Church in Longbow Village in northern Shanxi Province. The leading Catholic family of the village was killed and the priest was driven away. As far as Hinton could assess the situation in 1947, the Catholic Church was dead. Imagine his surprise then, when he returned to Longbow in 1972 to find the Church alive and well, though no priest had been in the village in 25 years. As he told the story to Fox Butterfield,[21] religious pictures were everywhere to be found, and the faithful packed the house and courtyard of a local carpenter who led prayer meetings. Hinton estimated that there were more Catholics in Long Bow Village in 1972 than there were when the communists came to power. We were to learn that such stories were not at all uncommon.

During this time, the Catholics inside China began to receive news of the outside world as well. As Father Ladany observed:

> For the first time Chinese Catholics learned about the renewal of the Church through the Vatican Council, received the text of the Mass in Chinese, religious books, holy pictures, news about missionaries they knew and news about the Church and the Supreme Shepherd in Rome. All this had a wide-reaching effect. The Church outside China, at least those who did not want to close their eyes and ears, learned about the extraordinary vitality of the faith of Christians in China, the courage of the faithful, so small in number, immersed in the ocean of non-Christians and facing an unfriendly government and hostile brethren.[22]

Word of the changes which had taken place in the Church spread quickly through China. Though the official Patriotic Church had continued to celebrate Mass in the old form using

Latin, many were eager to learn of the new post-Concillar liturgy. In the summer of 1984 I encountered an elderly gentleman from the PRC at the Trappist Monastery on Lan Tao Island (Hong Kong) where he was visiting his brother, a priest in the community. I remarked to the old man that the Mass in Chinese must appear strange to him. No, he said, he was quite familiar with this new liturgy which had been used in his village near the city of Shijiazhuang [Hebei Province] for some time. Missals printed in Taiwan and Hong Kong had brought the new liturgy to mainland China as soon as the new policies of openness to the outside world had permitted it. Indeed, it was not long before people began to talk of the liturgical differences—new Mass *vs*. old—as signifying the celebrants' loyalties to Rome or to the Patriotics.

Inevitably, one of the questions which arose as priests began to return to their churches was how one should regard the Patriotic priests. Bishops, priests, sisters and laypeople faithful to Rome had suffered terribly as we have seen. How should they regard their Catholic brethren who had chosen the path of cooperation with the government? The issue was complicated by the fact that even those who had tried to cooperate, or who had attempted to escape the role of martyrdom in the 1950s, had eventually suffered as well. China's Catholics now had a common history of suffering, though the Patriotics had suffered later, during the Cultural Revolution. It was not a question to which there were clear and simple answers, nor was it a question which would be quickly or easily resolved.

Bishop Tang, for example, noted that upon his release from prison, one of his priests told him, "You already know that you are no longer Bishop of Canton. Now Father Lau will be the Bishop and I the Vicar General." Playing the other priest's game, said Bishop Tang, he said to Father Lau, "Congratulations! So, now you are the Bishop," though inside he felt both "isolated and deserted."[23] Two priests, he noted, spoke together in a low voice about diocesan affairs so that he could not hear them. One priest he observed, "was not interested in anything and feared trouble," another had a "good heart" but "lacked courage." Yet another priest frequently took Bishop Tang to see the doctor. At first reticent, he began to speak more openly and told the Bishop, "We too suffered a great deal," during the Cultural Revolution. The lives of the priests were very poor, and many were sent to perform heavy labor.[24] Bishop Tang is an extremely gentle, forgiving and non-judgmental person. It is difficult to recall, over many conversations with him, that he ever volunteered an unkind evaluation of any of his Catholic brethren in Canton. Usually when questioned about a particular individual he will reply that the priest is, "a good man." Still, it is clear that throughout this period following his release from prison, he has regarded the fidelity of some of his priests more highly than others. This is a problem for the Church in China which would persist throughout the decade of the 1980s.

One obvious reason for the persistence of the problem is the fact that the basic issue, which had been the cause of the trouble from the beginning, itself had not been resolved. Namely: many Chinese Catholics wanted to practice their faith without governmental interference, and to remain faithful to the Holy Father in Rome. Nor had years, or decades, in prison done much to change the minds of those who survived the detention. In a sense, the problem had been put on hold for twenty years. Aside from the changes brought about by the virtual destruction of the institutional Church in China, the release from prisons and labor camps of people like Bishops Tang and Fan and Fathers Vincent and Francis Xavier Chu, simply put the problem right back to where it had been in the 1950s. These Catholics were no more willing to compromise their faith in 1980 than they had been when they were first arrested more than two decades earlier.

The atmosphere during these first years of the new openness, therefore, was not quite as joyous as it might have been. Though the prisons and labor camps were thrown open, the basic positions of the government/Patriotics and the Roman faithful had not changed in any fundamental way. The relationships remained extremely complex, unhappy and volatile. And if this situation was not easily apparent to those caught up in the China "fever" of the time, and in the heady atmosphere of openness and reform, those inside China quickly perceived that the old rules were still in force and that the road ahead would not be an easy one. Indeed, Father Vincent Chu told a foreign visitor to Shanghai in May 1980 that he fully expected to be re-arrested; one of his Jesuit brothers in Shanghai, Father Stanislaus Shen, had been arrested and returned to his labor camp in Anhwei Province the previous month in connection with an incident at the Marian Shrine at Zose.[25] True to his prediction, Father Vincent Chu was himself re-arrested several months later.

Even though the prisons and camps had been opened, and the priests freed, therefore, there still existed a kind of "catacombs" quality to religious life in China in the early 1980s. One received the very strong impression that religious activity, especially Roman Catholic religious activity, and most particularly Catholic activity which involved contact with foreigners, had about it an element of danger, so that certain things were better left un-said, un-done, or perhaps even un-thought.[26]

Religious Freedom Under Deng Xiaoping

The Third National Congress of the CCPA was convened in Beijing from May 22–30, 1980. This Congress had not met since 1962 and its re-convening was consistent with the policy of resurrecting the united front in Chinese politics, and with the reestablishment of the various local organs of the Religious Affairs Bureau, all of which had disappeared during the Cultural Revolution. The purpose of the meeting was to reorganize the Catholic Church and to establish political control over those religious activities and religious personnel which were slowly coming back into public life. It is important to remember in this connection that religious activity had not completely ceased during the Cultural Revolution; it had been driven underground. As there were no longer any formal institutions or places of worship in China during that time, all religious activity had, perforce, been conducted privately and in secret. The reopening of the churches and the reorganization of the CCPA, therefore, in addition to representing the return of religion to public life, may be seen as the government's attempt to establish control over these activities. Religious activities were to be permitted, but only in designated places, and only, as Bishop Tang found out, under the watchful eye of the agents of the state.

The Third National Congress of the CCPA was followed

immediately by a three-day meeting, the Chinese Catholic Conference, with essentially the same delegates participating.[27] The CCPA meeting was said to have been attended by some 200 bishops, priests, nuns and laypeople,[28] while the Chinese Catholic Conference was attended by 33 bishops, 105 priests, eight monks and nuns and 61 laypeople, a total of 207 participants.[29] At least four of the "senior bishops" appointed by Pope Pius XII were apparently among the 33 bishops participating in the second conference.[30] Both meetings adopted "open letters" which affirmed support for the "autonomy" and "independence" of the Church, and pledged to combat the "small minority of bad elements and foreign reactionary powers who fabricate miracles, spread rumors, stir up trouble, create division and carry out illegal activities under the guise of religion,"[31] positions and language which had changed little since pre-Cultural Revolution days.

The Conference also created two new structures, a 105-member National Catholic Administrative Commission[32] and a National Bishops Conference to deal with religious and pastoral matters; these organizations were identified as separate and distinct from the CCPA. Bishop Zhang Jiashu of Shanghai, elected by the Patriotics in 1960 to replace the imprisoned Bishop Ignatius Kung, was installed as head of both new organizations. The precise division of responsibility among these organizations was not entirely clear, though the CCPA was apparently to be removed from involvement in the operation of church religious affairs in order to concentrate on political matters and to serve as an intermediary between the Church and the government.

If this explanation of the role of the CCPA after its Third National Conference appears somewhat murky, the reality of this role, and the relationships among the various new religious organizations, has never, in my own experience, been much clearer. Nor is the matter clarified much when one sees on the gates of the churches two signs, one bearing the name of the church and the other reading *"Tian Zhu Jiao Ai Guo Hui"* [CCPA]. At least on paper, however, the CCPA was separated from the day-to-day operation of the church, and thus it was possible for priests and others to function freely without joining the CCPA. This may have been seen as an advantage by the government authorities who must have been keenly aware of the hostility and suspicion with which the CCPA had been treated in the past by large numbers of Catholics. Having said this, however, it must be emphasized that it is still the CCPA and the Religious Affairs Bureau (RAB) which constitute the constant governmental presence in church life in China. The other religious organizations meet only periodically to deliberate on the religious and pastoral work of the church while the CCPA and the RAB are always there, in the same building or down the road at the government headquarters. Moreover, all three of these church organizations feature interlocking control and overlapping membership. Consider, for example, the first officers of the newly-established organizations: Zhang Jiashu was president of the Administrative Commission and president of the Bishop's Congress while serving as vice president of the CCPA. Zhong Huaide was president of the CCPA and vice president of the other two bodies. Three other individuals served as vice presidents of all three organizations. One writer has described the important features of these three organizations as the "multiple memberships of their senior officials...and their control by the government."[33]

Here, also, a further word needs to be said about these various "Catholic" organizations in the PRC. Indeed, it is probably more proper to label them "organizations of Catholics" rather than "Catholic organizations." What is involved here is more than the mere splitting of semantic hairs. Bob Whyte, for example, writing of the Third CCPA Congress, asserts: "The Catholics obviously felt the need for a national church...."[34] One wonders how he, or others who might share the same view, arrive at such a conclusion. Certainly one cannot reach a conclusion about what Chinese Catholics feel they need from the activities of the CCPA. The Legion of Mary is a Catholic organization; the Knights of Columbus is a Catholic organization, but the CCPA is an organization of Catholics. The CCPA is organized and operated by the Chinese government. Its functions are identical to those of all the other mass organizations subsumed under the Patriotic United Front. It is constituted and maintained to serve the needs of the government, not those of Chinese Catholics or of the Catholic Church in China. The distinction made here is a fundamental one which is taught in every introductory course in comparative politics.

In democratic political systems, interest groups or associations organize freely, such groups arise spontaneously, the associations are voluntary, and perhaps most important, they are independent of the government. Freedom and autonomy are essential if the association is to be able to formulate and articulate the shared views of the members. Likewise, the group must have access to, and the right to possess, independent resources if it is to maintain its position of autonomy *vis-á-vis* the government. Obviously, none of these conditions is present in a Leninist state system. The CCPA is thus not a "Catholic" organization in any meaningful sense of the term; it is a political mass organization consisting primarily of Catholics, created by the government of the PRC, and operating under the direction of the government's Religious Affairs Bureau, which is itself overseen by the United Front Work Department of the CCP Central Committee.

Should there be any doubt about the nature of these power arrangements, the CCP Central Committee has been helpful enough to issue the *Chung-fa* [internal Central Committee] Document cited at the beginning of Chapter Two.[35] The *Chung-fa* Document refers throughout to the "religious problem" in China, and states that, "All places for religious activities should be managed by religious organizations under the administrative leadership of the government's Religious Affairs Department." Furthermore, "No religious organization or believer should do missionary work outside places of worship, spread theist propaganda or distribute tracts and other religious publications which have not been previously approved by the responsible government department." In addition, "All Patriotic religious organizations should accept the leadership of the Party and the government...."[36]

All of the principles contained in the *Chung-fa* Document were subsequently reaffirmed in a lengthy editorial published later the same year in *Hongqi* [Red Flag] the Communist Party theoretical journal.[37] What this important editorial revealed was that none of the Party's fundamental positions on religion had changed since the 1950s. The principles articulated in the two documents were, in fact, by now quite familiar: "[W]e communists are atheists and we advocate and will propagate atheism among the masses of the people."[38] "Furthermore, we must in no way allow anybody to use religion to oppose the Party's leadership and the socialist system or to use religion to carry out propaganda against Marxism-Leninism-Mao Zedong Thought."[39]

The editorial blames "leftist mistakes" in religious policy on the Cultural Revolution and declares that since the Third Plenum of the Eleventh Central Committee, "[T]he Party's correct principles and policies related to the question of religious work have been gradually restored."[40] In fact, as we have seen again and again, the policies which sought to eradicate religion in China go back to the Civil War period of the 1940s; they were not the products of the Cultural Revolution. Moreover, the basic principles which underlay those policies were explicitly reaffirmed in the party documents of the 1980s.

Both the *Chung-fa* and the editorial devote considerable attention to the role of religion in the effort of national construction and modernization. The language, in fact, is quite similar to that of Mao Zedong's famous 1940 essay "On New Democracy" which we discussed in Chapter Two. The Central Committee *Chung-fa* puts it this way:

> The world outlook of Marxism is in opposition to any kind of theism. But in political action, Marxists and Patriotic religious believers may, and what is more, must form a united battlefront in the common struggle for the construction of socialist modernization. This united front should be an important component of the large-scale Patriotic United Front which is led by the Party during the socialist era.[41]

In addition to bringing religious activities and personnel back under government control, therefore, the revival of the old notion of the United Front also helps to explain the adoption of the new policies of "religious freedom" under Deng Xiaoping. In the reform era following the Third Plenum of the Eleventh Central Committee, with the push to implement the "Four Modernizations," China's political leaders had apparently concluded that religious believers might be mobilized as a useful force in the development of the country. The *Hongqi* editorial states:

> In short, uniting both believers and the nonbelievers of religion among the masses to jointly strive for the construction of a modern powerful socialist country is the basic starting point and basic ground for us in carrying out the policy of freedom of religious belief and in carrying out all religious work.[42]

The same basic point is also emphasized in this way:

> Our comrades must understand that though in terms of world outlook Marxism runs counter to any theism, in terms of political actions, Marxists definitely can and must form a united front with religious believers to jointly strive for socialist modernization. This united front should become a very important part of the broad Patriotic United Front that is led by the Party during the period of socialism.[43]

Nor does the *Hongqi* editorial fail to take account of the fact that the concept of freedom of religion may have an important international dimension. In an era of increasing contact with and opening to the West, Chinese leaders acknowledged an awareness of the sensitivity of the religious issue, especially in the largely Christian Western nations upon whom much of China's economic modernization plans depended.

> At present, along with the daily increase in our international exchanges, the external contacts of the religious circles will also develop in a daily increasing manner and play an important role in raising our country's political influence....
>
> Facts have proven that when we have done the religious work at home satisfactorily, there will be no or very few loopholes for hostile foreign religious forces to take advantage of and the international exchanges in the religious field will be able to healthily and smoothly develop and play their due role.[44]

The *Hongqi* editorial also expressed a belief in the futility of force and violence as means of eliminating religion in society, a concept which we discussed earlier in Chapter Two:

> The idea and practice that treats religion as something we can eliminate once and for all by administrative orders or even by means of force, runs counter to the Marxist basic viewpoints on religious questions and is completely wrong and very harmful....

> [I]t is not only ineffective but also very harmful to use simple and forceful methods to handle the ideological problems of the people and problems concerning the spiritual world of the people, especially the problems of religious belief.[45]

It may well be that the views expressed by the party theoretical journal reflected an authentic belief in the ineffectiveness of the use of force and violence in the effort to control and eliminate religion in Chinese society. It is useful to recall, however, that the publication of this important statement on Party policy toward religion took place approximately six months after the arrests of Fathers Vincent and Francis Xavier Chu, seven other priests and several lay Catholics from the Shanghai Diocese for "counterrevolutionary activities."[46] In 1983, approximately six months following the publication of the *Hongqi* editorial, these priests were tried and sentenced to lengthy new prison terms for "counterrevolutionary crimes," specifically for their refusal to cooperate with the CCPA and for their persistent loyalty to the Holy Father in Rome.[47] Bishop Peter Joseph Fan Xueyan of Baoding, like the others, only recently released from a long imprisonment, was also re-arrested in 1983 and sentenced to ten years in prison for maintaining contacts with the Vatican.[48]

It may also be useful to remember, as the *Hongqi* editorial reminds us, that the basic aim of the party's religious policy, as it had been from the beginning, remained the "elimination" of religion from Chinese society, "once and for all."[49]

Having said this, however, it must be acknowledged that the religious situation in China in the post-Cultural Revolution environment was still much improved over the earlier period. Most priests and bishops, as well as religious brothers and sisters and lay Catholics, were released from prisons and labor camps, and only a few were re-arrested. Churches were re-opened and began to operate and to administer the Sacraments to the faithful, even if under the watchful eye of the state. Some property was returned to the churches with promises that more would be returned later. Seminaries were organized to train new priests. Many Catholics, such as Wang Xiaoling, were permitted to leave China and take up new lives abroad. Bishop Dominic Tang was allowed to travel to Hong Kong to receive medical treatment. From Hong Kong he travelled to Rome where Pope John Paul II named him Archbishop of Canton (*see below*, Chapter Ten).

Perhaps most symbolic of the improvement of the Catholic situation in China was the release from prison of Shanghai Bishop Ignatius Kung on July 3, 1985. Bishop Kung was released on a 10-year parole and became a virtual prisoner in his quarters under the care of the CCPA which would not permit him to receive foreign visitors. In January 1988, however, Bishop Kung was finally pardoned by the government and his political rights restored. Several months earlier, on November 17, 1987, Bishop Peter Joseph Fan had been released from prison on parole and returned to Baoding.[50] Also in early 1988, the authorities released Father Joseph Chen and Father Vincent Chu to return to Shanghai. Several other Shanghai priests including Father Stanislaus Shen and Father Fu Hezhou, who had been re-arrested in 1981, were also released but were said to have "returned to the places where they had been detained."[51]

Another old friend from these pages did not live to enjoy release from confinement. Father Francis Xavier Chu, who had been confined at the White Lake labor camp in Anhui Province, died on December 28, 1983 at the prison hospital in Hofei, Anhui. On April 4, 1984 in Hong Kong, Archbishop Dominic Tang and more than forty concelebrants, all wearing the red vestments signifying martyrdom, celebrated a Solemn Requiem Mass commemorating Father Chu who was described in the press as a "blessed martyr."[52]

In May 1988 Bishop Ignatius Kung was given permission to travel to the United States to receive medical care. Most assumed that the Bishop, already 87 years of age, would never return to Shanghai during his lifetime. He settled in Connecticut under the care of his nephew Joseph Kung. In May 1989, Bishop Kung met privately with Pope John Paul II in the Vatican. No account of the private meeting was published, but the Holy Father was said to be "very pleased" to meet the Bishop.[53] On June 2, 1990, two old friends met in Stamford, Connecticut for the first time in more than forty years. On that Sunday, Archbishop Dominic Tang concelebrated a Diamond Jubilee Mass celebrating the 60th anniversary of Bishop Ingatius

Kung's Ordination to the Priesthood and the 40th anniversary of his consecration as Bishop of Shanghai. Archbishop Tang's homily delivered on this occasion is reproduced as Appendix Two of this chapter.

In May 1991, the Vatican announced that in 1979 at his first Consistory, during the period when Bishop Kung was still in prision in Shanghai, Pope John Paul II had secretly, *in petto*, named Bishop Kung to the College of Cardinals. In June 1991, Ignatius Cardinal Kung journeyed to Rome to receive his Red Hat from the Pope.

All the good news, however, could not mask the fact that, as we have seen, many fundamental problems remained for the Catholic Church in China. Not the least of these problems was the persistent failure over more than 40 years to resolve the differences between the government of the PRC (and, thus, of China's Catholics) and the Holy See in Rome.

APPENDIX ONE
A Catholic Girl in Prison in China
by Margaret Chu, niece of
Bishop Kung of Shanghai
(Unpublished manuscript in the author's possession)

In 1949, I was in my early teens, full of hope dreaming of a great future with freedom, career, and love. Then, China turned Red.

According to communist teaching, I quote: "Religion is people's opium." Therefore, to be Chinese and a Catholic at that time was a very serious challenge. Suddenly, the Catholics had to decide whether to follow God or the government's anti-Catholic policy. To follow God meant prison. To follow the government meant security and a normal living. It was a difficult and painful choice. With God's grace, thousands of Catholics courageously chose God.

The leader of the Shanghai Catholic Diocese since 1950 was Bishop Ignatius Kung. (He was the bishop of three dioceses including Nanking, the old Chinese capital.) In the beginning of the communist regime, the government continued to give the Church certain freedom. They hoped to win Bishop Kung's cooperation to form a state-controlled Patriotic Catholic Church. They wanted him to cut off the church relations with the Vatican. After five years of increasing pressure, without success, the government changed its tactics. On September 8, 1955, Bishop Kung, together with thousands of priests, nuns and lay Catholics were arrested. The seminary was closed.

We had to attend brainwashing sessions every day. In these sessions the government wanted us to sign a declaration that Bishop Kung was the leader of the counterrevolutionary gang dedicated to overturn the communist government. We had to report on all religious organizations, the names of members and their activities. Those who buckled under pressure and signed the declaration were set free. They were restored to all jobs and educational privileges. But those who followed the Church were dismissed from their jobs. They were not allowed to attend the university and ended in prison.

I refused to participate and remained in complete silence. While they read their propaganda, I simply prayed in my heart. It worked for a short while.

The government gradually stepped up the pressure on us. Within two months, many of those priests who were still free signed a declaration supporting the government's action to charge Bishop Kung with high treason.

I was particularly shocked when I learned that my spiritual director, Father Aloysius Jin, cooperated with the communists. Father Jin was a very eloquent priest, the rector of the Shanghai Seminary, and had great influence among the Catholics. Soon after he was arrested, he recorded a tape to persuade loyal Catholics to support the government. This tape was used to broadcast in many prisons. Father Jin is none other than the current illicit Bishop of Shanghai of the Patriotic Catholic Association. That was indeed a great blow to the Shanghai diocese and to me personally. At a time when I needed spiritual support and consolation most, I was left entirely alone without any trusting priests.

After the September 8, 1955 mass arrest, we became a flock without a shepherd. Many Catholics including myself refused to receive Holy Sacraments from those priests who had publicly renounced the Church and betrayed the Bishop. At the same time, we had no spiritual support. We were lonely and isolated. We could only pray privately among friends.

We had no experience in political struggle. All we wanted was to keep our faith. We never wanted to oppose the government. We also never suspected that the government would even plant a spy among us. Because a spy came to us through the introduction of a good nun, we blindly trusted that spy. She joined every religious activity organized by us.

In the early morning of May 28, 1958, about ten persons from the Patriotic Catholic Association broke into my house. They grabbed my hands and feet and dragged me to a study meeting organized by the Patriotic Catholic Association.

There were many other Catholics dragged in the same manner as myself. The association wanted to brainwash us to think that we joined this meeting entirely on our own free will. They also carried out a smear campaign against the Church to force us to renounce the Pope. I was criticized, scolded, shouted at by many persons. I simply prayed my rosary quietly and ignored all the noises and insults thrown onto me.

I decided that my position should be God above all. I mediated on God's words to St. Peter, "You are the rock. Upon this rock I will build my church." I reminded myself that denouncing the Pope was the same as leaving Christ. I decided that I would rather die than leave God.

Three months after that forced religion study session, I was arrested and jailed on September 12, 1958. I was 22. It was the beginning of my 21 years in jail and labor camp.

My first reaction when I stepped into my cell was to nauseate. The cell was about 250 square feet housing some 16 prisoners. There was only one very small window. There was a strong smell from those cell-mates who obviously had not washed for a long time. Human wastes were collected in our cell. It was simply suffocating. I thought of my family at home and my brother Joseph in the United States. The pain of separation was immense. I was psychologically less prepared than I had thought.

After two months' waiting, without trial, I was sentenced to eight years imprisonment as a counterrevolutionary because I joined many religious activities. I was naive enough to think that since the government had what they wanted, they would leave me alone to serve my sentence. I thought my religious and psychological struggle was over. I thought I could enjoy God's grace in peace during my sentence. I was entirely wrong. My struggle had just begun.

After my sentence, I was sent to a transit jail waiting to be dispatched to the prisoner labor camp. We had seven persons in one cell with three beds only. Four slept on the concrete floor partly under the beds. It was winter. There was absolutely no heat. The cell was very drafty and freezing cold. We had two stone-cold meals a day. My first experience in stomach ache and cramps began in this cell.

Once, my family was allowed to visit me. While waiting in line, I said a few words with a Catholic. An inmate reported on me and, as a result, my scheduled visit with my family was abruptly cancelled. All prisoners were allowed to shower once a month, but Catholics were not allowed. But we Catholic prisoners still managed to communicate secretly among ourselves.

After staying in this transit prison for about a month, I was dispatched to a prison knitting factory about one hundred miles from Shanghai. My family came to say goodbye. From them I learned that two of my friends died shortly after they were sent to the camp. The news shocked me. I could not understand why they should all die shortly after they were transferred to the camp. What was the camp like?

In the prison factory, we worked eighteen hours a day, seven days a week. The drums would wake us up at four every morning. Before long, due to extreme fatigue, I lost my appetite. At night, I just collapsed in my bed without even washing my face. This routine kept on for one year.

A few days after I arrived at the prison, the officer asked me: "What is your crime?" I snapped back: "I did not commit any crime. I was arrested because I was a Catholic and tried to defend my faith." The officer became very angry and shouted: "If you did not commit any crime, why are you here?" I was stunned by his extreme anger and shut up. The whole factory was dead silent. Because of this incident, I discovered several Catholics. We quickly united. Among them was a girl named Tsou who had been turned in by a priest in the government-sponsored Patriotic Association. She was especially good to me. Unfortunately, after four years, she broke down mentally. The officer even used her mental condition as violation of prison regulations. They tied her up. They hung her up and beat her. They extended her sentence twice. Although she has now completed her time, she is still in the labor camp as of this date without proper care.

After one year, the government changed the eighteen-hour shift to ten hours. But there were two hours of political re-education every day. At year end, all of us were required to write a self-assessment on how our political thoughts had improved through labor. Those who refused to admit their crimes were often isolated from other prisoners.

Because I was a niece of Bishop Kung and because I had never admitted to my accused crimes, I had been under constant surveillance. However, I was always a model worker. My productivity was one of the highest among the groups. I followed all the regulations. I somehow succeeded in separating my work and my accused crimes as two separate issues. But all these did not earn me any leniency from my country.

Looking back, the prime of my life was robbed by eight years of hard labor and constant struggle sessions. Even though I knew I was doing all this for God, I despised and hated that camp which had no culture, no music and no love. I was tired and depressed by the endless brainwashing and struggle. I was totally homesick. At the same time, I realized that being released would not be the end of my problems. Ex-prisoners were social outcasts. I was condemned for life and would always be at the bottom of the social ladder. I thought of my brother Joe's invitation to go to the United States. But could that ever be possible? I was very tired and depressed. Oh Lord, please give me faith and hope.

Four months before my eight-year sentence was to have been completed, the cultural revolution started. The camp officers started surprise searches of all cells. Some years back, I came across a few verses which inspired me. I copied them on a little notebook. It was tucked away and forgotten. During a surprise search they found that notebook. They singled me out and made an example of me for other prisoners. They put me through many "struggle" sessions, even took me to the court. I was sure that my sentence would be extended. I was very alone. Most inmates were afraid of being near me.

On the morning of September 12, 1966, I was told that I would be transferred to another labor camp. I was stunned. This meant that my prison sentence would not be extended after all. Thank God! I took a deep breath and looked at the beautiful blue sky. Suddenly, everything became so beautiful.

I was not on my way home. No. I was simply transferred from a heavily guarded prison camp to a less secured labor camp. Rules in that labor camp were a little easier. We had wages— about US $6 a month. Out of the US $6, $3 were deducted for our food. Sounds like a real bargain, doesn't it? We had to buy all our personal necessities out of that remaining $3 each month! We had three weeks off to visit families each year.

Catherine Ho, who is now also in the United States, was with me in the same camp. In May 1968, two years after I was in this new camp, I received a parcel from my family. I told Catherine about this parcel. Immediately one inmate accused me of giving something to Catherine. I strongly denied that. I was dragged to the office. Without any investigation, the officer assembled the entire camp to start a struggle session against me. In the session, the officer suddenly asked me whether I had committed any crimes leading to my sentence. I was stunned. It then dawned on me that this struggle session was in fact prearranged. The parcel was only a pretence. Their real motive was once again to force me to admit all my accused crimes. So, I replied firmly: "I did not commit any crimes." Immediately two persons jumped on me and cut off half of my hair. He again asked: "Are you guilty?" I again replied: "No." Two persons then used a rope to tie my hands backward tightly. It was connected to a loop around my shoulder and underneath my armpits. It was knotted in such a way that a slight movement of my hands would cause intense pain. They ordered Catherine to stand next to me. The government often tried to alienate Catholics in that way. The struggle session lasted for two hours. Afterwards, they untied me and handcuffed me instead. The handcuffs became a part of me for the next one hundred days and nights.

After I was untied, I was so painful as if all my bones were broken. I had bruises all over. I was very indignant to be treated as such. I did not sleep that night. From then on, I washed and ate with my cuffs on. I worked in the field with my cuffs on. I was followed every minute. Anyone who dared to even smile at me would be punished. Working under 95 degrees in the field, I was not allowed even to wear a hat. I could not bathe or change my clothes with my cuffs on. My clothes would get soaking wet from perspiration, dried, only to get wet again. I smelled worse than a skunk. The parcel sent to me from home was returned by the camp. Every night there was another struggle session. Everyone was encouraged to insult me. I, in fact, became a prisoner again without a trial and without anyone outside knowing it.

I could not appeal. I could not escape. I was isolated. I was too sad to cry. I hoped I would die. I could not commit suicide.

But I could pray for the gift of death. So, when I was tortured, I hoped that I would be tortured more so that I could die suddenly. When I was ordered to carry things on my shoulder, I hoped that they would give me more to carry so that I could suddenly collapse. But, not only did I not die, I did not even get sick.

I spent my days and months working in the field with my hands cuffed. My sufferings became unbearable. Where are you, my Lord. I became somewhat annoyed with God. O Lord, for the last ten years I struggled and suffered. Haven't I already proved myself to you? Let me die, my Lord.

In the summer, we had two hours' rest at noon. Almost everyone took the opportunity to sleep. I was too distressed to sleep. In the field were wooden barrels used as toilets. All wastes were accumulated inside to be used later as fertilizer. The place smelled foul and was filthy beyond description. No one could go there longer than necessary. Certainly not the camp officers.

I found my haven right there in the stinky toilet. To me, it was quiet and peaceful. There, no one would come to accuse me. Once in a while, some kind people would secretly come with a wet towel to clean my face and rub my back—I couldn't do it myself because my hands were still cuffed. Several persons came to apologize for accusing me because they were under pressure. Their good intentions and sympathy moved me to tears.

When I was handcuffed in the beginning, I was the only target they attacked. They attacked me physically and verbally. Finding that I did not give in, they expanded their target to include the Catholic Church. They would use foul language to insult our Church, insult God and our Holy Mother. I was extremely saddened by the direct assault against our beloved God.

I prayed for my death, but it was not granted. I was afraid that I might not be able to endure much longer. I could no longer tolerate the foul language day and night against God and against Holy Mother. I finally admitted one of my accused crimes as written on the court paper. I admitted that it was counterrevolutionary to persuade children not to join the communist youth organizations and their religious activities. Nevertheless, that was enough for the camp officer to claim victory over me. My cuffs were finally off.

This episode of my being cuffed was only one incident. There were many, many others. For instance, there were times we did not have enough to eat. In desperation, we dug out the roots of a certain tree, ground them into powder and ate it.

In 1969, I was transferred to another labor camp. I harvested tea leaves and various vegetables. Frequently, I had to carry almost 150 pounds of vegetables on my shoulder. In the winter, I was ordered to the mountain about twenty miles away to gather firewood. Somehow, I began to prefer this kind of labor, although it was very hard. Being able to leave the camp in order to work in the mountain was quite an incentive.

Whenever I thought of the future, I became extremely depressed. I felt that I might never live to see the revival of the Catholic Church in China. I had nothing to look forward to. I was very, very lonely. Before long, several years had passed.

For six years my annual home visit privileges were taken away. In 1972, after fourteen years, I was finally allowed to visit home. When I was home in Shanghai, I discovered that the underground Catholic Church flourished. I was refused by the authorities to register as a resident of Shanghai. That meant I had nowhere to go but to return to the labor camp once my leave was up.

In the second half of 1974, I met Ignatius Chu who eventually became my husband. He was sent to jail three years before I was and for the same reasons. He too was transferred to hard labor. I knew him before, but had not seen him for some twenty years. We both grew much older. It must be God's providence that we met again. At that time conditions at the camp were a little better. We were allowed to talk to each other. After six months, we decided to get married.

At that time, I received from my brother Joe a copy of the approval of his petition for me to immigrate to the United States. Ignatius indicated his willingness to go there with me. Ignatius has a family of eight brothers. With the exception of his brother Father Michael Chu, a Jesuit, who was out of China when China turned communist, all the other seven were at one time or another in various jails for their faith. At that time, he still had four other brothers plus himself in the labor camps. It was most unlikely that his passport would be approved.

To marry Ignatius would jeopardize my chances of getting my passport. Ignatius would not want to drag me into his family situation. We wanted marriage. But I also wanted the United States. I wanted both. After much discussions and praying together, we decided to get married on February 11, 1976, on the Feast Day of Our Blessed Mother.

The marriage plan was a secret in the labor camp. We invited Ignatius' eldest brother, Father Francis Chu, also a Jesuit, to come to marry us. Father Francis was in another labor camp at that time. We both took home leave in February and hoped to get married in Shanghai. Father Francis also applied for permission to go home. Unfortunately, Father Francis did not receive the permission in time. By the time Father Francis finally arrived in Shanghai, we were back at our camps. So, Father Francis came to us. Ignatius and I faked sick that day and received permission to go to the clinic. Instead we went to the train station to meet with Father Francis. From there, we went to a small restaurant.

At the dinner table in the middle of a noisy restaurant, Father Francis took out a few soda crackers and a few drops of wine. He offered in secret a short Holy Mass and performed our marriage ceremony with our exchange of marriage vows. We were finally married before God. There were no flowers. There was no music, no guests, not even a ring. All we had was God's blessings. That was more than enough for us. After dinner, having taken Father Francis back to the train station, we went back to our separate dormitories, pretending that nothing had happened.

Here I would like to add that Father Francis died in prison in 1983 as a martyr after his second arrest. He was 70 years old. He spent a total of thirty years in prison and labor camp.

After my marriage, I started applying for my passport. But the officers of the camp refused to give me permission to proceed. In the meantime, my brother Joe started a letter-writing campaign. He wrote to the Public Security Department, Overseas Chinese Association, Reformation Department, Foreign Affairs Department and many others. Finally, in August 1978, I was contacted by the Public Security Department. But they rejected my passport application.

To test the attitude of the government toward us, we registered our marriage with the government and it was approved on October 3, 1978. Two and a half months later, U.S.-China relations were normalized. In July 1979, we were notified that our passport applications were approved.

On September 5, 1979, Ignatius and I walked across the border bridge and stepped onto the soil of freedom in Hong Kong. Ten months later, on July 10, 1980, Ignatius and I arrived in the United States, with my brother Joe waiting for us at Kennedy Airport. I started my second life.

September 1989
Tarrytown, New York

APPENDIX TWO
Bishop Kung—A Model for all Clergies
A Homily by His Excellency Most Reverend Archbishop Dominic Tang, S.J., the Archbishop Of Canton, China
On the occasion of the Diamond Jubilee of the Ordination to Priesthood and the 40th Anniversary as a Bishop of Bishop Ignatius Pin-mei Kung, Bishop Of Shanghai, China
(June 2, 1990, in Stamford, Connecticut, U.S.A.; an unpublished manuscript in the author's possession)

My dear Bishop Kung; my dear brothers and sisters in Christ,

Today, we gather here in this church, to thank God for giving China an outstanding shepherd, and a great priest, Bishop Kung. This is bishop's 60th anniversary as a priest, and also 40th years as a bishop. He is truly an inspiration for everyone, and a model for all priests.

My friendship with Bishop Kung did not begin today. It dated back some fifty years ago when I met him as Father Ignatius in Shanghai. You can, therefore, say that we are old friends. We are also followers of the same ideal. Bishop Kung served God by being obedient to God's will, and by being faithful to his duties as a priest. He is also very devoted to the young people.

Sixty years is indeed a very long time for anyone. And when we look at the life of Bishop Kung, half of these 60 years was spent alone and behind bars.

When I was in Shanghai, Bishop Kung was the principal of a Jesuit High School, devoted himself to education.

Then, there were alarming changes in China. Atheism spread like fire. Many priests in northern China were arrested. Most of the foreign bishops, priests and religious sisters were all expelled from China. You can imagine the atmosphere in China at that time. Looking through our human eyes, the future of the Church in China was helpless and horrifying. It was under such circumstances, that in October 1949, Father Ignatius Kung, accepted the episcopacy of the new Diocese of Shouchow and became its first chief shepherd.

We are all members of the One, Holy, Catholic Church, united under Christ. By Bishop Kung's sacrifice, the entire church has benefited. He has also set for us an example of obedience. Just as our Blessed Mother had replied to Angel Gabriel, "I am the servant of the Lord, let it be done to me as you say." Bishop Kung has accepted God's plan and the Holy Father's request without reservation.

Ten months later, in August 1950, Pope Pius XII appointed Bishop Kung as the Bishop of Shanghai. He is the first Chinese bishop in the Diocese of Shanghai. He also served as administrator of the Shouchow and Nanking Dioceses.

Shanghai is the largest city in China. At that time, it had a population of eight million. Shouchow is the famous Venice of the East, and Nanking is the old capital of China. Bishop Kung, therefore, became the bishop of three of the most important cities in China at a most critical time in the history of the Catholic Church in China.

By this time, in 1950, the communist government was already in complete control of China. Did Bishop Kung not realize that the persecution of the Church was imminent?

Bishop Kung imitated the spirit of Jesus when He prayed in Gethsemane before His passion, "Let it be as you would have it, not as I." Bishop Kung completely disregarded his own personal safety. He became the spiritual leader of the largest diocese of China, and started his journey towards Calvary.

In a short five years, the Shanghai diocese flourished and became full of life under his good leadership. He was firm and caring. He gave all that he had for the salvation of souls and for the greater glory of God. He had the whole diocese completely united under him. Bishop Kung's name soon spread throughout China. All the dioceses modeled after the work of the Shanghai Diocese. He was particularly loved and admired by all young people, students from the University and High school.

It was, therefore, apparent to the enemy of the Church that something must be done about this Bishop Kung. On the night of September 8, 1955, Bishop Kung, 23 priests and over 300 Catholics were arrested. The next day, thousands of people wept when they read the front page headline on *The People's Daily*, "Counterrevolutionary Ignatius Kung was arrested...."

One day of misery is painfully long. Bishop Kung spent thirty years in jail, one day at a time, for 11,000 days. He was completely cut off from the world, had no spiritual support such as Holy Mass or spiritual books, and had very little material support.

How many people in the Catholic Church in China also spent twenty to thirty years in the same way? And, as I am speaking to you now, how many of our brothers and sisters in Christ are still without freedom in China, suffering persecution for their faith?

As recently as last November, the bishops in China, who are loyal to our Holy Father, set up "The Bishops' Conference of Mainland China." Bishop Fan, whose name is familiar to many you, was elected president. As a result of this open declaration of loyalty to His Holiness, the government arrested the bishops and priests who have taken part.

Therefore, the Diamond Jubilee we celebrate today is not just another Diamond Jubilee. Bishop Kung has inspired thousands of Chinese Catholics, and millions around the world, during the last forty years. In Bishop Kung, we can witness the mystery of God's plan and the power of God's grace in China.

Please, let us all pray for Bishop Kung, for his continued health, so that he can give greater glory to God.

I beg you to remember the Catholic Church in China in your prayers, so that China will once again submit itself to Blessed Mother, Queen of China.

God Bless all of you.

NOTES

1. "Communique of the Eleventh Plenary Session of the Eighth Central Committee of the Communist Party of China." Adopted August 12, 1966. Myers, Domes and von Groeling, *Chinese Politics, op. cit.,* 279.
2. "Chairman Mao Meets the Revolutionary Masses," *Peking Review* (Beijing), no. 34, August 19, 1966.
3. See for example, Liang Heng and Judith Shapiro. *Son of the Revolution.* New York: Alfred A. Knopf, 1983; Nien Cheng, *Life and Death in Shanghai*, New York: Grove Press, 1986.
4. "Resolution on Historical Questions." Adopted by the 6th Plenary Session of the 11th Central Committee of the Communist Party of China. *Xinhua*, Beijing, June 30, 1981. In *Foreign Broadcast Information Service—China* (FBIS-CHI), July 1, 1981, K16.
5. An example of this was the famous Da Zhao in Huhehot, Inner Mongolia, a Ming Dynasty period Sino-Tibetan style monastery which I visited in 1982 only to find that it had been turned into a hat factory and its Great Hall of the Sutras converted to a warehouse. I have written elsewhere of the several days which I spent looking for the 100-year-old Catholic Church of St. Francis of Assisi in Xi'an, Shaanxi Province. The Church building proper had been returned to the local Catholics but it was almost impossible to locate because a meat processing plant had been built directly in front of it during the Cultural Revolution. See, James T. Myers. "The Catholic Church: An Eyewitness Report." *Commonweal*, October 7, 1983, 525ff. Even as late as the summer of 1990, the external ornamentation of the St. Ignatius Cathedral at Ziccawei [Xujiahui] in Shanghai had not been repaired or replaced.
6. *Xinhua*, Beijing, August 31, 1966; SCMP, September 6, 1966. Also see, Desmond Forristal, *The Bridge at Lowu: A Life of Sister Eamon O'Sullivan* (Dublin: Veritas, 1987). Bush describes the sisters as French. Fr. Bernard J. Shields, S.J., gives them as seven French and one Irish [private correspondence with the author], while Fr. Angelo S. Lazzarotto describes them as one French, and the others from Canada, Italy, Switzerland, England, Poland, Greece and Ireland. [Private correspondence with the author.]
7. See Richard C. Bush, Jr., *Religion in Communist China, op. cit.*, 165–167. Bush gives Sister Eamon's age as eighty-five. Fr. Angelo S. Lazzarotto, however, citing Fides News Agency reports, gives her age as fifty-nine. [Private correspondence with the author, January 1991.]
8. *Xiaoling: Memoirs*, 112–114.
9. *Xiaoling: Memoirs*, 148–149.

10. Unpublished manuscript in the author's possession.

11. I have these statistics from a prolonged series of interviews with the dean of the Faculty of Law (a program which had not existed before 1980) at Shanxi University, Taiyuan, Shanxi Province, August–December 1982.

12. See Angelo S. Lazzarotto. *The Catholic Church in Post-Mao China.* Hong Kong: Holy Spirit Study Centre, 1982, 17 *ff.*, 43 *ff.* Also *cf.*, Bob Whyte. *Unfinished Encounter op. cit.*, 344–345.

13. *Xiaoling: Memoirs*, 178.

14. *Tang: Memoirs*, 135.

15. *Ibid.*, 137.

16. Interview with Archbishop Dominic Tang Yi-ming, S.J. Our Lady of Mepkin Trappist Monastery (South Carolina), May 25, 1986.

17. *Tang: Memoirs*, 139.

18. *Ibid.*, 142.

19. *Ibid.*, 144–145.

20. See James T. Myers. "The Catholic Church: An Eyewitness Report." *Commonweal.*, *loc. cit.*

21. Fox Butterfield. *China: Alive in the Bitter Sea.* New York: Bantam, 1983, 423.

22. L. Ladany, S.J. *The Church in China Seen in December 1983.* Hong Kong: privately circulated. 4.

23. *Tang: Memoirs*, 140.

24. *Ibid.*, 140–144.

25. Private correspondence in the author's possession.

26. I have written elsewhere about the very unpleasant confrontation with various university and party authorities which resulted from my eventually successful attempt to meet a Catholic priest who was teaching at the university where I lived during part of 1982–83. See James T. Myers, "The Catholic Church: An Eyewitness Report." *Commonweal*, (New York), October 7, 1983, 528ff.

27. For a detailed discussion of these meetings see, Angelo S. Lazzarotto. *The Catholic Church in Post-Mao China, op. cit.*, 35–38. Also *cf.* L. Ladany. *The Catholic Church in China, op. cit.*, 35–36; Bob Whyte. *Unfinished Encounter, op. cit.*, 346–347.

28. *Xinhua*, Beijing, May 22, 1980.

29. *Xinhua*, Beijing, May 31, 1980.

30. Father Lazzarotto gives them as Francis Han Ting-pi [Shanxi], Paul Teng Chi-chou [Sichuan], Mathias Duan In-ming [Sichuan], and Archbishop Francis Wang Xueming [Inner Mongolia]. There were in addition to these men, five other "senior" or legitimate bishops still living at the time of the conference: Bishops Dominic Tang and Ignatius Kung who were still in prison (though Bishop Tang would be released one week following the end of the conference), and Bishops Anthony Chow Wei-tao [Shaanxi], Peter Joseph Fan

Xueyan [Hebei] and Melchior Chang K'o-hing [Hebei], all of whom were out of prison and enjoying some degree of personal freedom. See: *The Catholic Church in Post-Mao China, op. cit.*, 71, note 16.

31. *Ibid.*, 36; Ladany, *The Catholic Church in China, op. cit.*, 36–37.
32. This body is also sometimes referred to as the National Catholic Church Affairs Committee or the National Catholic Religious Affairs Committee.
33. Gerald Chan, "Sino-Vatican Diplomatic Relations: Problems and Prospects," *The China Quarterly* (London), December 1989, 821.
34. Bob Whyte. *Unfinished Encounter, op. cit.*, 346.
35. A Document of the Central Committee of the Communist Party of China, *Chung-fa* (1982) no. 19: "The Basic Position on and the Policy Toward the Religious Problem During the Socialist Period in Our Country." *Issues & Studies*, Taipei: Institute of International Relations, August 1983, 72–90.
36. *Ibid.*, 82–83.
37. "Our Party's Basic Policy on Religious Questions During the Period of Socialism," *Hongqi* editorial, Beijing, June 1, 1982; FBIS (JPRS 81504), August 11, 1982, 1–13.
38. *Ibid.*, 5.
39. *Ibid.*, 6.
40. *Ibid.*, 5.
41. *Issues and Studies, loc. cit.*, 80–81.
42. FBIS, *loc. cit.*, 6.
43. *Ibid.*, 8.
44. *Ibid.*, 10.
45. *Ibid.*, 3, 6.
46. *China: Prisoners of Conscience in the People's Republic of China*. New York: Amnesty International, 1987, 4.
47. *Ibid.*, 5, 36–37.
48. *Ibid.*, 15–16.
49. See above, note 44.
50. *National Catholic News Service*, Peking [Beijing], February 2, 1988.
51. *National Catholic News Service*, Shanghai, August 9, 1988.
52. *Sunday Examiner*, April 6, 1984.
53. *National Catholic News Service*, Vatican City, May 12, 1989.

TEN

ROME AND BEIJING
ON THE ROAD TO RECONCILIATION?

May the great and wise people of China, who first received the faith
from without, seek, as true Chinese, to live that faith in full communion with the universal Church, to the joy and enrichment of all.

Pope John Paul II
Seoul, Korea
May 6, 1984[1]

On April 28, 1981, Bishop Dominic Tang Yi-ming, recovering
in Hong Kong from major surgery several months earlier,
made a brief journey to Manila at the invitation of Cardinal
Jaime Sin. From Manila he flew to Rome, arriving on April 30,
to make his *ad limina* visit to the Holy Father. This was the first
time he had had an opportunity to make such a visit since his
appointment as apostolic administrator of Canton thirty years
earlier. On June 5, 1981, Bishop Tang was informed by Vatican
officials that the Pope had decided to name him Archbishop of
the Canton Diocese. Bishop Tang, declaring his unworthiness,
accepted this post in writing.[2]

On June 11, Bishop Yang Gaojian, speaking for the CCPA,
denounced the appointment as "illegal," and accused the Vatican once again of interference in the sovereign affairs of the
Catholic Church in China. "The Holy See," said the CCPA
statement, "has always adopted a hostile attitude toward the
Chinese people; it has resorted to various kinds of means to
subvert and sabotage the New China."[3] Several other official
attacks on the Archbishop followed, and on June 22 a meeting

of some seventy Catholics in Canton, presided over by the head of the Canton city CCPA, "dismissed" Dominic Tang from his office as Bishop of that diocese.

What had been seen by many as a possible opening for the betterment of relations between Beijing and Rome had come to an unhappy end. Archbishop Tang decided to remain in Hong Kong.

The Case of the Archbishop

Several months after his release from prison in Canton, Bishop Dominic Tang was diagnosed as having cancer. At the urging of members of his family living in Hong Kong, he applied for permission to leave the country for medical treatment. Before this permission was granted, he was summoned from the hospital by the local CCPA officials to attend a meeting at the Shek Shat Catholic Cathedral. The meetings, which were held on October 8 and 9, 1980 addressed basically two questions: does the diocese of Canton need a bishop, and is Dominic Tang Yi-ming worthy to be that bishop? Approximately fifty to sixty people took part in the discussions which included priests, sisters, lay Catholics and representatives of the CCPA. At the end of the deliberations, the local Religious Affairs Bureau declared, "As the members of the meeting have unanimously agreed that Tang Yee-ming [Tang Yi-ming] should be Bishop of Canton, our government also agrees to this."[4]

Following the October meetings, Bishop Tang returned to the hospital where he remained for about one month. He then took up residence at Shek Shat and resumed his pastoral duties while awaiting permission to leave China for medical treatment in Hong Kong. Permission to leave the country for one year finally arrived in early November, and on November 5, 1980, the Bishop made the short journey to Hong Kong.

Following surgery, Bishop Tang began a several-month period of recovery at the home of his sister-in-law, Mrs. Ruby Tang. He eventually established his residence at Wah Yan College, a Jesuit school for boys in Kowloon.

In February of 1981, Pope John Paul II began a tour of Asia which included stops in the Philippines, Guam, and Japan. On February 18, in a meeting with overseas Chinese at the

Apostolic Nunciature in Manila, the Pope delivered a message to the Catholics of China.[5] Perhaps in response to the anti-foreign emphasis of the "Independent" or "Patriotic" Church in China, the Pope placed special emphasis on the patriotism of Chinese Catholics and on the contributions they might make to national construction. "A genuine and faithful Christian," said the Pope, "is also a genuine and good citizen," and a "good Chinese Catholic works loyally for the progress of the nation."[6] "The Church," said the Pope, "seeks to respect the traditions and cultural values of every people. There is, therefore, no opposition or incompatibility in being at the same time truly Christian and authentically Chinese." The Church, in fact, "encourages her members to be good Christians and exemplary citizens dedicated to the common good and to the service of their fellow man, and collaborating through their personal efforts to the progress of their country."[7] There was no official reaction from Beijing to the Pope's remarks.

The Holy Father made it known that he would like to see Bishop Tang either in Manila or in Japan,[8] but as the Bishop was still not entirely recovered from his surgery, he was not able to make the journey. Instead, Cardinal Agostino Casaroli, the Vatican Secretary of State, made a brief visit to Hong Kong to greet Bishop Tang on behalf of the Pope. Before the Cardinal's departure from Hong Kong, he and Bishop Tang each issued a statement and they conducted a joint press conference. Cardinal Casaroli expressed the hope that the Vatican might be able to engage in a direct dialogue with the Chinese government.[9] As to the central question of the Vatican's continued recognition of Taiwan, the Cardinal suggested that there existed many diplomatic ways to solve the Taiwan question.[10]

The day following the press conference, Bishop Tang reports that Cardinal Casaroli made two requests of him: He wanted the Bishop to "contact the Chinese government [Peking] and to build a bridge," and he asked Bishop Tang to go to Rome to meet the Pope.[11]

Following his return to Rome, Cardinal Casaroli made additional statements to the press concerning the China situation. The episcopal ordinations which had taken place in China without Vatican approval, said the Cardinal, could be considered "valid" as they had been performed by bishops who themselves had been validly consecrated. The ordinations were, however, considered by the Vatican to be "illegitimate" in that they had not been carried out "according to canonical legislation." He added, however, that what was presently considered to be "illegitimate" could, under certain conditions, be made "legitimate" again.[12]

It seems clear from these events that the Holy See perceived an opening for the betterment of relations with the PRC. And there seems to be no doubt that Bishop Tang was considered the "bridge" between the two sides. The Bishop was, after all, a faithful Roman Catholic; no one could doubt this, as he had spent 22 years in prison for his fidelity. In addition, he was not only the legitimate Bishop of the Canton Diocese, he had been accepted as Bishop of the diocese by the local Catholics in Canton, by the CCPA, and by the Religious Affairs Bureau of the government. Surely it was not unreasonable to believe that he might serve as a go-between in some attempt to open a dialogue between Chinese state authorities and the Vatican. The precise explanation for what happened next, however, is not entirely clear.

As indicated above, Bishop Tang flew to Rome, arriving on April 30, 1981. At one o'clock that day, Bishop Tang was received by Pope John Paul II. The Pope gave him a gold Bishop's ring which had been saved for him as a memento of the Second Vatican Council which met while the Bishop was in prison. Photographs were taken, and then the others present withdrew. Bishop and Pope spent about thirty minutes together in private conversation. Bishop Tang has not provided us with any account of the substance of that conversation other than to indicate that the Pope, "showed his concern for me."[13] There was a second official audience with the Pope later that day, and then dinner in the papal apartments where the Pope presented Bishop Tang with, "many medals, rosaries and other sacred articles."[14]

The Bishop visited religious sites in Rome, celebrated Mass in St. Peter's and celebrated Mass in Chinese over Vatican Radio for broadcast to the PRC. Bishop Tang also visited the Embassy of the PRC in Rome where he registered as the "Bishop of

Canton." He was received by the second secretary as the ambassador was in Beijing. When the secretary learned that the Bishop intended to travel to several other countries, he invited him to call on the Chinese embassies there if he should require assistance.[15]

From Rome Bishop Tang went to Paris, Lourdes, Dublin, New York, San Francisco, Lisbon and Madrid. He returned to Rome on the evening of June 4, 1981. On June 5, Bishop Tang was summoned and informed that the Pope had decided to name him Archbishop of Canton. This title was, in fact, his due, as prior to 1949, each provincial capital in China had been an Arch Episcopal See. The announcement of the appointment was made the following day.[16]

Here, the issue becomes a bit complex. At the time of Bishop Tang's consecration as a titular bishop in 1951, the Canton Diocese was under the care of an apostolic administrator, Bishop Deswaziere, who was bishop of another diocese. There was, in other words, no residential bishop in the Canton See. Bishop Tang succeeded Bishop Deswaziere as apostolic administrator of the diocese. It was only after his release from prison that Bishop Tang was designated residental Bishop of the Canton Diocese by the Patriotic Church. There is some reason to believe that it was in the context of this latter development, as a gesture of goodwill on the part of the Holy See, that the Pope made his decision to name Bishop Tang Archbishop of Canton. The announcement of the appointment stated that Bishop Tang had been "promoted to the metropolitan See of Canton of which till then he had been the apostolic administrator."[17]

The precise motives for this move on the part of the Holy See have never been made clear, though it has been widely assumed that the Pope's promotion of Bishop Tang was intended to be a friendly—not hostile—gesture toward the Chinese government. It is not known if there had been some prior communication between Beijing and the Vatican the results of which were misunderstood, or if perhaps the entire incident was the result of a failure in oblique communications and a misreading of signals. Whatever the intended motives of the Vatican move, the result was a serious blow to the betterment of relations between the two sides. The Chinese, as we have seen, denounced the appointment as "illegal," attacked the Vatican for interference once again in the internal affairs of the PRC, and attacked Bishop Tang personally in rather harsh terms.

The official Chinese response to the appointment, as indicated above, came from Bishop Yang Gaojian, one of the three individuals who serve as vice presidents of the CCPA, the Administrative Commission of the Catholic Church and the National Catholic Bishops' Congress.[18] Bishop Tang was accused of engaging in activities which harmed the dignity of the Chinese Catholic Church, and the statement asserted that the Bishop's behavior "cannot be tolerated." Bishop Yang Gaojin further vowed that the day was long since past when the Catholic Church in China could be controlled by the Holy See.[19] Several days later, in Canton, the decision was taken, under the direction of the local CCPA, to strip Bishop Tang of his position as Bishop of the Canton Diocese. So vehement was the Chinese reaction to the Pope's action and to the new Archbishop personally, that Archbishop Tang decided to remain in Hong Kong. As of this writing, he has been there nearly ten years now, maintaining a relatively low profile, and hoping one day to be able to return to his diocese.

There is no doubt that many observers were shocked by the intensity and hostility of the Chinese reaction to the Pope's elevation of Bishop Tang to the position of Archbishop of Canton, especially as it was widely perceived to have been an act of goodwill on the part of the Holy See. Clearly, however, the Chinese did not see it in that way. This, then, leaves us with the question, what might the Chinese demand and accept of the Vatican in order to improve relations between the two sides?

The Chinese Position

It is difficult at the outset to know whom to rely on to articulate the position of the Chinese side in this dispute. Should one quote the government's statements, or those of the CCPA, the Administrative Commission and the Bishop's Congress? Though it is difficult to discern any important differences between the Chinese government and the three Catholic groups, the question remains, at least in theoretical form, who speaks for China's Catholics? Indeed, the question itself reveals a part of the problem: this is not simply a religious question, it is also—perhaps predominantly—a political question. Church affairs, activities, and decisions are not directed by religious institutions which are independent of the government. All permitted religious activities are carefully overseen by the government through the various levels of the RAB and the CCPA. On the other hand, there is little evidence, other than impressionistic and anecdotal evidence, which provides any testimony as to what Chinese Catholics themselves think about the Pope, the Patriotics and relations of the Chinese government and the Holy See. This latter point—the views of the ordinary Chinese Catholics, including clergy, and particularly of those who might oppose official or CCPA positions—is certainly not insignificant and we shall return to it later.

In the final analysis though, because they do represent the "official" Chinese view, all that is really available to us to evaluate the subject of Sino-Vatican relations are the published official statements of the Chinese government and those of the officials of the CCPA and the government-controlled church organizations.

The Chinese authorities have continued to insist on "two basic principles" in the area of Sino-Vatican relations:

1) The Vatican must sever the so-called "diplomatic relations" with Taiwan and accept that the People's Republic of China is the sole legitimate government of China.

2) The Vatican should not interfere in the internal affairs of our country, including non-interference in the religious affairs of our country.[20]

The quotations above are taken from an interesting document, known as the "1989 Number Three Document," which surfaced in Hong Kong in the summer of 1989. The document provides a summary and analysis of a report entitled "Strengthening the Work Concerning the Catholic Church Under the New Situation," issued jointly by the United Front Work Department of the Communist Party Central Committee and the Religious Affairs Bureau of the State Council. The 1989 Number Three Document is interesting, not because it breaks any new ground, but because it reaffirms in rather unambiguous language the basic positions expressed by the PRC since the 1950s. Also, the report addresses the issue of the "underground" Catholic Church in China, a topic we shall return to later.

The first condition always put forward by the Chinese government for the improvement of relations with the Holy See is that the Vatican should break diplomatic relations with Taiwan. The Vatican is presently the only state in Europe which maintains full diplomatic relations with the Republic of China on Taiwan. This demand is fairly straightforward: either the Vatican has full diplomatic relations with the Republic of China on Taiwan, or it does not. Either it recognizes the People's Republic of China as the sole legitimate government of China, or it does not. In the real world of diplomacy, however, there are multiple paths to the same result. Though the Vatican has maintained diplomatic relations with Taiwan, the Vatican's "embassy," the *nunciature* in Taipei, the capital of the Republic of China on Taiwan, has not been headed by an ambassadorial-level *pronuncio* since 1971. From that year onward, the *nunciature* has been headed by a relatively low ranking *charge d'affaires*. If this downgrading of the Vatican's diplomatic representation in Taipei was intended as a friendly gesture to the PRC, as most believe it was, the government of the PRC has not responded in kind. Indeed, they continue to insist, as the report quoted above indicates, on the breaking of diplomatic relations between the Vatican and Taiwan as a *prior* condition for any improvement in relations between Rome and Beijing.

Though the "two Chinas" issue is a complex one in international law, diplomacy, and organizations, this complexity has not prevented most of the advanced nations of the world from devising formulas for dealing with it. The United States, for example, broke diplomatic relations with the Republic of China on Taiwan in 1979, and exchanged ambassadors with the PRC. This has not, however, prevented the United States from engaging in a full range of contacts with Taiwan in the ensuing years. Both nations established private organizations which function as embassies in Taipei and Washington. A number of other nations have adopted the same formula. A way was found for Taiwan (which still considers itself to be the government of

China) to compete in the Olympic Games in Los Angeles and in Seoul, and in the Asian Games as well, including the Asian Games held in Beijing in 1990. There are ways, therefore, around the "two Chinas" problem, assuming that the parties involved want to seek out those ways.

There are, of course, problems for the Vatican which would result from the breaking of relations with Taipei. Consideration would have to be given as to how such a move would impact on the Catholics of Taiwan. The Holy See would probably also want to consider the effect such a move would have on those Catholics in China who have remained faithful to Rome and who have suffered for this fidelity. In the end, though, this is probably a problem which is soluble, though it is certainly not one for which there are either quick or easy answers. One further big question which remains to be answered, however, is whether the government of the PRC would want to have a permanent papal representative in Beijing, even if the Vatican should meet the most stringent prior conditions which the Chinese might demand. On this point there is no clear answer, though one suspects that such a presence might be unacceptable to at least some elements of the Chinese leadership.

The second set of Chinese demands, those involving "non-interference" by the Vatican in Chinese affairs, are not so easy to pin down. Precisely what do the Chinese mean by "interference?" Statements on this topic vary greatly. Central to the problem of interference is usually said to be the self-consecration of bishops by the Chinese Church. The Chinese authorities and spokesmen for the CCPA and other church organizations have consistently insisted that the Vatican should have nothing to do with the selection of bishops for the Church in China. As with the "two Chinas" question, however, here too a number of formulas have been advanced which would allow the two sides to compromise if they should genuinely desire to do so.[21]

A related point usually raised in connection with the self-consecration of bishops is the matter of the excommunications announced by the Holy See at the time of the first illicit episcopal ordinations in China in 1958. We have already considered this point briefly in Chapter Eight. There is no doubt that the censure of excommunication was mentioned in the case of these ordinations, though there appears to be no evidence of a "decree" of excommunication having been issued. It is frequently asserted that Pope Pius XII had "threatened" both the consecrators and those who received the consecration with excommunication.[22] There was, in fact, no formal decree of excommunication. Nor was there precisely a "threat" of such. At the time of the ordinations in 1958, the Congregation of Propagande Fide in Rome, the body which has jurisdiction in such matters, sent telegrams to China calling attention to the decree issued by the congregation of the Holy Office on April 9, 1951. The decree stated, "The bishop of whatever rite or dignity who confers episcopal consecration on a clergyman who has not been nominated by the Holy See, or expressly confirmed by the same, and also the person who receives such consecration, even though under duress, are subject *ipso facto* to excommunication *specialissimo modo* reserved to the Holy See."[23] These matters were treated at length by Pope Pius XII in his 1958 encyclical *Ad Apostolorum Principis*, whereas with the Propaganda Fide statement, the Pope does not declare that any individual has incurred excommunication.[24] While it cannot be denied, as some writers have suggested,[25] that the matter of the excommunications remains a sore point with some Chinese Catholics, it is not clear that there are actually excommunications which need to be lifted.

Beyond the question of the self-consecration of bishops, however, the concept of "non-interference in the religious affairs" of China becomes rather murky. What, exactly, do the Chinese authorities have in mind with this demand? In the most general sense, the Chinese authorities seem to want the Holy See to accept the government-controlled Church in China without complaint or reservation: to accept the bishops, to accept the Patriotic priests, to accept in the fullest sense a Catholic Church in China which is truly independent and autonomous. As to the question of what sort of influence, if any, the Pope might have in this independent church, the Chinese position is not entirely clear. In contrast to the earlier position that Chinese Catholics could obey the Vatican in "matters of dogma and morals,"[26] Chinese spokesmen have more recently generally insisted on total hierarchical independence. One of the most articulate spokesmen for this official position has been Jin Luxian, a former Jesuit who was elected by the Patriotic Church first as auxillary Bishop and then Bishop of the Shanghai Diocese. In a well-publicized address delivered in West Germany in 1986, Bishop Jin asserted that all local Catholic Churches and all bishops, including the Bishop of Rome, should be equal:

> A diocese is a local church in the full sense of the word; a regional, a national, a continental church is likewise a local church. Cologne is a local church as is Shanghai. The diocese of Rome is likewise a local church as are the Italian church, the Asian church, the European church, the Slav church.
>
> The relationship between the local churches must therefore be: *koinonia*, communion, mutual love, respect, help, no crude interference. No local church should oppress other churches.[27]

These remarks were delivered by Bishop Jin when he was still auxillary Bishop of the Shanghai Diocese, and at a time when he insisted that he was not a member of the CCPA. Subsequently, he was elected Bishop of the diocese and became president of the Shanghai CCPA. At a study meeting for members of the CCPA in 1988, Bishop Jin sounded much the same theme:

> Our church is not a Patriotic church, but a Catholic church which is in union with the universal church. Our church is very influential. Rome highly esteems our three million Catholics in China. It fears we may influence the whole world because the Catholic Church throughout the world is demanding from Rome freedom to govern the local church. Consequently, Rome wants to oppose us and cut down our influence.[28]

The full text of this important address is included as Appendix One at the end of this chapter.

Other Chinese officials have not attempted to couch their views in such sophistocated rhetoric. In an interview given in February 1990, Lu Junqi, Chief of the Catholicism Section of the State Council's Bureau of Religious Affairs, was asked what laws had been broken by Catholics who had recently been arrested [see below]. He replied, "It is illegal for them to be loyal to the Vatican. They should abide by state laws and follow principles of independence."[29]

One further point which Bishop Jin addressed in his remarks to the Shanghai CCPA, and a topic addressed in the Number

Three Document as well, is the Vatican's support for those Catholics, especially priests and bishops, who have remained loyal to the Pope. Even more important, perhaps, is the official distress with what the Chinese authorities see as the Vatican's support for the "underground" Catholic movement in China, a movement which has grown sufficiently large in recent years that it can no longer be ignored.

The Roman Catholic Faithful

One of the results of the opening of China to the outside world since 1979–1980 has been the tremendous amount of contact Chinese Catholics have had with Catholics from abroad. Chinese Catholic churchmen have traveled the world attending meetings, seminars and the like, though this sort of travel and contact has been limited to trusted clergy such as Bishop Jin. More important, perhaps, has been the steady stream of Catholic visitors to China. Cardinals and bishops have visited China since 1980, as well as a small army of priests, religious and lay Catholics. What these visitors have seen of the Church in China has to a considerable degree been shaped by what they were looking for, though sometimes it has also been limited by what they were permitted to see. Not all visitors have been equally well prepared to observe the situation of the Church in China, or of religion and religious freedom in general, under the special political conditions which exist in a political system like that of the PRC. Thus, reports on the condition of the Church carried back out of China by these observers have varied greatly.

One point which has been clear to experienced observers, however, is the existence of large numbers of Chinese Catholics, clergy and laity, who have remained faithful to the Holy See in Rome. Of course, such fidelity is what got most of them put into the prisons and labor camps in the first place, so one does not expect to find these faithful Catholics announcing their fidelity indiscriminately to strangers. There have been many visitors to China, however, who have returned to places which they know—especially Chinese priests who have returned to their ancestral homes—or visitors who have returned to see people they knew, or individuals who have somehow gained the trust of the local Catholics. Few such visitors to China have come back without moving stories of the faith and of the fidelity of large numbers of Catholics to the Holy Father in Rome.

The "catacombs" quality of much of religious life in China has thus given rise to something of a dispute as to the size, or even of the existence, of such a community of Catholic faithful. One scholar, for example, writing recently in a major academic journal, put it this way:

> Some observers say that the Chinese Church is split into an open church which defies the authority of the Pope and the "underground church" whose followers supposedly "remain loyal" to him. However, others reject this dichotomy, saying that such an alleged "schism" does not exist, nor is it helpful for the rapprochement between the Chinese Church and the universal Church.[30]

Helpful or not, it is pointless, even foolish, to deny the existence of this "loyal" church in China. But the problem is not even as simple as two competing churches, one loyal to Rome, the other under the control of the Patriotics. The Catholic Church in China is a church of at least four parts.

There are, first of all, devoted and committed members and adherents of the CCPA. As far as we can tell, two of the leading spokesmen for the official church, Bishop Aloysius Jin Luxian of Shanghai and Bishop Michael Fu Tieshan of Beijing, who is also married and in office, are examples of such CCPA loyalists.

Second, there are priests and bishops who have cooperated with the CCPA, but who remain loyal to Rome. Many such examples are known to church-watchers in Hong Kong as well as by personal contacts with visitors to the PRC. A number of priests called by CCPA election to serve as bishops have sent word through Hong Kong to request permission from the Holy See to accept consecration. I had a long interview with one such Bishop (though he did not know that I knew the story of his consecration) and saw on his finger the episcopal ring which had been sent to him by the priest in Hong Kong, who had served as the intermediary with Rome.[31]

Underscoring the point of the loyalty to Rome of many Patriotics, there came to light in the fall of 1988 an extraordinary statement by Bishop Ma Ji of the Ping Liang Diocese in Gansu Province. Bishop Ma was ordained a bishop in March 1987 by

Patriotic Bishop Zhang Wenbin of the Daili Diocese of Shaanxi Province.[32] Bishop Ma was a member of the CCPA, of the Administrative Commission, and of the Bishops' Conference. On August 14, 1988, the Feast of the Assumption, he sent to the various religious and governmental departments concerned, a statement denouncing the "three organizations"—the CCPA, the Bishops' Conference, and the Administrative Commission—and announcing his resignations.[33] Bishop Ma indicted the three organizations on five points: 1) Many of the leaders of the three organizations have violated the rule of celibacy. These people were described by Bishop Ma as "proud and arrogant" men who had "trampled under foot" the rules of the Church and the vows they made to God. 2) The most powerful leaders of the three organizations "deny the primacy and authority of the Pope, Bishop of Rome and successor of St. Peter," the man chosen by Jesus as the leader of the twelve apostles. 3) The CCPA claims to be a "bridge" between the government and the people, but the "unfaithful" behavior of its leaders has caused a "counterreaction" among the people to the appeals to love the country and love the Church. The malefactors controlling the CCPA, said Bishop Ma, "are holding the chalice with their right hands while their left hands are embracing their wives." Believers, said the Bishop, "need only a little common sense to see through their aims and intentions." 4) The CCPA is an instrument of "class struggle" left over from the 1950s. It is irrelevant in the 1980s, but only the CCPA cannot "yet see the light of reform." What we still see, said the Bishop, "is the same old faces standing in the front line of the struggle movement." The leading members of the three organizations "relentlessly impose their infidelities on the heads of the Catholics." 5) The matter of property confiscated from the Church in the 1950s has been very badly handled. The three organizations are no help to the Church at all. "All the Patriotic Associations, Religious Affairs Committees, Episcopal Conferences do nothing to help. It is better for them not to exist than for them to have the name of their existence."

It is interesting to note that the Bishop did not attack the Chinese government in his statement. On the contrary, his remarks suggested that the Chinese Catholics would be better citizens without the existence of the three organizations. And he affirmed his support for the "Four Cardinal Principles"—what he called the Four Basic political principles—of Deng Xiaoping's reform movement. [These are: 1) the leadership of the Communist Party, 2) adherence to the Socialist road, 3) the people's democratic dictatorship, and 4) Marxism-Leninism-Mao Zedong Thought.]

The Bishop's remarks suggest a serious problem within the CCPA. The power of these three organizations, according to Bishop Ma, "in each place, is every day becoming weaker and more fragmented: these bodies are increasingly isolated and paralyzed. They have lost their attraction and become very unwelcome." The full text of this interesting and important statement is reproduced as Appendix Two of this chapter.

Third, there is a large group of loyal Catholics, largely lay people, though also including some priests and religious, who have not associated with the CCPA, but who have also not openly opposed the organization. There are non-CCPA priests whose loyalty is to Rome but who continue to celebrate Mass in churches which are under the control of the CCPA. Likewise there are large numbers of loyal Catholics who continue to receive the Sacraments in these churches but who avoid receiving them—especially the Sacrament of Reconciliation (confession)—from those priests whom they regard as unreliable.[34]

Finally, there is the underground Church which is not only loyal to Rome, but defiantly so. In the past there has been some dispute as to the existence of this underground Catholic movement, or of its significance if it did exist. There can be little doubt any longer that such a movement does exist and that it is growing. The 1989 Document Number Three devotes considerable attention to the underground movement which it says has seriously affected "social stability." Document Number Three gives this definition of the movement: "The underground forces of the Catholic Church are the Holy See, the bishops secretly appointed, the priests ordained by these bishops, and the leading persons directed by them." The authors of Document Number Three even distinguish between the underground activists and those grouped under point three above, those disaffected loyalists who are not underground activists:

> One should pay attention to distinguish the underground force and those of the clergy who on account of their belief in the Pope are estranged from us. One should also distinguish between the activists of the underground force and those Catholics who have been influenced and controlled by them. The majority of the mass of Catholics should be united through painstaking work. The activities of the underground forces should be watched in all places.

Bishop Ma, in his attack on the "three organizations," also made reference to the underground movement. "The division within the Church in Gansu Province," he said, "is very great and well-known: it becomes more extensive and serious. The power of the 'underground' believers is now well-known and has won the trust and support from most of the Catholics."[35]

Shanghai Bishop Jin Luxian, in his address to the CCPA quoted above, also expressed great concern about the underground movement:

> Now, inside the country, in some regions, the power of the "underground" element is very strong. In Hopei [Hebei] Province, there are nearly 1 million Catholics. But the Catholics who belong to the "underground" Church are more than those who follow us. There are also "underground activities" in Tianjin, Shansi [Shanxi], Shensi [Shaanxi], Gansu, etc., and these are spreading southward.[36]

Bishop Jin complained that, while Catholics go to pray at the Three Holy Shrines at Zose [Sheshan], "they do not want to go into the Church," which is controlled by the CCPA.[37] Bishop Jin criticized the Holy See, claiming that the Pope "supports the underground Church and has appointed many underground bishops. According to what I know, there are nine underground bishops in Hopei [Hebei]. In Foochow [Fuzhou] there is someone who calls himself the 'big bishop' of four provinces. In many other places, he has also secretly appointed underground bishops."[38] If Bishop Jin's figure of nine underground bishops is correct for Hebei Province, it is indeed extraordinary as there are only four government-approved bishops in the province.[39] Many observers claim, in fact, that there are more underground bishops than there are those bishops approved by the government.[40] The number of China-appointed bishops is usually given as approximately fifty for the 139 reorganized dioceses.[41] The precise number of underground bishops is unknown, but one Catholic source places the number at fifty to sixty, and suggests that the number "continues to increase."[42]

The underground Church, then, is not a mirage or a figment of an over-active imagination. Moreover, it is apparently perceived as a significant problem by China's civil and religious authorities.

New Confrontations

In September 1988, Cardinal Jozef Tomko, prefect of the Vatican Congregation for the Evangelization of Peoples, sent to the bishops of the world a letter and a confidential document entitled, "Directives on Some of the Problems of the Church in Continental China." The document, which was prepared at the direction of the Pope and approved by him, was said to, "reply to some requests which Chinese bishops have repeatedly made of the Holy See."[43] Cardinal Tomko's letter advised that contacts between foreign and Chinese Catholics be marked by "fraternal charity," but cautioned against actions by visitors which would seem to imply recognition of the legitimacy of the CCPA. The document reaffirmed the Catholic position on the primacy and authority of the Pope as successor to St. Peter, and addressed the three questions raised by the existence of the "independent" Patriotic Church: The excommunication of the China-apppointed bishops, the validity of sacraments administered by Patriotic priests, and the legitimacy of the newly-opened seminaries operated under the control of the CCPA.

On the first point, the document repeats the formula discussed earlier, that the ordinations do not appear, *per se*, to be invalid, but that they are considered gravely illicit, and that those involved have incurred a *latae sententiae excommunication* reserved to the Holy See. The matter of such *latae sententiae* or "automatic" excommunications has been the subject of considerable controversy, especially as they remain publicly ineffective until they are "declared." They remain, that is, in essence a matter of conscience: those involved "know" that they have been excommunicated, though no formal decree has been issued.[44]

On the second point, the document presumes that the sacraments administered by Patriotic priests are valid, but Catholics are directed "to look for priests who have remained faithful."[45]

On the question of the legitimacy of the seminaries, the document reaches no firm conclusion. It suggests, rather, that if there is no other way for the formation of candidates to the priesthood, including private training, then candidates could be sent to CCPA-controlled seminaries, but only if the "general orientation and formation imparted there follow the teaching and directives of the Church." The document adds that the situation should be evaluated "according to local circumstances," including an evaluation of the individuals who direct the seminaries.[46] This cannot be said to amount to a very strong endorsement of the CCPA-controlled seminaries in China.

Cardinal Tomko's document, though issued as "confidential," became quickly known and circulated around the world, including China. As might have been expected, the Chinese authorities did not react favorably to this Vatican directive. In May 1989, approximately eight months after the document was issued, Anthony Liu Bainian, a vice president of the Church Administrative Commission, told the press in Hong Kong that issuing the document "was not a sensible move," and that it "invited bad consequences."[47] The official called on the Vatican to renounce the document, asserting that such renunciation, "may be perceived as the Vatican's concrete step indicating its good will to improve bilateral relations."[48]

In another interesting development in May 1988, Pope John Paul II elevated Bishop John Baptist Wu Cheng-chung of Hong Kong to the rank of Cardinal. Hong Kong had not previously had a cardinal; no other Chinese had been named a cardinal since the death of Cardinal Yu Pin in 1978. Cardinal Wu, a native of Guangdong Province, who has served as a priest from many years in Taiwan, was seen as a natural bridge-builder to the mainland church. Bishop Jin, however, said in an interview in Hong Kong that he believed the appointment, "showed the Vatican misunderstood the situation in China."[49] And in his address to the Shanghai CCPA, Bishop Jin declared:

> In the future we shall be "one country, two systems." Hong Kong governs Hong Kong, mainland China governs mainland China. We

respect each other, we do not interfere (with) each other, we do not belong to each other. Wu Cheng-chung cannot be a member of the mainland China Episcopal Conference, so how can he carry out a function as a bridge?[50]

Cardinal Wu's usefulness as a bridge-builder may, therefore, be somewhat questionable. It will be interesting to see how the relationship develops after the PRC assumes control over Hong Kong in 1997.

The year 1989 was a year of great turmoil in China with events leading up to the bloody clash between demonstrators and the People's Liberation Army in Tiananmen Square on June 4. It was a year of important developments for the Catholic Church as well. Let us recall that Bishop Ma's attack on the "three organizations" was made in mid-August 1988. Cardinal Tomko's document was issued in September 1988 and was apparently rather quickly circulated inside China. Bishop Jin's rallying call to the Shanghai CCPA, which we have cited above and in Appendix One of this chapter, was delivered in December 1988. In March 1989, the Party Central Committee and the State Council of the government issued the 1989 Document Number Three.[51] The reader will remember that the 1989 Document Number Three asserted in no uncertain terms the "independence" of the Catholic Church in China from the authority of the Holy See. At the end of March 1989, the Chinese Bishops' Conference met in Beijing. In contrast to the clear message of the Number Three Document, the bishops agreed on three points: 1) the Pope must be recognized as the head of the Church, 2) the Bishops' Conference should take over direction of the affairs of the Church in China, and 3) married bishops should no longer be allowed to be members of the Bishops' Conference or of the Church Administrative Commission.[52]

This extraordinary development, taken together with later events, was indicative not only of the level and extent of disaffection with the CCPA management of church affairs, but also of a belief that a new atmosphere of openness permitted such dissent from clearly articulated party and government positions. We would later see the same attitudes regarding the possibilities for dissent played out on a much larger stage with the massive demonstrations by students and others in Tiananmen Square during May and early June 1989.

Some time around March 1989, a document began circulating in China which recorded an interview with Bishop Peter Joseph Fan Xueyan of the Baoding Diocese of Hebei Province. Bishop Fan had been paroled from prison in November 1987. In the interview, Bishop Fan addressed the question of the validity and legitimacy of the CCPA-run Catholic Church in China. The Bishop took a much harder line than had Cardinal Tomko's Congregation for the Evangelization of Peoples, asserting, for example, that Catholics who receive the Sacraments from Patriotic priests commit sin.[53]

As might be expected, not all of the confrontation was rhetorical. On April 18, 1989 some 5,000 police and public security troops raided underground Catholics in the village of Yutong, near the city of Shijiazhuang in Hebei Province. The target of the raid, which was described as a "savage bloodbath," was a group of some 1,500 loyal Roman Catholics who reside in the village.[54] These Catholics had apparently erected a large tent on the site of the Catholic Church which had been destroyed during the Cultural Revolution. Masses had been conducted there every day despite the efforts of the local authorities to put an end to the practice. Government officials at first were silent about the event, but later confirmed that the attack had taken place. Anthony Liu Bainian, the government spokesman who protested the Cardinal Tomko document, denied, however, that there had been heavy casualties among the villagers.[55] Amnesty International reported that 32 Catholics were arrested in the raid. They also reported two villagers beaten unconscious by the police who had still not recovered consciousness by late June, and were not expected to live. The same organization reported widespread arrests throughout Hebei Province during this period, with nineteen people arrested in the Handan Diocese, nineteen others arrested in the Xingtai Diocese, and twenty arrested in the Shijiazhuang Diocese. All of the arrests were apparently made in connection with underground Church activities.[56]

The spring of 1989 was a period of great turmoil in China. People around the world watched, some with hope, all with fascination, the building confrontation in the center of Beijing during the month of May, and all witnessed as well, the tragic denouncement of those events. It is, therefore, all the more surprising that, in the aftermath of the bloody clash in Tiananmen Square, a group of Catholics should plan to meet in a clandestine conference for the specific purpose of defying the government's long-standing fiat mandating independence from Rome for the Catholic Church in China.

On November 21, 1989, a group of underground bishops and priests gathered in an unauthorized meeting in the village of Zhangyi, Shaanxi Province. The purpose of the meeting was to establish a Bishops' Conference which would be in full union with the universal Church and with the Holy See in Rome. That a meeting such as a clandestine Bishops' Conference could take place in a political system like that of the PRC is truly remarkable. A meeting of this kind represents an independent, autonomous, and spontaneous association of participants for the purpose of expressing their own interests. We have earlier discussed the fact that in political systems such as the PRC, all such "interest groups" are organized, penetrated, and controlled by the government. The meeting also represents the breakdown of a system of internal control in the PRC which would, in the past, have rendered such a clandestine gathering virtually unthinkable.

There is no evidence that the bishops gathered at the suggestion of the Vatican; on the contrary, it appears that Vatican authorities may have cautioned them against the meeting.[57] Nevertheless, the bishops asserted that, "[I]t is our duty to meet and to create a bond among ourselves; this is essential for the unity and survival" of the Church in China.[58] The conference named three leaders for its new organization: Bishop Peter Joseph Fan of the Baoding Diocese, Bishop Dominic Tang Yiming, S.J. of the Canton Diocese and Bishop Ignatius Kung Pin-mei of the Shanghai Diocese. None of the three was, in fact, available to serve in an active leadership capacity. Bishop Tang was living in exile in Hong Kong, Bishop Kung was living in the United States, and Bishop Fan was arrested again on December 11 and taken away from his residence, possibly for an "inspection tour"[59] of the region. He was reportedly released again in March 1990 but remained under police surveillance.[60]

The government reacted angrily to the meeting. Though the internal control system might have been weakened, it had not disappeared. Participants began to be rounded up in December, and continued to be arrested throughout February. It is probably the case that a number of the arrests which Amnesty International reported from Hebei Province during this period were connected with the clandestine Bishops' Conference. Arrests were reported in the press in January and February, but the government said nothing about an unauthorized Bishops' Conference. The meeting was reported in the Hong Kong *South China Morning Post* which, along with several other sources, reported the arrests of more than thirty priests and bishops who participated.[61] In April 1990, Amnesty International detailed the cases of some 26 Catholics who had been arrested over the previous several months, fifteen others who were arrested earlier, and six who were under house arrest.[62]

The decade which had begun with the opening of the prisons and labor camps and the release of Catholic prisoners, thus ended with the arrests of Catholic leaders and open defiance of the government and the CCPA by Catholics faithful to the Holy See. The cautious optimism with which many observers had viewed the prospects of a reconciliation between China and the Vatican and between the Chinese Catholics and the Holy See, had been replaced by doubt and by the realization that any such true reconciliation would be a long-term process. Prospects for reconciliation had been complicated as well by the unexpected growth and militancy of the underground Church, leaving both the government of the PRC and the Holy See with a very sticky and complex set of problems to unravel.

How all these forces would eventually play out would be anyone's guess. It was clear, however, that no final resolution of the problem was to be quickly or easily found.

APPENDIX ONE
Address to the Shanghai C.C.P.A.
by Bishop Jin Luxian
December 1, 1988
(*Sunday Examiner*, Hong Kong, March 10, 1989)

My brothers and sisters. Today we gather together in this place. As the Bishop of Shanghai Diocese and the president of the Patriotic Association of the locality, it is a great joy for me to talk heart-to-heart with you. I think there is not such a great number of members in other dioceses as in ours.

The first word I want to say is: "Thank you. Thanks to all the leaders. Thanks to all the working-members of the diocese and the Patriotic Association!" Since September 8, 1955, the apostolic work of the Catholic Church in Shanghai, as well as all over the country, has been in a very difficult situation. That the Catholic Church in China has become what it is today is due to your efforts and correct guidance given during these past thirty years. History will prove this judgment to be correct. When the Cultural Revolution began, the Church and the people throughout the whole country suffered very much. Even Mr. Lu Wei-du, etc., who followed closely the footsteps of the Communist party and the People's government from the time of the Liberation, was also "struggled." After the Third Plenum (1978), opposition ceased and normal religious life was restored. Up to the present moment, more than churches have been re-opened in the diocese. East-China Zone Seminary was established. The training of postulants for women's religious congregation was begun. Guangqi Press, Catholic Intellectuals Association, etc. were established one after the other. We have also built a clinic, a chapel to house the remains of the dead, and a foreign languages school. All these achievements have been esteemed by the Church outside, and praised by the Church inside. This flourishing situation was achieved through all your efforts. Therefore, I repeat again, "Thank you."

These developments are expanding all the time and many other things are waiting for our attention. For example, there are many more churches to be re-opened, catechism instruction to be given to young people, other social services to be established. We must also help the faithful to adapt themselves to the present situation, to make them fit to help the progress of China, to hasten the Four Modernizations, to make more contribution in the material and spiritual fields. We must not, because of the above-mentioned achievements, rest on our laurels. Also, at the present time, our self-governing Church is facing a severe challenge. Now, it is the time of reform and openness but there is danger to the traditional culture and morality. People are only concerned for money. The religion of worshipping money and materialism has taken root in many people's hearts. Unhealthy values corrode the mind of the people. Most of the young people pursue material enjoyment and neglect the spirit.

Also, there is a small group of people inside the church in China which, because of their hatred of communism and socialism, secretly contact outside organizations and carry out secret activities under the cover of religion. In order to destroy our real achievements, they have deceived some of the faithful. In order to achieve their purpose, they use any means to invent untruths in order to slander us. In the past, we were taught: "When you are living peacefully, you should be ready for danger; when you are at peace, you should also prepare for danger." Now, we are living in danger, if we delude ourselves into thinking there is peace and not want to face the reality. If we only want to live in peace, then there would be danger added to danger.

The second word I want to say is, "To face the facts and take the right means." The important thing is for us to face the reality of our situation, building ourselves up. Our situation is still good. But danger certainly exists also. If we do not look at the danger in the right way, we will suffer from it. We have to govern the Church well. We ourselves must be the ones to govern the Church. If we do not govern the church and govern it well, other people will surely take over this work and govern the Church themselves. Now, inside the country, in some regions, the power of the "underground" element is very strong. In Hopei Province, there are nearly one million Catholics. But the Catholics who belong to the "underground" Church are more than those who follow us. There are also "underground activities" in Tianjin, Shansi, Shensi, Gansu, etc, and these are spreading southward. Before "September 8," there were 120,000 Catholics in Shanghai. The 20,000 Catholics in Chongming were also incorporated in Shanghai diocese. So, there should be 104,000 Catholics in Shanghai. But this number of Catholics did not go to church at Christmas. Before, there were 10,000 Catholics in Xu Jiahui, but how many go to church now? Some Catholics go to pray at the Three Holy Shrines of Zose but they do not want to go into the Church. Some people are working actively at Jin-shan, Soochow, etc. and make those Catholics who began to go to the church not go any more. One or two people of the "underground" can do very much. What about ourselves who are so many? Are we who form the "visible" Church not so energetic as those of the "underground?" We should see that this danger is a real one.

The enemy attacks and slanders the Shanghai diocese. For example, they spread rumors against Bishop Zhang but their purpose was not to attack him but to overthrow our independent, self-governing, self-supporting Church. Now, there is someone aiming to destroy the authority of the head of our diocese. Is he really attacking me? His intention is rather to overthrow the strength of the lawful patriotic activity of the independent, self-governing, self-supporting Church. On the surface, Shanghai diocese looks calm but in fact, the "underground" movement is carrying out a preparatory work. They have completed their sentences in the labor camp and return to Shanghai but they do not join the diocese. These people are very "united" and are working together. They are nearly eighty years old but they still endure every hardship and continue to work. We must not feel that the days are peaceful. The Vatican uses this kind of strength to oppose us.

The Patriotic Association also faces problems of organizing its activities. Previously, you contributed very much to restoring the Church. Now, you should put first the important work of expanding and protecting the Church. I hope all of you will complete the glorious new task with greater efforts than in the past.

The present tensions cannot be separated from the global situation. Moreover, they cannot be separated from the situation following our country's openness. Our Church is not a Patriotic Church, but a Catholic Church which is in union with the Universal Church. Our Church is very influential. Rome highly esteems our three million Catholics in China. It fears that we may influence the whole world because the Catholic Church throughout the world is demanding from Rome freedom to govern the local Church. Consequently, Rome wants to oppose us and cut down our influence. The present situation is the situation of the end of the 20th century. Every country demands from the Church pluralism, nationalism, and localization. But the Pope in Rome demands absolute obedience under his—one person's—directive and control. Now, every country is establishing Episcopal Conferences. The instruction we received in the past was that Jesus gave His divine power to St. Peter alone. The Bishop of Rome is the successor of St. Peter. The other apostles have no successors. But even before the Vatican Council II, many theologians no longer taught this. They described the Church as the new people of God on its pilgrimage.

The Vatican Council II document "Lumen Gentium" describes the old people of God as Israel which was formed by the twelve sons of Jacob. The Church, the new people of God, also comes down from the twelve Apostles. The successors of the College of Apostles are the Episcopal Conferences. Bishops—apostles. Each bishop should exercise authority. Vatican II explained this point of theology clearly. But the Pope fears this teaching about the Church developing from the twelve Apostles with each country protecting the rights of its church. It uses as its means, the Episcopal Conferences. Episcopal Conferences are meant to balance the absolute and autocratic power of the Pope. But the "monarchists" do not agree. They want the Pope to make the Episcopal Conferences into a consultative committee, not a body with its own authority. Recently, the Holy See issued a document, saying that the Episcopal Conference is only a consultative committee. The Asian Episcopal Conference was the first one to oppose this. Then the American Episcopal Conference also opposed it. Their solemn and just stand won support from the Church all over the world. This struggle is continuing. But the bishops who have been consecrated during the past few years are conservative. The former rector of Notre

Dame University told me that he had said to Pope John Paul II, "In the 16th century, the Pope made a mistake and lost England, East Germany and North Europe. Now, you are making a mistake and losing the Church in China. The influence of the Church is very great. They now choose and consecrate bishops themselves; you should approve them. We Americans also want to choose and consecrate bishops ourselves."

Now, in the Church, the progressive elements and the conservative elements are fighting each other. The cry of every country which wants to be nationalist and independent is becoming louder. Nowadays, it is not enough for the Pope to say "Yes" and everything will fall into place. The Pope's words are opposed everywhere and this opposition is becoming more widespread and outspoken. The Pope of Rome spends his days with great anxiety. Previously, people had not realized this. But now it is different. In Austria, when the Pope appointed a very conservative bishop and auxiliary bishop, the Catholics in Austria held a demonstration-procession. This situation expressing the desire to be independent is widespread. The Pope has a special esteem for the Church in China. According to his words, he wants to restore a relationship with China and asks for the past to be forgotten. The Pope of Rome has never admitted that he has made any mistakes. But the words he uses now are very uncharacteristic. He still wants to treat China in the same way as in the 1940s and 1950s. On the one hand, he says that he wants to restore a relationship with China and on the other hand, he still recognizes Taiwan. He does not want to break from Taiwan. Furthermore, he supports the underground Church, and has appointed many underground bishops. According to what I know, there are nine underground bishops in Hopei. In Foochow, there is someone who calls himself the "big bishop" of four provinces. In many other places, he has also secretly appointed underground bishops. Rome, on the one hand, says that it would not support the underground Church and hopes that it will show itself openly. But on the other hand, it continues to give much money to the underground Christians.

Some people still hold onto the 88-year-old Kung Pin-mei and want him to receive approval from Rome and come back to carry out a new mission. To sum up, their two hands are ready to go two ways. If the negotiations succeed, they would put Kung aside. If the negotiations do not succeed, they will still carry on supporting him. If they do not use Kung, they will use someone else. This shows that the Vatican is playing a game of double-dealing. On the one hand, Rome shows an attitude of trying to improve its relationship with us. On the other hand, it tries hard to help the underground destroy us, who are the official Church. Their slogan is, "Village surrounds city." After surrounding the cities, they will gather all their strength to fight against Peking and then fight against Shanghai. If we do not make any effort, thinking we have gained much credit and supposing that the situation is good, then they will take advantage of us when we are off our guard. Therefore, there is much to be done in the future by our Patriotic Association. We have to know the situation very clearly and have a policy. Previously, because we did not know the situation well or have any policy, the "September 8" happened. Rome thought the communists would not last long. They thought that after a few years, the nationalists in America would return to China. So they asked the former missionaries who were expelled from China to stay in Hong Kong, Macau, and Taiwan, and be ready to return to China. They asked us to resist the communists with all our strength. Some leaders of the Church in China did not understand the situation. In 1951, when I came back to China from abroad, I went to Wang-Jia-du to see Bishop Kung. After kissing his ring, he immediately asked "When will they actually come back?" I said, "After 1957, 1958!" He said it was too long, he could not wait so long. Then, Kung, etc. was the first to stir up the students to oppose and resist the government. Mayor Chen Yi invited him to go to see him but he refused. But when the French Consul invited him for dinner, he accepted.

Now, the Pope has appointed Wu Chang-chung to be cardinal. Some foreign priests coming from overseas were amazed. But the Pope wants him to be the bridge to China. This also is the result of not knowing the situation. When I was in Hong Kong, I said to Cardinal Wu Chang-chung and to the journalists, that we have "one country, two systems." This principle will not change. In the future, we shall be "one country, two systems." Hong Kong governs Hong Kong, mainland China governs mainland China. We respect each other, we do not interfere with each other, we do not belong to each other. Wu Chang-chung cannot be a member of the mainland China Episcopal Conference, so how can he carry out a function as a bridge?

Recently, there was news that the Pope will go to South Korea in 1989, and then he will go to Macau to discuss the problem of China. This shows that the Pope does not understand the situation. With whom will he discuss? How can he discuss? What will he discuss?

We, as members of the Patriotic Association, need to have a very clear understanding of the situation. Otherwise we cannot guide the good Catholics. We have taken the right line in the past. But today the situation is different. I am very busy. Every day I have to read all kinds of newspapers and listen to radio broadcasts. Because I have no time to study, I have made some mistakes and also caused others to make mistakes. Of course, today it is not one person who is guiding the Church but a number of persons governing the Church in a democratic way. We have to love our country. Today, to understand the situation clearly, the important thing is to support the decision of the three church organizations and believe firmly that the government will overcome all difficulties. We have to take the lead in showing confidence that difficulties will be overcome. We have to develop our ideas in harmony with the work of the Patriotic Association.

The work of our Patriotic Association is to contact all the Catholics. We must not be satisfied with finishing with the past and looking forward to the future. We must not be satisfied with speaking about our own experiences. We should see our own inadequacies and should learn from others. We should get accustomed to making contact with all the faithful. There are more than 100,000 Catholics. How many are we in contact with? We have to have our ideas prepared. When there are rumors, we must refute them and retaliate. Otherwise, it will be the same as giving our consent. We must also solve the problems of the faithful. Some other Patriotic Associations have done this very well. We should learn from them. Our efforts are far from satisfactory; the Catholics who go to church are few. There are many reasons for this: some are very busy, others are old and sick, some are still afraid. We should work with patience and delicacy. We should focus our efforts on making contact with the faithful, giving them the correct line of thought. We should be active and put our work first. It is no use giving help when the fire has already destroyed everything, but we should do our work before that happens. When we see the first sparks of a fire, we should make ready. We should inform and help one another. Very often we do not inform and help one another, so we lose our strength. After traveling round the world and seeing many things, I feel that our country is really very good. For the moment, the present enthusiasm for going abroad is only temporary. As the country makes progress, those who study abroad will come back.

The other point is our self-development. As working members of the Patriotic Association, loving the country has a special meaning for us, and we have to help the Church become better. The ideal of the Patriotic Association is to govern the Church well. We are the Catholic Patriotic Association, we are not any other kind of Patriotic association. So the members of the Patriotic Association should put loving the Church in the most important place. Each member should be a fervent Catholic. Otherwise, he had better join another Patriotic organization!

You cannot deceive the people. Priests must be good priests, bishops must be good bishops. This is a basic requirement. So we have in front of us the problem of personal renewal: To love the country and also to love the Church. Recently, a leader of the Protestant Church wrote to another leader, saying, "Protestants inside China and outside China do not have a good impression of the Protestant Three-Self Movement." Therefore, we hope to improve the popular idea of the Patriotic Association. The members of our Patriotic Association are basically good. But in some places inside China and outside, people look at us in a different way, and make our faults prominent. As members of the Patriotic Association, we must give a good impression to those inside and outside the country. Otherwise, it will be a great disadvantage in promoting our activities.

Some people try to slander us, to misrepresent us. The Patriotic Association is needed to help them. Someone said to me, "It is needed today and it will be needed still more tomorrow." It is not enough just to have some old priests and some inexperienced young priests; the Patriotic Association is needed to help them. Someone said to me, "If you want me to go back to the diocese, first of all, bring the Patriotic Association to an end." I certainly did not agree with this. I answered him, "We need the Patriotic Association. We do not need you on your own." Even if in the future, the relationship between China and the Vatican is restored and improved, we must still value the Patriotic Associations. The members of the Patriotic Association should appreciate what they are and try to improve themselves. I solemnly declare in the name of Shanghai dioceses that the Patriotic Association is our most important helper. The more enemies oppose the Patriotic Association, the higher we should raise the banner of the Patriotic Association. In front of us is the work of self-development. We must renew ourselves all the time and continue to raise our standards. Now we are in a time of reform. The situation of the world is evolving, including the area of relationships with the Vatican. The true rulers of the Church are the faithful. And the members of the Patriotic Association represent the most distinguished elements of the faithful. Today I am just "casting a brick to attract jade" just offering a few commonplace remarks by way of introduction so that others may come up with valuable suggestions. We shall say more later when there is an opportunity.

APPENDIX TWO
My Statement
by Bishop Ma Ji of the Ping Liang Diocese
Gansu Province, August 14, 1988
(*Sunday Examiner*, Hong Kong, February 24, 1989)

People still have living remembrance of experience of religious affairs in society after Liberation, something not easily forgotten. The Catholic Church at that time, suffered great tribulation and was in danger of being wiped out during the Cultural Revolution. After the Third Plenum of the Party's Eleventh Central Committee, it is still struggling in the midst of great tribulations. External pressures have ended but the division within becomes more serious everyday and more apparent everyday. This causes very knotty problems for the government's religious policy, problems which seem impossible to solve. The division within the Catholic Church in Gansu Province is very great and well-known: it becomes more extensive and serious. The power of the "underground" believers is now well-known and has won trust and support from most of the Catholics. But the power of the so-called Chinese Catholic Episcopal Conference, Chinese Catholic Religious Affairs Bureau and the "Patriotic Association" (we shall simply call them the Three Organizations) in each place, is everyday becoming weaker and more fragmented: These bodies are increasingly isolated and paralyzed. They have lost their attraction and have become very unwelcome, for the following reasons:

1) Some of the most important leaders of the Three Organizations have abandoned the most essential and basic teachings of the Catholic Church. The chief characteristic of the universal Catholic Church is that its leaders, bishops and priests, have to be seriously and carefully considered and tested before they accept their office. Then they have to make a solemn promise to God that they will persevere in keeping chastity throughout their whole life, that they renounce marriage to live in chastity and willingly serve the Church until death. But now, some of these church leaders have publicly abandoned these rulings. They have given up their vows and trampled them underfoot. They have married and have children. But they still go up to the altar to celebrate Mass, to pray and give absolution to others. They are so proud and arrogant, putting on the appearance of righteous people. This situation began to evolve during the 1950s, when an extreme left policy was being carried out. But now, at the end of 1980s, this situation is still in existence and not corrected. At that time, because of the threat of the extreme leftist policy, the faithful dared not say anything, although they were angry about this development. But now, it is the time of reform, of socialism's greater development, so the situation of religion in society has radically changed. Believers can organize activities publicly, they can speak more freely, they dare to express different opinions and to put an end to disordered behavior and wrong situations. Therefore, seeing the wrong-doing of some of these leading members of the Three Organizations of the Chinese Catholic Church in abandoning the Church's precepts, the whole country has expressed its silent denunciation and public disapproval. We agree that this is perfectly correct and necessary: There is no alternative. No, we also unitedly ask these leading members of the Three Organizations—the married bishops and priests—to take the initiative to resign, to give up all their titles and offices. They must be forbidden to wear religious vestments in carrying out the public liturgy in all the churches. We appeal to the Three Organizations to eliminate completely this element which no longer has any religious significance.

2) The most powerful elements of the Three Organizations arrogantly and freely deny that St. Peter is the leader of the twelve Apostles chosen by Jesus. They deny that St. Peter is the Rock of the Church and that Jesus has built His church on St. Peter, the Rock. Thus it follows that they deny the primacy and authority of the Pope, Bishop, and Rome and successor of St. Peter. They deny that the Pope is infallible when he proclaims a dogma which all Catholics must believe. They give up entirely the principles of the Catholic Church and weaken the precepts and doctrines of the Church. They have lifted up the schismatic banner of the Chinese Catholic Church: "To get rid of the control of Vatican," "and to resist the penetration of

foreign religious powers." They openly declare to the whole world that they deny that the Pope's office as successor of St. Peter gives the right to govern the Catholic Church throughout the world. This rebellious attitude of the leading members of the Three Organizations of the Chinese Catholic Church makes all the faithful Catholics readily stand up to protect the inviolable integrity of the Church's teaching. They are obliged to oppose and have nothing to do with this kind of major rupture and betrayal. The Catholic Church of China has consequently diverged into this present situation of division which is becoming more extensive and more serious as time goes on, causing countless complicated problems for the apostolate.

The basic reason for this split is that the leading members of the Three Organizations of the Chinese Catholic Church adulterate and betray the teaching of the Catholic Church. If these problems are not solved very soon, it will certainly have very harmful consequences on the apostolate, making the leadership half-hearted and indifferent. The bad name of the married bishops and priests, the leading members of the Three Organizations of the so-called Chinese Catholic Church, is well-known inside by the people and outside by the world. Those who belong to that group and have relationship with them also feel embarrassed, and find it hard to speak in their defense.

3) The unfaithful behavior of the leading members of the Three Organizations greatly affects the Patriotic Association's claim to be a bridge. People make propaganda that the Patriotic Association is a political organization of the people, that it serves as a bridge between the government and the Church. But during these thirty years, what believers can see the function of a bridge in the appearance and behavior of these married bishops and priests? They keep a tight grip on the Patriotic Association of the whole country and of every province, city and village. They are "holding the chalice with their right hands while their left hands are embracing their wives." What function as a bridge can they carry out? Believers only need a little common sense and discernment to see through their aims and intentions.

How should believers react to them? They can only keep a distance from them and fear their influence (as they would the devils or ghosts). How could believers possibly listen to their propaganda about loving the country and loving the Church? During these thirty years, they have caused a counterreaction to the appeal of loving the country and loving the Church, a reaction which is much stronger than any response to it. If they were not so strongly upheld by the government, they would have long ago been spurned by the people and would no longer be in existence. As long as they exist, the Catholic Church in China cannot be united. The religious policy of the government will become more and more complicated and impossible to implement. The prestige and good standing of the Party and of the government amongst believers, both inside China and all over the world, will be lessened. For these reasons, we consider that this is the time to solve the problem of this organization: The solution should not be put off.

4) The movements of anti-imperialism and patriotism, the emergence of the Three-self Organizations inside the Catholic Church were all part of the massive campaign of class struggle, anti-imperialism, anti-colonialism, and anti-feudalism at the beginning of the 1950s. It was a movement against foreign imperialism and colonialism in our country's religious and cultural life. Since the Opium Wars, the foreign powers used Western culture and religion to impose their will on China and to incur great guilt in their treatment of the Chinese people. At that time, the movement of anti-imperialism and patriotism inside the Catholic Church took an extremely leftist character. All the foreign missionaries were treated as imperialist elements. All the Chinese priests were treated as struggle instruments and running dogs of the imperialists. Everywhere, the Patriotic Association was the instrument of this struggle-campaign. Consequently, the activities of the Patriotic Association were very well-known by everyone. Their activities had a very great effect on everyone; the people cannot forget this and the very mention of the "Patriotic Association" makes them turn pale.

Now, in the 1980s, the situation of China in the world has greatly changed. Everything has taken on a more human tone. The No. 1 enemies of the people all over the world, American imperialism and Japanese imperialism, have all disappeared. All the old ideas, which were supposed to be inviolable in the 1950s, have been put into the museum. The Thirteenth Plenary of the Seventh People's Congress appealed for "reform, to put reform in every sphere of life." The economic, political, cultural, educational, and every other system is being subjected to spectacular and dynamic reform. The Party and government are now separated; likewise politics and business. The first stage of socialism proposes to establish a socialism with Chinese characteristics, etc. The forbidden zone of "theory" has been opened up. There only remains the "signboard" of the Catholic "Patriotic Association," still hanging high above the heads of all the Catholics. It seems too sacred to touch. Only the Catholics, who are under this heavy signboard of the "Patriotic Association," cannot yet see the light of reform and the new openness, cannot hear the good news of reform and openness, cannot smell the breath of reform and openness. What we hear is still the extreme leftist slogans of the 1950s. What we see is still only the same old faces standing in the front line of the struggle movement. The leading members of the Three Organizations of the Chinese Catholic Church relentlessly impose their infidelities on the heads of the Catholics. Under the Party's slogan: "To reform, to put reform in charge of everything," our heads and minds become clear and we dare to express our views. We will never accept such behavior.

5) At the beginning, when the "Patriotic Association" was established, the cadres of the Religious Affairs Bureau made propaganda and many promises to believers and priests with honeyed and sweet words, putting forward their arguments time and again with ostensibly good intentions, saying "how important it is to establish the Patriotic Association," "how beneficial this will be in practice," etc.

Finally, in the provinces, cities, and villages, the Patriotic Association was successfully established. Most Catholics and priests loyally obey the government and follow its directives.

But, until the end of the 1980s, practical policy in dealing with the landed property of the Catholic Church was very poor. The "Number 188 Document" of the Central Party Office was just like a stone dropped into the sea which disappeared and was never heard of again. In fact, the State Council of the Central Government has clearly pointed out that the practical policy regarding the landed property of religious communities should be dealt with in a special way: "On principle, in dealing with the landed property of a foreign church, it is not for the government to take it back, but according to the development of the Patriotic religious organizations, it should gradually become the possession of the Church in China." "According to the present situation, the time has come for the transfer of the landed property of the foreign churches. It is clear that they belong to the Church in China." "If the rent-income of religious communities is substituted by the government giving money to religious ministers for their living expenses, it will seem as if we have confiscated the landed property of the Church, and will have a bad influence on the government-dominated church. It will also seriously hinder the firm policy of self-support. It will be very unhelpful both politically and in our relationship with the outside world. Therefore, dealing with the rent and properties of religious communities is not a simple economic matter but a political matter, and part of a very important overall policy." "It should be seen from the viewpoint of politics, dealing with it as a special case." "Give back entirely to religious communities their house-properties. If there is no possibility of giving them back, they should pay them back in currency."

This policy of the Central State Council of the Party has not been given enough attention by the people. People do not hear anything more about it. We Catholics believe the party and believe the central policy with sincere hearts but what we experience is completely contrary to what we expect. People do not take the policy of the Central Party and State Council as guiding principles. They act as if they had their own independent rights, they oppress people with their power. They use as an excuse the fact that the country is poor. They use the government's financial deficits as their reason. They exercise their power over the helpless Catholics. The lands and house properties of the Catholic Church become worthless. Not one cent is paid for houses which have been confiscated and used for twenty or thirty years. Very little money is given for houses which have to be pulled down. A house, whether it is good or bad, is worth only $200–300 dollars, even though the government says: "Pay back entirely the house property of the original church of the Catholic Church." The supervisory unit puts the seal on the matter and that is the end of it. They are very satisfied. If any chapels still exist, only the right of property is recognized but the chapels may not be used. They are so kind as to point out a solution for us: Pull the chapels down, or rent or sell them. They also change the appearance of the original buildings of the Catholic Church, embellish them a little, and then sell them as units for approximately $108,000, exorbitantly high prices! But they will only pay the Catholics about $300 for one house as compensation. It is not possible to give all the examples one could. What principles are being followed in this unjust treatment? What reason for this "special treatment" for the lands and buildings of the Catholic Church? The government does not want to have the name of confiscating church properties, but in fact they have confiscated them. They really put us in the situation of having nowhere to go and no people to ask for help. The Patriotic Association, Religious Affairs Committees, and the Episcopal Conferences do nothing to help. It is better for them not to exist than to have the name of their existence. There are plenty of facts to prove the truth of this. Those provinces which do not have these organizations can carry out a very successful religious policy. I wish that those who are in charge of implementing the religious policy of the government would go out and walk around and see these things for themselves.

To sum up all the above-mentioned arguments, we request to be treated from now on in the same way as everyone else. With the identity of ordinary people and as belonging to a Catholic diocese, we fulfill all our lawful obligations and should enjoy all the lawful rights which belong to us. We support the four basic political principles and the policy of reform and openness. As regards all the titles and offices of the present local

Patriotic Association and the Patriotic Association of the whole country, we respectfully dismiss them. We can govern our Church ourselves. We can carry out our religious ceremonies in caves or huts.

The land and house properties of the Church have been taken over by the government. The churches and houses which they have repaired are like pieces of bronze which cannot be given back. This is a problem which has not yet been solved. It seems that it will still exist in the year 2000. The landed and house properties of the Church belong to the Church, they cannot be surrendered. The civil law of the People's Republic of China, Chapter 5, Civil Right Number 77, clearly affirms: "The lawful properties of social communities, including religious communities are protected by the law." Therefore, I send this letter to the Three Organizations of the Chinese Catholic Church and all those departments which deal with religious affairs. I express my own standpoint and opinions. If there is anything in this contrary to the law, I myself take all the responsibility.

NOTES

1. Pope John Paul II. "Wishes for the Chinese People." Seoul, Korea, May 6, 1984; Elmer Wurth, M.M. *Papal Documents Related to the New China 1937–1984* (two volumes). Maryknoll, NY: Orbis Books and Aberdeen, Hong Kong: Holy Spirit Study Centre 1985, 179.

2. *Tang: Memoirs*, 160–164.

3. *Xinhua*—English, Beijing, June 11, 1981.

4. *Tang: Memoirs*, 147–148.

5. Pope John Paul II. "True Christians and Authentic Chinese." Manila: February 18, 1981, in Elmer Wurth, *M.M. Papal Documents Related to the New China. Loc. cit.*, 138–141.

6. *Ibid.*, 139. For a discussion of these events also see, Angelo S. Lazzarotto, *The Catholic Church in Post-Mao China, op. cit.*, 127–131.

7. *Ibid.*, 139–140.

8. *Tang: Memoirs*, 157–158.

9. See, Angelo S. Lazzarotto, *The Catholic Church in Post-Mao China, op. cit.*, 130–131.

10. *Ibid.*; Also see, *Tang Memoirs*, 158–159.

11. *Tang: Memoirs*, 159.

12. See Angelo S. Lazzarotto. *The Catholic Church in Post-Mao China, op. cit.*, 131.

13. *Tang: Memoirs*, 161.

14. *Ibid.*.

15. *Ibid.*, 161–163.

16. *Tang: Memoirs*, 163–165. Also see, Angelo S. Lazzarotto. *The Catholic Church in Post-Mao China, op. cit.*, 132–133; L. Ladany. *The Catholic Church in China, op. cit.*, 38–39; Bob Whyte. *Unfinished Encounter, op. cit.*, 440.

17. Quoted by Angelo S. Lazzarotto. *The Catholic Church in Post-Mao China, op. cit.*, 133.

18. For a discussion of the interlocking structure of leadership of these three organizations see, Gerald Chan. "Sino-Vatican Diplomatic Relations: Problems and Prospects," *The China Quarterly, loc. cit.*, 820–822.

19. *Xinhua*, Beijing, June 11, 1981. Also see Angelo S. Lazzarotto. *The Catholic Church in Post-Mao China, op. cit.*, 133–136, for a detailed discussion of the Chinese response of the appointment of Bishop Tang as the Archbishop of Canton.

20. "Thoroughly Implement the 1989 No. 3 Document of the [General] Office of the Party Central [Committee] on Strengthening the Work Concerning the Catholic Church under the New Situation," unpublished document in the author's possession.

21. A number of such scenarios are suggested in, *The Catholic Church in*

the People's Republic of China. Leuven, Belgium: Pro Mundi Vita International Information and Research Centre. Pro Mundi Vita Studies, no. 15, June 1990, 33–34.

22. See, for example, Gerald Chan. "Sino-Vatican Diplomatic Relations," *The China Quarterly, loc. cit.,* 819.

23. "So-called 'Excommunication of Patriotic Bishops,' April 1958," Elmer Wurth, *M.M. Papal Documents Related to the New China, op. cit.,* article #5, 48.

24. Pope Pius XII. *Ad Apostolorum Principis.* June 29, 1958; in *Ibid..,* article #6, 51–61. This issue is discussed at length in Geoffrey King, S.J. "The Catholic Church in China: A Canonical Evaluation," *The Jurist,* Washington, D.C.: Catholic University 49, 1989, 69–94.

25. See, *ibid.,* 69; also see Gerald Chan. "Sino-Vatican Relations," *loc. cit.,* 819.

26. See above, Chapter Seven.

27. The original German version of this address was published in *China Heute,* (Divine Word Fathers). May-June, 1986. An English translation was published in *Tripod,* (Hong Kong: Holy Spirit Study Centre), No. 36, December 1986, 36–53. I have an English translation in manuscript form courtesy of L. Ladany, S.J. Citations are to this manuscript version. For an analysis of Bishop Jin's address see L. Ladany, *The Catholic Church in China, op. cit.,* 77-81.

28. *Church Bulletin,* Shanghai, no. 7, December 1, 1988, 5–11. Translation in *Sunday Examiner,* Hong Kong, March 10, 1989, 10–11.

29. "Official Confirms Arrests of Catholics," AFP—English, Hong Kong, February 8, 1990. In FBIS-CHI-90-027, February 8, 1990, 14–15.

30. Gerald Chan. "Sino-Vatican Diplomatic Relations," *The China Quarterly, loc. cit.,* 817, note 15.

31. Naturally, much such information is received in confidence, so that the names of those involved cannot be revealed. Many of these stories are sufficiently well-known, however, that I suspect much of the China-watching Catholic community abroad could quickly identify at least the identity of the priest who gave the bishop his ring.

32. *Sunday Examiner,* Hong Kong, February 24, 1989. The newspaper report incorrectly identifies the Dali Diocese as being located in Gansu Province.

33. The text of this statement was first published outside China in a Catholic newspaper, *Shantao Weekly,* Kaohsiung, Taiwan. A number of translations have subsequently been published and the document has been widely circulated. The English citations here are from a translation published in the *Sunday Examiner,* Hong Kong, February 24, 1989, 10–11.

34. See, L. Ladany. *The Catholic Church in China, op. cit.,* 55–57.

35. *Sunday Examiner, loc. cit.,* February 24, 1989, 10.

36. *Sunday Examiner, loc. cit.,* March 10, 1989, 10.
37. *Ibid.*
38. *Ibid.*
39. Gerald Chan, "Sino-Vatican Diplomatic Relations," gives a listing of the names and dates of consecration of all fifty-one government-appointed bishops, *op. cit.,* 832–836.
40. See, for example, L. Ladany. *The Catholic Church in China, op. cit.,* 71.
41. See above, note 39. The precise number varies from time to time, of course, as a result of deaths and new consecrations.
42. Pro Mundi Vita Studies, *The Catholic Church n the People's Republic of China, op. cit.,* 20.
43. This document, though issued as "confidential" circulated widely within a relatively short time. Citations here are to the Pro Mundi Vita Studies, *The Catholic Church in the People's Republic of China., op. cit.,* 23. Though the document was said to have been circulated in September 1988, the copy which I obtained from Fr. Bernard J. Shields, S.J. in Hong Kong, bears the handwritten notation "maggio [May] 1988."
44. This issue is discussed at length in Geoffrey King, S.J. "The Catholic Church in China: A Canonical Evaluation," *The Jurist, loc. cit.,* 89–91.
45. Pro Mundi Vita Studies. *The Catholic Church in the People's Republic of China, op. cit.,* 23.
47. *National Catholic News Service.* Hong Kong, May 18, 1989.
48. *Ibid.*
49. Beatrice Leung, "Chinese Bishop Says Cardinal in Hong Kong Could Create Problems," *National Catholic News Service.* Hong Kong. July 19, 1988.
50. *Sunday Examiner, loc. cit.,* March 10, 1989, 10.
51. The unpublished copy of this document which is in my possession is dated May 9, 1989, but it calls for the "implementation" of the directive which was "recently sent out." Other sources have given the date of the original directive as March 1989. See, Pro Mundi Vita Studies. *The Catholic Church in the People's Republic of China, op. cit.,* 25. The Italian translation of the document, which I have courtesy of Fr. Angelo S. Lazzarotto, gives the source of the document as the United Front Department of the Party Central Committee and the Religious Affairs Office of the State Council, and the date of December 24, 1988. This source further notes that the document was "issued" by the Secretariat of the CCP Central Committee on February 23, 1989.
52. *Ibid.,* 26. The bishops would almost certainly not have seen the "Document Number Three" at the time of their meeting. However, their position was in opposition to the clear and consistent government policy which they would soon see reaffirmed in "Document Number Three".

53. *Ibid.*, 20–22.
54. "Catholics Said Killed, Injured, Arrested in China Attack," *National Catholic News Service*. Hong Kong. April 27, 1989.
55. "China Church Official Says No Casualties in Raid on Catholic Village." *National Catholic News Service*. Beijing. May 4, 1989.
56. Amnesty International. *People's Republic of China: Catholics Imprisoned in China; Recent Arrests and Long-Term Prisoners*. London, April 1990, 7–8.
57. Pro Mundi Vita Studies, *The Catholic Church in the People's Republic of China*. *op. cit.*, 27–28. There are several rather detailed unpublished accounts of this meeting which have reached Hong Kong. I have two courtesy of Archbishop Dominic Tang and Fr. Bernard J. Shields, S.J.: "Message to Bishops, Priests and Lay People of Taiwan, Macau and Hong Kong, Brought by a Catholic From Mainland China on January 1, 1990," and "Do Not Let The Mainland Church Fight The Battle Alone, " which also contains a list of those arrested at the conclusion of the meeting.
58. *Ibid.*, 27.
59. Such "inspection tours" became somewhat common in the aftermath of the Tiananmen confrontation of June 4, 1989. Many of the intellectuals who were rounded up by the government were taken on these tours to demonstrate to them the progress China had made during the ten years of reform. Party authorities apparently believed that if the dissidents saw with their own eyes the results of the reform policies, especially in the rural areas, they would conclude that these authorities were wise and able rulers of the nation.
60. See Amnesty International. *People's Republic of China*. April 1990, *op. cit.*, 6.
61. "Mainland Catholics Seek More Religious Freedom," *South China Morning Post*. Hong Kong. April 3, 1990; in FBIS-CHI-90-016, "Three More Catholic Leaders Arrested," Jan. 23, 1990, 18–19; FBIS-CHI-90-014, "Chinese Leaders Reportedly Arrested," January 22, 1990, 26; FBIS-CHI-90-027, "Officials Confirm Arrests of Catholics," February 8, 1990, 14–15.
62. Amnesty International. *People's Republic of China, op. cit.*

ELEVEN

THE FUTURE OF THE CHURCH IN CHINA

> But the monopoly of all power will not be enough. There remains the old Adam. Unless they can remake the fallen nature of man, the self-elected gods cannot make a heaven of the earth.
>
> Walter Lippmann,
> *The Public Philosophy*[1]

The fate of the Catholic Church in China over the years since 1949 has been closely linked to the twists and turns in Chinese domestic politics. Though the Church has never been treated generously, there have been times of relative calm in which the policies of the government toward religion have been relatively less oppressive. The period since the return to power of Deng Xiaoping in 1978 might be described as such a period. There have, of course, been the clashes with the underground Church which we have described, and the continued imprisonment of the most unreconstructed of the Roman loyalists, but this period has not produced the scale of bloody confrontations which characterized the 1950s.

A somewhat less generous assessment of this period might also point out that most of the biggest loyalist troublemakers from earlier days have been eliminated from the scene. Many were killed or died in prison or in labor camps. Some were released and allowed to leave the country. Some were released only to be re-arrested. In all cases, these loyalists were no longer available to serve as leaders in the opposition to the government and the CCPA. Still, the reform policies of the period of the "Four Modernizations" under Deng Xiaoping have resulted, in general, in policies toward religion and toward the Catholic Church which are less brutal and less repressive than those of the worst years of the 1950s and 1960s. Though the communist government has throughout remained hostile, the day-to-day treatment of the Church has thus shifted with the ebb and flow of domestic political events.

Given the high degree of volatility in Chinese politics, there is no reason to believe that the future course of events will be much different. Policies toward the Church will probably continue to be a reflection of the ideological balance of forces in the domestic leadership structure. But the events of 1989, which culminated in the showdown at Tiananmen Square on June 4, appear to have introduced a new element into the equation. It is now perhaps the case as well that the future of the Church in China is closely linked to the future of the Chinese political system itself. This is no place to attempt an in-depth analysis of the future of the Chinese political system, but perhaps a few suggestive comments may be useful in view of our attempt to link the future of the Church to the fate of that political system.

On the one hand, if the Chinese authorities—specifically, the leaders of the Chinese Communist Party—are able to maintain strong internal, central political control over the activities of the Chinese people, the Catholic Church is probably in for continued hard times ahead. If, on the other hand, as we have already suggested, the level and degree of political control is diminished, and if this development should countinue or even accelerate, then the possibilities for the Church are likely to be quite different. We suggested earlier that already groups within China perceive possibilities for dissent from clear government policies, which previously did not exist. Indeed, the level and degree of central control which exists in a number of areas in China today is considerably less strict than has been the norm throughout most of the life of the PRC.

In the case of the Church, for example, there are areas where the local bishop is receiving substantial assistance from abroad and operating more or less independent of any direct government interference or control. Local officials who might interfere are apparently sympathetic to the bishop or choose to ignore those activities which are not strictly in accordance with established government policy.[2] In other areas, the CCPA and the more orthodox government authorities attempt to maintain a strict degree of control over the activities of the Church. Thus we can already see substantial differences in the application of formal, announced government policies toward the Church from one area of China to another.

This weakening of central control is not the result of deliberate policy decisions taken by the national leadership, it is the unintended consequence of an attempt to decentralize decision-making in recent years. This line of policy has been controversial within the leadership precisely because of the weakening of central control which it has brought. In the same way, Deng's "black cat-white cat" approach to Marxist ideology has been upsetting to his more orthodox colleagues because it creates confusion about the ultimate values of the regime and its future goals. The revolution, after all, was not fought to make China a bastion of market capitalism. Moreover, this casual treatment of ideology, combined with policies encouraging partial decentralization and marketization of the economy, have given rise to the mistaken hope or expectation on the part of many observers, including many Chinese intellectuals, that China was committed to political liberalization and a move toward Western-style democracy. Thus we saw the appearance of the "Goddess of Democracy" in Tiananmen Square and the shock expressed by many, inside and outside of China, when the government resorted to deadly force to put an end to the demonstrations.

In addition to these political problems, China faces a host of other practical problems—social, economic, spiritual, and environmental, to name a few—which are so intractable that any future leadership is going to find them difficult to solve. Included among all these very serious problems is the elementary political problem of keeping the regime together and avoiding disintegration.

The future of the Catholic Church, therefore, is likely to be deeply affected by how the domestic political drama is played out in at least these three problem areas: leadership, ideology, and organization or performance.

Leadership

When we consider the armed assaults against the underground Church, the killing in Tiananmen Square, the harsh crackdown which followed the demonstrations of summer, 1989, and the ensuing nationwide effort to subject Chinese intellectuals to ideological re-education, we must ask: what happened to Deng Xiaoping, the moderate reformer on whom so much hope rested? Much of the hope for improvement in relations between Beijing and Rome was aroused by an image of Deng as a moderate reformer which was very much encouraged by the Western press since the time of his re-emergence as China's top leader in 1978.

This image of Deng emerged during his years as an opponent of the radical policies of Mao Zedong and his followers. But while Deng may not have been a believing Maoist, he never ceased to be a fairly orthodox Leninist. That is, while he opposed the more wildly radical policies of the Maoists such as the Great Leap Forward and the Great Proletarian Cultural Revolution, at the same time he always maintained the necessity for the centrality of Communist Party control.

The flaw in the popular image of Deng has been a misreading of his opposition to Maoist radicalism. What Deng has been is an ideological risk-taker, willing to sacrifice this or that tenet of Marxism-Leninism-Mao Zedong Thought in order to achieve his ends. In this sense Deng has been more practical-minded or more pragmatic than the more ideologically rigid Maoists. But Deng's "heterodoxy" was linked to policy questions and did not extend to the area of organization. Deng has, for example, been more willing to rely on material incentives to motivate workers and peasants, in contrast to the Maoists' reliance on ideological agitation and exhortation. And Deng has been more interested in moving the nation ahead economically than he has in building the New Communist Man. Thus, for example, we see Deng willing to endorse the concept of limited marketization of the Chinese economy. Nowhere, however, has Deng Xiaoping suggested that any institution other than the Communist Party should lead in the process of modernization, nor has he given any indication that the ultimate goal of his modernization effort was anything other than the building of socialism and communism.

In view of the fact that Deng has never given any indication that it was his intention to move China in a direction even remotely resembling Western-style democracy, one wonders how he could have been so completely misunderstood. One would have supposed, for example, that Chinese students and intellectuals at least would have recalled that Deng was the Party General Secretary during the One Hundred Flowers episode, and one of the chief Party triggermen during the ensuing Anti-Rightist campaign. More recently, Deng used the Democracy Wall movement of 1978-1979 against Hua Guo-feng, and then smashed the movement when it had served his purposes. Even more surprising, perhaps, was the fact that the image of Deng as a moderate persisted into the spring and summer of 1989, in view of the fact that it was the same leadership and same army which had only recently put down with deadly force the demonstrations in Lhasa, the capital city of Tibet. Perhaps it is true that hope springs eternal in the human breast, though in reality, no one should have been surprised by the results of the confrontation in Tiananmen Square on June 4, 1989.

If Deng Xiaoping is not the leader who might lead China to a more open and liberal era, does such a leader or group of leaders exist in China? It is probably impossible to answer this question except to say that there is no evidence of the existence of such a group at this time. Deng was usually described as the head of a "liberal" faction which was opposed by "conservative" elements, though it is not entirely clear how orthodox Marxists and Maoists were transformed into conservatives. And Deng was applauded for promoting younger, better educated, and more technically competent leaders such as Premier Li Peng, a Soviet-trained engineer. But Li Peng became one of the chief villains of the Tiananmen Massacre, so it is no longer clear how one should regard the younger generation of communist leaders.

Still, many continue to hope that the future may bring forth leaders who are a substantially different breed from those who have traditionally risen to the top of the Communist Party. One Catholic group, for example, has boldly asserted, "A younger, more moderate leadership will gradually appear in China."[3] It is a hope which one hears increasingly expressed by China-watchers in the aftermath of Tiananmen. Younger leaders will surely appear as mortality claims the older generation of revolutionaries, but whether the career path by which leaders claw their way to the top of a Leninist-Communist bureaucracy will produce leaders who are more moderate, remains to be seen. We should at least be aware that other, less hopeful, possibilities also exist.

Ideology

Despite the fact that the "liberalization" of the Deng era has given rise to the hope or expectation that China might move toward a more open, pluralistic, even democratic political system, the actual limits of post-Mao ideological debate in the top levels of Party leadership have been extremely limited. As suggested above, there has been no hint from the "liberal" faction—including Deng, Hu Yaobang and Zhao Ziyang, the latter two now widely regarded as the most "liberal" of the communist leaders—that China would move to abandon the Four Cardinal Principles [leadership of the Communist Party, adherence to the socialist road, the people's democratic dictatorship and Marxism-Leninism-Mao Zedong Thought]. The two most important of the cardinal principles remain the leadership of the Communist Party and the reliance on Marxism-Leninism-Mao Zedong Thought. No one in a position of authority has seriously suggested abandoning these principles.

What then have been the sources of contention in the top ranks of the party leadership? The ideological problems have come from a belief on the part of the more cautious or "conservative" Party leaders that the reform policies of the Deng Xiaoping group might threaten these basic principles of communist rule, even though the reform group professed to support these principles. And in this case, we might judge the conservatives to have been correct. Deng's policies of reform and opening to the outside world apparently did lead a large number of people to believe that China was moving in a direction of liberalization that Deng and his allies never intended for it to move.

The explanation for this misunderstanding is actually rather simple. Deng and the reformers saw correctly that the modernization effort required a loosening of ideological control in order to promote the innovation which was necessary to respond to the ever-changng empirical world. But the innovations which resulted from the loosening of ideological control proved to be unacceptable to the Party leadership. One such innovation, for example, asserted that the problem with China's lack of development lay in the system itself. That is, Marxist-Leninist systems do not work very well. They provide neither a high standard of material well-being, nor a sufficient degree of political freedom. This is a contention which is now widely accepted as valid. Looking at the history of these systems, such an assertion makes a good bit of sense. It is potentially, therefore, a rather useful innovation. But is this innovation either useful or acceptable to those in power who still possess the capacity and the instruments to apply the ultimate sanctions of torture, deprivation and death?[4] The innovation, after all, demands that those in power should step down (this was precisely the call issued by the demonstrators in Tiananmen Square), and that the system should be scrapped.

The problem is further complicated if the legitimacy of the political leadership is also dependent upon maintaining the coherence of a sanctioning ideology (Marxism-Leninism-Mao Zedong Thought) which claims to represent "scientific" truth, and is, therefore, directly threatened by any innovations which challenge that coherence and "truth."

The leaders of China are thus caught in what appears to be an impossible dilemma. The very sources of innovation which hold out the promise of the sort of future which China's leaders profess to want, and which they clearly require in order to get where they want to go, are in the end unavailable to them. By giving to the social institutions and to the intellectuals who are a part of them the freedom which is necessary for them to randomize their behavior and to innovate, the coherence of the legitimizing ideology will be threatened. Conversely, by bringing the intellectuals under the control of that ideology, the principal sources of innovation will be shut off.[5]

There is, therefore, very little room in a system of this kind for the development of the sort of pluralism, based upon independent social institutions, which would be required for the appearance of anything approaching true religious freedom of the sort found in the Western democracies. The Communist Party will continue to attempt to dominate all such institutions in the society to the extent that they are able to do so.

Performance

It is, perhaps ironically, in this last assertion that some possibilities for religious freedom have appeared. The Party will continue to attempt to dominate, but has its capacity to do so been significantly weakened? We suggested above that some possibilities for escaping the domination of the Party have begun to appear in what might be described as the "cracks" of a political system which is in very deep trouble.

There can be no doubt that, in addition to its specifically political problems, China is suffering a deep spiritual malaise. The country's leaders recognize this problem and discuss it publicly. Widespread corruption among government officials, including Communist Party officials, is but one manifestation of this problem.[6] This spiritual malaise may also account for the reported tremendous increase in interest in religion in the recent past. Some of the more optimistic observers believe that Christians in China now number 50 to 60 million, all but a small fraction of whom have become Christians in the last decade. This tremendous growth, whether 50 million or less, has been primarily attributable to the work of Protestant evangelical groups, though all observers agree that the number of Catholics has increased as well.

This spiritual malaise has infected Chinese intellectuals in a special way in the wake of the Tiananmen killings and the subsequent course of political re-education to which they have been subjected. In a long journey through the PRC in the summer of 1990, as political re-education classes were nearing completion, one was struck by a sense of disaffection, even ennui, among students and academic colleagues which was almost palpable. No constructive future for the Chinese nation is possible without these people, but to re-capture their hearts and minds will be a very difficult—perhaps impossible—task for the current regime.

There are other serious problems as well: rapid population growth, insufficient food output, disappearance of agricultural land, and environmental degradation, to mention a few of the more difficult ones. The failure to solve any one of these problems could prove fatal to China's modernization plans, fatal to the survival of the regime, or both.[7]

In recent years, China's population has been growing at a rate of about 1.5 percent per year. This is not a terribly high rate by the standards of the developing world, but with a base population in excess of 1.1 billion, China is adding to its population by about 16.5 or 17 million new mouths each year. The Chinese State Statistical Bureau now speaks in terms of a terminal population size of 1.5 or even 1.8 billion, numbers so large as to be almost inconceivable. How the political system might care for such an immense population is difficult to imagine.

Add to this the fact that in recent years agricultural land has been disappearing at an alarming rate due to erosion, desertification, urbanization, road-building, and the like. China is already a land-poor nation, having only about forty percent as much land under cultivation as the United States. Moreover, grain supplies have not yet exceeded those of the peak year of 1984. Food can, of course, be bought from abroad, and the Chinese have been buying foodgrains, but the hard-earned foreign exchange used in that way is not then available for capital investment at home.

If these basic problems of people, land, and food were not enough, the government of the PRC also faces a deteriorating educational system, especially at the lower and middle levels, and particularly in the countryside where basic education is most needed. Major infrastructure problems await solution, including an inadequate highway system, insufficient railway capacity, and energy shortages. Environmental degradation has been accepted as a price of modernization, but China now faces serious shortages of fresh water, and must eventually deal with massive pollution of the air, soil, and water which will require uncounted sums of scarce financial resources even to slow down, much less eradicate.

All of these problems must be attacked with financial resources squeezed from a gross domestic product (GDP) which is among the lowest in the world on a per capita basis. China's 1990 per capita GDP amounted to no more than US $350–400; the total national budget for that year was aproximately US $75 *per capita*.

Can China solve these problems with a political system which is crippled by corruption and inefficiency, and with a belief system in which almost no one believes? It seems unlikely that the present regime will be able to do so. Increasingly, one sees China-watchers predicting the "death" of the communist system in the PRC. One famous Sinologist, for example, with an excellent record for accurate prediction, has recently published an essay entitled, "Four Ways Communism Could Die in China."[8] It is difficult to disagree with his very perceptive analysis.

It is possible to imagine several scenarios in which this end comes rather quickly, yet it is also possible that the death rattle of the present system could linger for quite a long time. China is still largely a rural, peasant nation; the concerns of Beijing and Shanghai intellectuals have little relevance in the Chinese hinterland. In this regard, it is useful to recall that with all the problems which China has confronted during the reform era of Deng Xiaoping, the quality of peasants' lives has, for the most part, been substantially improved. Indeed, it is no small achievement that the regime has significantly improved the standard of living, especially in housing, for 700 million or so rural Chinese. This improvement must be regarded as a significant force for stability of the current regime, even in the face of the massive problems which we have laid out above. Even so, this positive force is likely only to delay the end of the regime, not to prevent its coming.

Whither the Church?

How is the Church likely to fare in this period of uncertainty which lies ahead for China? The answer to that question obviously depends upon what form future Chinese political arrangements assume. The death of communism does not necessarily imply the rise of democracy. The future may be very bright indeed, but it is also possible that whatever replaces the present system in China may be just as bad, or worse, in terms of a decent regard for personal liberty, political freedom, and human rights. One thing we can probably predict with a fair degree of certainty, is that the successor regime is not likely to have the strong built-in ideological hostility to religion which characterizes the communist system. Whether the successor regime is a strong central system or some sort of federation of regional centers of power remains to be seen, as does the question of whether this regime will be friendly to the Church. It is even possible that, in the event China breaks up into regional centers of power, the treatment of the Church may vary greatly from one area of the country to another.

Whatever political form the future takes, the past has demonstrated that the Church has a tremendous capacity for survival. The basic needs which religion satisfies in human lives have not been met by Marxism-Leninism-Mao Zedong Thought. Nor, despite the drives, campaigns, slogans, and near complete control of information for four decades, have the communist leaders of China succeeded in remaking the "fallen nature of man." Recognizing this fact, the *China Daily* complained that farmers had been willing to accept "science" as it pertained to farming, but in other matters related to "birth, death, age, illness, and marriage," the people continued to "cling to feudal superstition and outmoded custom."[9] There may be more important human concerns than birth, death, age, illness, and marriage, but it is difficult to imagine what they might be. Any belief system which fails to deal with such fundamental concerns of the real human condition is not likely to displace one which does.

The leaders of the PRC, armed with "scientific" Marxism-Leninism-Mao Zedong Thought failed to understand this basic point. Believing that they could more or less rapidly transform the Chinese people according to the Maoist revolutionary image, and that they could eliminate "superstition" from Chinese society, they failed to understand the stubborn resistance of the Catholic faithful, and the joyful acceptance of suffering and martyrdom which characterized the lives of so many of those imprisoned and brutalized. They could not understand of the faith of men like Bishops Kung, Tang and Fan, and of teenage girls like Wang Xiaoling and her Catholic friends, even in the face of decades of re-education in the doctrines of Marxism-Leninism-Mao Zedong Thought.

Faith, a gift of the greatest possible value, is a strange and powerful thing. In a curious way, it can give power to the most powerless. The great power of the state could, and did, kill large numbers of people. But this power could not finally destroy an idea. And in the end, who can be judged really to have triumphed in the bitter and bloody contest between church and state?

The leaders of China might have understood more clearly the terms of the contest if they had for a moment put aside Marx and read St. Bernard of Clairvaux (1091–1153). Bernard surely spoke for all those Catholics who defied the efforts of the government to change them:

Our trials are wings that carry us to God.

NOTES

1. Walter Lippmann. *The Public Philosophy*. New York: Mentor Books, 1955, 69.
2. This information is from private correspondence in the author's possession.
3. Pro Mundi Vita. *The Catholic Church in the People's Republic of China, op. cit.*, 9.
4. I owe a great debt to my friend Professor Morse Peckham who has developed this idea in several works over a number of years. See especially, Morse Peckham. *Explanation and Power*. New York: The Seabury Press, 1979. I have attempted to develop this argument with specific reference to China in, James T. Myers. "Socialist Spiritual Civilization and Cultural Pollution: The Problem of Meaning," *Issues & Studies*. Taipei: Institute of International Relations vol. 21, no. 3, March 1985, 47–89.
5. I have attempted to develop this argument more fully in, James T. Myers. "China and 'Germs' of Modernization," *Asian Survey*, Berkeley: University of California Press, vol. XXV, no. 10, October 1985, 981–997.
6. I have attempted to develop this point in depth in, James T. Myers' "Modernization and 'Unhealthy Tendencies,' " *Comparative Politics*. New York, January 1989, 193–213.
7. We have attempted to develop this argument more fully in, James T. Myers and Donald J. Puchala. "Some Demographic Constraints on Chinese Economic Modernization," *Issues & Studies*. Taipei: Institute of International Relations, vol. 24, no. 10, October 1988, 116–145.
8. Jurgen Domes. "Four Ways Communism Could Die in China," in George Hooks, ed. *The Broken Mirror: China After Tiananmen*. London: Longman, 1990, 46–472.
9. *China Daily*, Beijing, November 10, 1982, 4.

Index